PLEASURE AND EFFICACY

Pleasure and Efficacy

OF PEN NAMES, COVER VERSIONS, AND OTHER TRANS TECHNIQUES

GRACE E. LAVERY

PRINCETON UNIVERSITY PRESS
PRINCETON & OXFORD

Published by Princeton University Press
41 William Street, Princeton, New Jersey 08540
99 Banbury Road, Oxford OX2 6JX

press.princeton.edu

Library of Congress Cataloging-in-Publication Data

Names: Lavery, Grace E., author.
Title: Pleasure and efficacy : of pen names, cover versions, and other trans techniques / Grace E. Lavery.
Description: Princeton : Princeton University Press, [2023] | Includes bibliographical references and index.
Identifiers: LCCN 2022056604 (print) | LCCN 2022056605 (ebook) | ISBN 9780691243924 (hardcover) | ISBN 9780691243931 (paperback) | ISBN 9780691243955 (ebook)
Subjects: LCSH: Transgender people. | Gender transition—Social aspects. | BISAC: LITERARY CRITICISM / LGBTQ+ | PSYCHOLOGY / Human Sexuality (see also SOCIAL SCIENCE / Human Sexuality)
Classification: LCC HQ77.9 .L39 2023 (print) | LCC HQ77.9 (ebook) | DDC 306.76/8—dc23
LC record available at https://lccn.loc.gov/2022056604
LC ebook record available at https://lccn.loc.gov/2022056605

British Library Cataloging-in-Publication Data is available

Editorial: Anne Savarese & James Collier
Production Editorial: Jaden Young
Jacket/Cover Design: Heather Hansen
Production: Lauren Reese
Publicity: Jodi Price & Charlotte Coyne

Jacket/Cover Credit: Photograph by Kristina Paukshtite

Parts of "Trans Realism and Its Referents" were originally published in different form in *Critical Inquiry*/University of Chicago Press, 2020.
Parts of "The King's Two Anuses" were originally published in different form in *Differences*/Duke University Press, 2019.
Parts of "Picaresque and Pornography in The Old Curiosity Shop" were originally published in different form in *Please Miss: A Heartbreaking Work of Staggering Penis*/Seal Press, 2022.
"Fear of Commitment: Adorno Castrating Brecht" was originally published in *Victorian Literature and Culture*/Cambridge University Press, 2020.
Parts of "On Being Criticized" were originally published in different form in *Modernism/Modernity*/Johns Hopkins University Press, 2018.
Parts of "The Egg and the Essay" were originally published in different form in *Trans Studies Quarterly*/Duke University Press, 2020.

This book has been composed in Arno Pro

10 9 8 7 6 5 4 3 2 1

"Do not think that one has to be sad to be militant, even though the thing one is fighting is abominable. It is the connection of desire to reality (and not its retreat into the forms of representation) that possesses revolutionary force."

—M. F., 1977.

CONTENTS

PROSPECTUS

THIS BOOK MAKES TWO CLAIMS, the second dependent upon the first, about gender transition as it has been experienced and represented in the modern period, roughly 1850 to the present. "Gender transition" is a somewhat euphemistic term with certain advantages over "sex change," but certain disadvantages as well: I use them roughly interchangeably, to refer to (1) any kind of process by which a person may make changes to their body on the grounds of transsexual or transgender ideation; (2) any kind of process by which a person may make changes to their legal or social personhood, such as by changing names or requesting to be referred to by new pronouns; (3) any kind of psychic reorientation by which a person may come to understand themselves as belonging to a different sex class, including a new, fictive, imaginary, or negative class, than the one to which they were assigned at birth. I make no ontological distinction between binary and nonbinary presentations of transition, but where nonbinary presentations appear in this book, they are inevitably associated to some degree with *sex* as a system of somatic classification. I therefore exclude such transitions as are concerned *solely* with gender, and not with sex at all, from my discussion—primarily because I have not seen such transitions represented in the literature I have studied.

This will appear to some as an unnecessarily broad way of defining an experience that, after all, affects few people to such a degree that they reorient their entire lives around it. Yet while transsexual commitment in its most profound form is a relatively rare phenomenon in the archives I have been examining, various degrees of transsexual ideation, orientation, or experimentation are much more common. Indeed, according to the reading of psychoanalysis I advance here, they are not merely common but practically universal. I therefore bypass entirely the question of whether a historical figure such as George Eliot—assigned female at birth, but relatively committed to a masculine pseudonym which we still use—"is" "trans"; insofar as a given person adopted a masculine pseudonym, that person transitioned; to the degree that Eliot's writing explores the viability of identifying with a masculine or male position, then it may be said to be exploring the possibility of transition. These historical inclusions are especially necessary given the bizarre and ahistorical arguments of contemporary antitrans historians such as Jane Clare Jones and Selina Todd, who argue that nobody transitioned before "the late twentieth century."[1] The attempt to isolate trans experiences from history serves the political goal of isolating trans people from the LGBT communities among which they (we) have lived, loved, and fought for more than a century and a half.

This book's first claim is that representations of transition in the modern period have exhibited a profound ambivalence concerning the ontological condition of the transsexual—whether or not the transsexual now belongs to the sex class into which the transition has sought to place them—and that this ontological conundrum has determined the characters of both antitrans oppression and the civil rights claims with which trans people have usually confronted it. This problematic has emerged strangely entangled with the history of psychoanalysis: though Freud wrote about transsexuality rarely (and, in his notes on the Schreber case, characterized the condition as psychotic), by the end of his career the related conditions of "penis envy" and "castration complex" had become more or less definitive of neurosis and therefore not merely universal, in the sense that everyone has them, but the "bedrock," as Freud calls it in *Analysis Terminable and Interminable*, of the neurotic subject's latent condition. While Freud died shortly after writing that paper and therefore had no chance to further develop his understanding of a primary universal transsexuality, later readers of psychoanalysis, especially those following Lacan, have explored the ontological implications of Freud's insights in a variety of ways. Yet, partly because of Lacan's idiosyncratic understanding of the therapeutic function of psychoanalysis, critics have yet to grapple fully with the *pragmatic* dimension of Freud's understanding of castration complex / penis envy (which I conjoin thus because, ultimately, Freud understood them as variant presentations of the same condition). So, by considering the context in which transsexuality presented to Freud as a peculiar type of ontological foundation, I aim to restore to view the therapeutic apparatus that psychoanalysis was to have been.

My second claim derives from the first: in the face of the ontological problematization of transsexuality, a trans feminist strain of embodied thought (or praxis) has sought to enable trans life by sidestepping ontologization and, rather than asking what the transsexual *is*, instead developing techniques by which transitions might be more fully effectuated. This trans pragmatism affirms in all places that transition *works*, that despite expectations, it *is possible*, and that it *happens*. The politics of trans pragmatism has consisted of a resistance to the ontologizing demands of medicalization, pathologization, and even liberal accounts of irresistible LGBT interiority, and the development of methods for passing (the acrobatics of the penile tuck, for example), for cultivating pleasure (the trans-specific sexual techniques documented in contemporary zine culture), and for evading various forms of racial and sexual surveillance. As an essentially pragmatic philosophy, the trans cultivation of technique has been neither "essentialist" nor "anti-essentialist," insofar as those terms have organized much of the political content of feminist thought since the 1970s. Nonetheless, trans women especially have figured as the scapegoat for a critical branch of feminist thought which understands reproductive capacity (in the biological rather than Marxist sense of the term) as the sole grounds of the oppression of women.[2] Though this branch of "trans-exclusionary radical feminism" ("terf") was relegated to the sidelines of feminist organizing from its inception in the early 1980s until the last few years, since the so-called trans tipping point of circa 2014, antitrans feminism has suddenly become a massive cultural force, aligned with religious and social conservatives in the pursuit of trans-exclusionary social policy. While terfism seeks the full ontologization of transsexuality along essentially liberal lines, trans pragmatism operates as an informal but global mutual aid society, with trans people online swapping practical tips for evading state capture in much the same way as their Victorian and early-modernist forebears.

The book advances these claims in two sets of essays and an epilogue, which have been organized to pursue the argument in its logical sequence but also to explore the generic and cultural logics by which these historical and political conditions have become knowable, both to trans people and to the world at large. The first sequence of essays, "How to Change Sex Like a Pragmatist" (part 1), draws on the perhaps unexpected traditions of philosophical and literary realism to sketch out a logical grounds for transition, exploring a number of canonical treatments of sex, volition, and technique in George Eliot, Sigmund Freud, Ernst Kantorowicz, Charles Dickens, Theodor Adorno, and Alfred Tennyson. The second sequence, "How to Survive Negation" (part 2), begins to demarcate some of the generic lineaments that transition has engendered, albeit that in some cases the literal referent of transsexuality seems rather remote: cultural criticism as theorized by Matthew Arnold, the queer essay since Sontag, the serial killer narrative, and the stoner neo-noir. Finally, in the book's epilogue, I examine the trans cover version as a distinctive musical genre of transition, glancing back over Kevin Rowland's album *My Beauty* and the output of the indie record label V/Vm Test Records to reinterpret the Kantian condition of subjective universality that governs both this book's method and the condition of many of its objects.

The book therefore covers a long cultural history and does not move chronologically. My excuse for the historical breadth is that the book covers, broadly, the history of the modern transition, from the age of George Eliot and Fanny and Stella to the post–tipping point antagonisms of online culture.[3] The excuse for the progression is, as I've said, that I have preferred to organize my work logically rather than chronologically. The work moves between media and genres—it involves poetry, creative prose, criticism, philosophy, fiction, cinema, pop music, pornography (textual and video), and memes. Although this multigeneric breadth is not intended, in itself, to make an argument, nor is it surprising: since transition, by design, takes people out of one genre and deposits them in another, it is no surprise that a cultural history of gender transition will also provide, by accident, a history of genre transition.

I would like to take this opportunity to thank the many readers and writers who have made this work stronger. My Berkeley colleagues Judith Butler, Ian Duncan, Nadia Ellis, Eric Falci, Catherine Flynn, Anne-Lise François, Josh Gang, Mark Goble, Steve Goldsmith, Steve Justice, Celeste Langan, Andrew Leong, Colleen Lye, Maura Nolan, Kent Puckett, Juana María Rodriguez, Damon Young, and Hannah Zeavin have all responded to some of this work in various ways, and all have contributed to it. I am especially grateful to the graduate students with whom it has been my honor to work and who shape my thought reciprocally: Alex Brostoff, Emma Eisenberg, Mary Mussman, Jessy Nyiri, Kevin Stone, and Emily Sutton. Colleagues outside of Berkeley have generously shared their thought and care too: Dylan Burgoon, Ronjaunee Chatterjee, Martha Feldman, Beth Freeman, Nat Hurley, Cliff Mak, Sharon Marcus, Meredith Martin, Kyla Wazana Tompkins, Kara Wittman, and many more. I want to offer a special note of gratitude to my old friend Mat Paskins, who is a careful and trustworthy reader, and for whose judgment I have been grateful in composing this work, as others.

I have presented writing from this project at the Universities of Harvard, Yale, Princeton, Oxford, Cambridge, Chicago (twice), Toronto, California at Irvine, and Brown, as well as at the San Francisco Center for Psychoanalysis (twice); I am grateful to all for their generous and nourishing engagement. I would especially like to thank the various psychoanalysts, training analysts, and psychoanalytic colleagues who have helped me with this work, in particular Lisa Buchberg, Patricia Gherovici, and Mitch Wilson. I would also like to thank my comrades in solidarity working for queer and trans liberation and for the abolition of state technologies of punishment on and off campus, both in the Cops off Campus movement and in the broader movement for police and prison abolition. I write in and for my community of sisters, siblings, lovers, and comrades—though I speak a language taught to me in school, in some cases I speak of things I learned outside. Thank you to all those who have taught me techniques of pleasure over the last decade, as I have made several important transitions—to my femmes on top, to my trans with plans. Working with Princeton University Press for the second time has been a pleasure, and I extend my gratitude to the editorial staff, Anne Savarese and James Collier, the production editor, Jaden Young, and to Rei Terada and the other reader for their careful reviews of this book. Nothing in my life would be possible without my lodestar, my husband, Daniel Lavery. During the final stage of this book's composition, I developed a post-viral brain fog, which created unexpected challenges in completing the edits. I am therefore especially thankful to my friend, colleague, companion, comrade, and quondam, Cliff Mak, who helped enormously with that frustrating and difficult work. This book has many interstitial dedicatees, remnants of the plural scenes of its composition and transmission. In its entirety, it's for Lily, who has crafted for and with me new techniques, which it falls to the lover to learn.

INTRODUCTION

How to Brainwash Yourself

I BEGAN TO TAKE feminizing hormones in January 2018, after many, many years of delay. The day that I took my first dose of spironolactone, to suppress my testosterone, and estradiol, which supplemented my endocrine system with estrogens, I did not believe that doing so would help me—indeed, I believed that I was ruling something out, and that I would shortly thereafter be able to put aside, if not the drive to transition, then at least the notion that anything might be accomplished in real life that might manifest that drive. Instead, what I learned was that altering the levels of my estrogen and testosterone profoundly, overwhelmingly, and completely transformed my experience of the world and of myself. The central fact, which my experience has ratified over and again in the years since I began hormone replacement therapy, is that it has been possible for someone who merely *wanted to have been* a woman, to indeed *become* one—a metamorphosis from present perfect to present continuous, as utterly fantastical as an Ovidian fabliau.

That transformation has reshaped my intellectual and political commitments. How could it not? I began to question why, indeed, this transformation had seemed so impossible, despite the evidence of trans people writing about their experience for over a century—though, of course, the introduction of *the hormone* as the major vehicle of somatic change was a more recent phenomenon. How had I, who had read widely and enthusiastically in queer theory, failed to take seriously the fundamental ontology upon which my own life was being refounded? What I came to realize was that a lot of the work I had read, while written by queer critics and activists unquestionably supportive of trans people as a verifiable social fact—indeed, as trans people's only allies in a world implacably committed to our eradication—was nonetheless stridently hostile to the claims trans people tended to make about ourselves.

Eve Sedgwick, for example, the indispensable advocate of queer allyship and universality, argued in 1990 that "virtually all people are publicly and unalterably assigned to one or the other gender, and from birth," and that therefore gender is not especially "apt" for critical deconstruction.[1] Sedgwick, as Jules Gill-Peterson has noted,[2] would go on to see gender-affirming care of children as an attempt to eradicate gay children—an argument that is now being marshalled by Republican lawmakers across the United States and the United Kingdom as an argument for the abolition and criminalization of transgender care. While I was editing this book—i.e., since I first wrote the previous sentence—the following has happened: bills preventing trans athletes from participating in collegiate athletics have been introduced in Washington, Wyoming, Utah, Arizona, Oklahoma, Minnesota, Iowa, Missouri, Wisconsin, Illinois, Tennessee, Louisiana, Michigan, Indiana, Ohio, Pennsylvania, Delaware, North Carolina, and Georgia;[3] trans kids were prevented by law from using school bathrooms in Alabama, while similar bills were introduced in Tennessee, South Dakota, and Arizona (the reason there aren't more is that it was already banned in many places);[4] bills criminalizing the provision of transgender care to minors were introduced in Arizona, Iowa, Oklahoma, Tennessee, Louisiana, Alabama (which act specifically criminalizes such procedures as are "intended to alter [the] appearance of gender"), and New Hampshire (which treats transition-related care under an existing child abuse provision);[5] similar bills were repeatedly introduced and vetoed in Kansas;[6] a bill characterizing and criminalizing transition as "genital mutilation" was passed in Idaho;[7] and attempts were made to outlaw transition itself in Arizona, Iowa, Missouri, and Tennessee by the removal of existing provisions for legal sex changes.[8]

I began to understand my work as contesting what I saw as the *impossibilization of transition*, which I took to be a governing structure of much contemporary thought, both queer and str8. And in order to track the social reproduction of that procedure, I used my training as a literary and cultural critic to investigate the historical origins of skepticism about the efficacy of a sex change and to interpret the literary and cultural genres that that skepticism produced, which I tend to think of as *romances of intractability*. A romance of intractability is a narrative or argumentative procedure—perhaps, following Wayne Booth, a "rhetoric"—that endows a given historical problematic with value in proportion to how difficult it is presumed to be to solve it: if, for example, one finds the notion of using hormonal transition to solve one's problems "too easy," one is engaged in a romance of intractability.[9]

The idea that insolvable problems are much more appealing than solvable ones, to such an extent that we change some of the latter into the former—the better to ruminate on their splendid insuperability—has yielded literary themes for many authors. Franz Kafka is one of the mode's maestros. Consider this piece of microfiction, "The Next Village," written sometime between 1917 and 1923:

> My Grandfather used to say: "Life is amazingly short. Now, looking back, it is so jumbled up that I can hardly understand how a young man can make up his mind to ride to the next village without fearing that–even without any unfortunate accidents—the span of a normal, happy life won't prove long enough for such a ride."[10]

The story is, to be sure, hard to summarize, its meaning hard to glean. The story begins with the disappearance of an utterance, or even of a grandfather, since we cannot be sure whether the "used to" indicates the grandfather's death (or muteness from some other cause) or a change of heart on the specific question of the brevity of life. This question, indeed, has bearing on the grandfather's adage itself, since perhaps his own life has been long enough (like Marianne Dashwood's in Jane Austen's *Sense and Sensibility*) that he has lived to see his own commitments reversed. Or perhaps short enough that he simply died. But this comical impossibilization of the eminently possible will be familiar to readers of Kafka's work: it appears in "The Great Wall of China" as part of the famous "Imperial Message" section, in which the Emperor's messenger is unable to escape the palace grounds during a lifetime's journey, or "Before the Law," from *The Trial,* in which a "man from the country" waits a lifetime to gain access to an infinitely deferred judicial authority. Each of these stories produces a wildly dilated temporal disorientation, in which the achievement of basic tasks takes on the quality of Zeno's Arrow Paradox: impossible because requiring the traversal of a space whose interior is, by the nature of interior space, infinite.

Yet the short story also offers us something other than this kind of goofily mind-blowing speculation: it suggests that the problem derives from the subject who "can hardly understand," rather than from the world itself. As in Zeno's paradox, the arrow *does* reach its destination; the young man *does* ride to the next village, and however difficult the divisibility of space may be to contemplate, there is also something irreducibly silly about the contemplation. Key to Kafka's romances of intractability, then, is the suspicion that the pseudo-problems which detain us in literature have, elsewhere, rather straightforward solutions. Since an important purpose of this book is to encourage my readers to relinquish the undoubted appeal of such ruminations, I will generally prefer to examine such conundrums as I *do* encounter from the perspective of what I have tended to call "pragmatism"—a term, of course, with many meanings. I tend to follow the classical formulation of Charles Sanders Peirce: "Consider what effects, which might conceivably have practical bearings, we conceive the object of our conception to have. Then, our conception of these effects is the whole of our conception of the object."[11] The truth-value of a proposition is equal to its necessary effects. While I do not, in this book, get into debates with "gender critical" thinkers, whose ideas fall outside the scope of a feminist, liberationist work of theory, I would suggest that Peirce's maxim might clear up much of the fogginess around the metaphysical definitions of "woman" that have become contentious: a trans woman is a woman if and only if she is referred to as a woman; likewise an absolutist definition of women deriving from gamete size (or chromosome, etc.) is useful only if it accurately encapsulates the word "woman" as it appears in use. Since plenty of people *do* use the word "woman" to refer to trans women, for whom many of those reductive characteristics do not apply, the latter definition is of limited use.

I am aware, too, that by marking my commitment to a Peircean stripe of pragmatism here, I may be at risk of blurring a distinction between method and object that, in general, I aim to keep quite separate. Broadly speaking, I *adhere* to pragmatism, but I don't study it; I *study* Freudian psychoanalysis, but I don't adhere to it. Certainly I hope to recover aspects of Freudian thought and other methods of analysis insofar as I believe they can be put to political use. However, I am not in this book offering a normative account of any individual method, but rather pointing to some of the conceptual difficulties that have arisen from the collisions of psychoanalysis, feminism, and trans embodiment. My only normative method is the nonmethod of trans liberation—for which, as it happens, I believe psychoanalysis may indeed be more useful than its reputation would suggest.

I don't consider most of the theoretical questions raised by the claim that one has changed sex to be solvable in the terms in which they are posed; certainly, and I hope obviously, I don't believe that I have dispelled them. Yet as I investigated the history of the romance of intractability, I also discovered a feminist counterhistory of technique, of tricks and techniques passed on by women to women that comprises a body of knowledge written in the margins of history. These devices emerge to spite the notion that the most dignified response to the psychic suffering of women and queers is pious acceptance, yet they do so without congealing into a generalizable system of rationality, and indeed are as hostile to technorationality as they are to the counsel of despair. The archive of technique appears as a nonorganic, nontotalizable, inductively organized sequence of attempts to improve the lives of women and queers, accredited on the basis of their efficacy, not their elegance, and certainly not on their conformity to macro-epistemic schemes of knowledge. These auxiliary knowledges, the One Weird Tricks of modernity, are the focal point of this study, and while they are not all defensible—the two I am going to discuss in this introductory essay were written by an imperialist eugenicist and a manipulative charlatan—they offer us ways to think of collective modes of redress and, most importantly, the *real* difficulties that emerge to impede transition and mobility once one relinquishes the certainties of depressive pessimism.

That nonsynthesized compendium of techniques, upon which the attention of my book has been trained, I call "realism." Though this is certainly a usage at odds with other contemporary uses of that overburdened word, I derive my sense of realism from George Eliot, a Victorian novelist who typifies the term, and whose work—as we shall see—strives to learn, of a given situation, what *works* in amelioration. Temperamentally resistant to Romantic claims of either revolutionary or conservative types, but no less skeptical, finally, of the mid-Victorian celebration of "reform" as a historical metanarrative, Eliot's novels, as well as essays, are replete with pragmatic devices to be assessed on the basis of their efficacy. Eliot intended the novels themselves, indeed, are not to be read exactly as *descriptions*, but rather as *protocols* for social improvement: the purpose of each sentence of Eliot's novels is to cultivate empathy and thereby, little by little, to effectuate a more empathic world.[12] In *The Rhetoric of Fiction*, Booth dwells on this as one of the typical features of realist fiction; more narrowly, in *The Antinomies of Realism*, Fredric Jameson sees it as an individuating feature of Eliot's bad faith, ultimately amounting to a refusal to take a position.[13] Yet I plan—following Sedgwick, as it goes—to read realism as far as possible without paranoia and without fear that the knowledge schemes into which it attempts to induct me are either totalizing (they do not explain everything) or hostile (they will not make my life worse).[14] But if I confess to attempting to animate, within realism, the erotic frisson that might derive from the fantasy of being *brainwashed*, I will feel myself safe because George Eliot was, unquestionably, a trans author, and transition, whatever else it may be, can hardly escape the condition of brainwashing, and those upon whom it does its work would hardly wish it to.

Readings of nineteenth-century literature and culture occupy a central role in my analysis here, and close to the core of this book is an attempt to better understand the genres, theories, and aesthetic categories that readers of nineteenth-century literature tend to group together as "realism"—and not just to understand, but also to allow the political and aesthetic commitments of our own moment to be challenged by those of the past. The nineteenth century might be understood as the century of *technique*: the word first came into use in the 1820s, the historical moment immediately succeeding industrialization, when what Marx and Engels called the "charm" of preindustrial labor was still recent enough that its absence could be felt.[15] Yet indeed, within the dominant masculine strain of romanticism resisting the banalizing isomorphism of industrialization, it was not technique but its antithesis that ensured the freedom of man from the enslavement of the factory: in John Ruskin's brief polemic, "The Nature of Gothic," to take the most famous example, it was the very imprecision of Gothic architecture that demonstrated the free minds of the laborers who built the great Gothic cathedrals.[16] Masculine crafts, like the masculine bodies that produced them, were to be admired because they resisted technique—they demonstrated that true beauty was brute, that it came from a place of nonknowledge, of pure, unsullied roughness. Centuries of sexualized violence extending back and forth from that romance of masculine roughness give feminists ample reason to mistrust the evocations of freedom derived from R(/r)omantic constructions of the preindustrial worker.

Although this Romantic opposition to technique was dispersed across Victorian literature and culture, it was confronted and in many cases overwhelmed by utopian new frameworks for deploying technique *against* the interests of the ruling classes. Among these, for example, we could count Matthew Arnold's insistence on the technical precision of cultural criticism against both the liberal utilitarians, for whom criticism in general was a feminized luxury, *and* the Romantics, who saw cultural criticism as an impediment to the spontaneous overflow of human emotion.[17] (Meanwhile for Arnold, as for many of the other figures I discuss in this book, technique does not stanch affective flux—indeed, technical expertise is a necessary condition for discharging it.) George Eliot, meanwhile, took the novelist's technique of representing truth in fiction as the central plank of a broader ethics in which the care taken in representing the motives and interior life of another can generate, through the processes of identification and displacement, a nourishing sympathetic relationship between real beings.

In that sense, this work comprises a set of meditations on what it means *to know how to have a good time.* Such an assessment presupposes two premises, neither of which we conventionally take for granted: that following certain procedures will produce a good time, and that those procedures can be known in advance. These premises comprise the central problematic of *Pleasure and Efficacy,* in which I explore techniques of pleasure-giving and -receiving, which I take to be both essential to the possibility of trans feminist thriving and roundly suppressed by patriarchal epistemologies as well as antitrans feminist activism. The goal of *Pleasure and Efficacy* is to center feminists' attention on the devices—the "one weird trick your doctor doesn't want you to know"—by which we can create anew our own bodies, communities, and politics. In so doing, I aim to refresh Michel Foucault's call in 1977 to "withdraw allegiance from the old categories of the Negative (law, limit, castration, lack, lacuna), which Western thought has so long held sacred as a form of power and an access to reality," and instead rebuild our world with our own knowledge-practices, trained not on what satisfies, intrigues, or expresses, but solely on what *works.*[18]

Pleasure and Efficacy moves between the development of new genres and rhetorics of technique in nineteenth-century literature, and contemporary (i.e., contemporary to the decades prior to the publication of this book), mass-cultural reproductions of the older opposition between masculine roughness and feminized craftiness. Of all of the figures upon which that opposition has been brought into material reality, none is more persistent nor more ruinous than that of the transsexual woman, whose body might be—and frequently is—represented as the site of a literal conflict between latency and labor, for control over the organizational meaning of flesh itself. This book explores the trans woman's body as both a figure and a participant within this conflict, exploring (for example) the slippage between accounts of trans women as *accidentally men* and as *devious women* in arguments about trans women's right to participate in women's sports. And it develops a historical understanding of the figuration of the trans woman as, in all cases, an example of technique winning out against natural aptitude in the diagnostic and cultural genres in which trans women have appeared: those of autogynephile, serial killer, and invert (represented in this book by the music of Kevin Rowland, the character Buffalo Bill from Thomas Harris's *The Silence of the Lambs,* and the writing of Matthew Arnold). I therefore both draw historical connections between classical sexology and a contemporary text like *The Silence of the Lambs* and explore the logical necessity of those connections, the configuration of the transsexual woman as both the archetype and the confounding disproof of modern theories of labor.[19]

We are primed, in many ways, to hear such a call as vulgarly utilitarian—as, perhaps, an extension of the morbid bootstrap logic of murderous neoliberal fantasy. Queer theory has after all consistently emphasized the necessity of what Jack Halberstam calls "the queer art of failure," the ontologized form of which is "depression" as outlined by Ann Cvetkovich or "the depressive position," as Eve Sedgwick commends Melanie Klein's mode of reparative reflection; of what Eric Stanley and others have called "gay shame," designed to repudiate the triumphalism of white gay liberalism; of "looking backwards," as Heather Love calls the melancholic appeal of gay historiography; and of various other forms of broken, sad, disenchanted, and negatively oriented psychic, political, affective, and aesthetic formations.[20] So an exhortation to *focus on what works* might hit less as an invitation to utopia and more as yet another course correction into Gradgrindism, with its cudgels of standardized testing and routinized labor in markets lacking any protection.[21]

Yet for trans women, resigning oneself to the queer art of failure can feel alarmingly like the standard assurance that transition is impossible or asymptotic and that one might better spend one's effort accepting one's own eminently theorizable self-difference than learning how to apply eyeliner effectively. *You better work, cover girl,* the slogan of RuPaul's famous 1993 hit "Supermodel (You Better Work)," is both a self-consciously realist assessment of how to pass and therefore survive in a world in which the lives of Black trans women are murderously obliterated, *and* an invitation to demand more than mere survival—to articulate, and create with one's own Black trans body, the denied pleasures on the other side of survival.[22] The "work" RuPaul has in mind, after all, is neither manual labor nor office drudgery—"wet your lips and make love to the camera"—it's the work of desiring and being desired, of fucking and being fucked. Sex work, femme work—and also, crucially, the work of a single technique. Don't work harder—wet your lips.

Clearly, technique is not a morally innocent notion—something so enormous and all-encompassing could hardly be so. In this book we will encounter figures whose own understandings of technique were haphazardly constructed—Ernst Kantorowicz, for example, a Jewish German-American medieval historian whose formulations of academic freedom laid the groundwork for distinguishing that concept from mere "free speech," but whose own commitment to anti-Communism had led him, by his own account of his pre-emigration life in Germany, to enable and participate in fascist violence.

These consequences of *optimization* must be accounted as part of a history of technique. On the other hand, the romantic enchantment of techniquelessness one finds in Victorian aesthetics has produced horrors on no smaller scales: the workplace rapeocracy which depends, in its own way, upon Ruskinian notions about the freedom of the masculine worker, whose redress requires some—however ambivalent—labor towards the restitution and governance of institutional authorities, if only in the minimal—but not uncontroversial among some of the aforementioned queer theorists—position that Title IX protections are worth defending.

In other words, the "techniques" to which this book draws readers' attention are not Taylorized recipes designed to produce predictable effects, as though the whole of social relations could be brought under laboratory conditions. They are the skills acquired through practice, conveyed against and athwart the interests of capital, with which feminists, queers, and trans people have made our lives not merely possible, but pleasurable. Not sex tips you learn from *Cosmo*, then, but those you picked up from an ex in college; earnest attempts to teach the apparently unteachable—new ways of feeling, of experiencing embodiment, of relating with others. These are the very techniques that patriarchal exhortations to the untechnical delirium of the rudely masculine craftsman have taught us to neglect, and whose history and value I seek once more to excavate.

In the remainder of this introduction I will discuss two exemplary texts spanning the century between 1850 and 1950. These are not to be taken as congruent or as pointing to the same politics of technique or even the same style of technique. Their very eclecticism is part of the historical point—that the rhetoric of technique has been, since the mid-nineteenth century, both ubiquitous and hard to isolate. However, for all their differences, both of these examples do three things: first, they construct a complex address to the reader in order to persuade her that something transformative is happening to her consciousness in the very act of reading; second, they attempt to deploy that force in order to subordinate to the regime of technique a psychic outcome hitherto placed beyond its reach; and third, they all draw on the narrative structure of realism in order to engender the changes that they depict. In the first example, the very notion of sexual pleasure itself is rigorously subordinated to a series of learnable techniques, and sex transformed from a supposedly spontaneous collision of bodies into a site of labor and skill; in the second, an anonymous voice works to instill in the reader a quasi-religious experience, with the goal of countermanding a putatively primal—indeed, materially determined—drive. These two texts, then, are *Married Love* by Marie Carmichael Stopes and the anonymously authored *Alcoholics Anonymous*.[23]

winning and wooing

To position oneself as the imagined ideal reader of *Married Love*, published in 1918, would be to imagine oneself as someone unaware, for example, that a single seduction of a lover does not precipitate her physical arousal in ongoing perpetuity. Yet the outlandish clumsiness of the text's oafish antagonist is only one of the many forms of ignorance that Stopes illuminates in a book that has been called "one of the first modern best-sellers," "the most read book on sex of its time, perhaps of any time," and, less accurately, "the first sex manual for women."[24] (Less accurately because, as we shall see, not only is the male reader consistently addressed by the narrative speaker of *Married Love*, but his interest is positioned as prototypical.) The ignorance in which sex was shrouded Stopes presumed, with cause, to be absolute, not only because her bourgeois readers did not know the differences between sexual acts, experiences, desires, and body parts, but because they could not describe that which they *did* know. In the words of Stopes's contemporary and fellow abortion activist Stella Browne, "the conventionally 'decently brought-up' girl of the upper and middle classes, has no terms to define many of her sensations and experiences."[25] *Married Love* thus apportions to itself an enormous and weighty responsibility: to endow a generation of householders, whom the eugenicist and imperialist Stopes understood as noble sires of Empire and whiteness, with a sexual vernacular fit for their racial and class position. In his brief foreword, Professor Ernest H. Starling, offers a justification for the publication: "it is better to acquire knowledge by instruction than by a type of experience which is nearly always sordid."[26]

As Laura Doan has shown, a major part of the educative contribution of *Married Love* was Stopes's original theory of the periodicity of female sexual desire: that is, the notion of a relationship between the menstrual cycle and sexual desire, which Stopes developed first from self-observation, encouraging her women readers to self-observe and report.[27] That research, in turn, informed research into the hormonal basis of menstruation in the decade after *Married Love* was published: throughout the 1920s, endocrinologists worked to extract and synthesize the three estrogens—estrone in 1929, estriol in 1930, and estradiol in 1936—research that might also form a basis for the untested-but-widely-reported claim by trans women that they experience menstrual cramps. Another important aspect of Stopes's technique might also be approximated to techne in the more familiar sense: her interest in, and commercial development of, contraceptive technologies: she developed a series of rubber diaphragms and sold them under her own brand name, "Racial," and also offered advice on contraception and home abortion, the two topics on which she received the most voluminous correspondence.[28] Stopes's writing on domestic contraception adopts, as many of her readers have noted, a hominess that recalls the tone and genre of Isabella Beeton's *Book of Household Management*.[29] "Buy a fine-grained rubber sponge," she says in the follow-up, *Wise Parenthood*, "and cut it to a circle about the size of your palm, or a little (not much) smaller, and about the thickness of your own thumb . . ."[30]

Yet none of this is quite what the pseudonymous reviewer M.D.S. meant when referring to Stopes as an "expert in the technique of married life" in her review in the *Woman's Leader* in 1923.[31] That expertise, which is the one that drove readers to *Married Love*, did not derive from either Stopes's impeccable training as a paleobotanist nor her side hustle as an inventor, but from her experience of sexual practice. Yet if it is easy enough to guess at the referent of the phrase "technique of married life"—sexual skill—it is far harder to excavate from the book itself any such tidbits; there is nothing encyclopedic, nor even especially normative, about the book's many descriptions of satisfying sexual intercourse, and nothing that can easily serve as an analogue or forerunner to the genre of "sex tips" that historians sometimes trace back to Stopes. For its swooniness—the first chapter begins, "Every heart desires a mate"—Paul Peppis designates *Married Love* as an example of "sentimental modernism," but even sentimentality, as capacious an affective structure as it is, hardly accounts for the jarring mixture of medicalized candor and tender evasiveness with which Stopes approaches each discussion of mucus membranes. To a reader familiar with Freud's *Three Essays on the Theory of Sexuality*, first translated into English in 1910, Stopes's work might well have appeared glossy, euphemistic, and vague: A. A. Brill's translation of Freud speaks candidly of a variety of sex acts, "sexual aims," "sexual objects," and the like—while Stopes's imaginative field is wholly restricted to the presence or absence of the female orgasm within the scene of heterosexual married copulation.[32] (Stopes herself was evidently powerfully ambivalent about psychoanalysis, describing Freudian practice as "filthy in the extreme" in her 1926 book, *Sex and the Young*, but nonetheless her close friend Jessie Murray, who wrote the preface to *Married Love*, was instrumental in the foundation of the London Medico-Psychological Clinic, an important British landing strip for psychoanalytic thought.)[33] More pressingly for these purposes, one might contrast *Married Love* with the trans woman Jennie June's *Autobiography of an Androgyne*, published the same year and while similarly couched in the euphemistic Latin of the medical establishment, remarkably candid about sex acts—coining a Latin phrase, in fact, to describe the penetration of June's inguinal canals, the trans sex practice Mira Bellwether called "muffing."[34]

The phrase with which Stopes discloses the "technique" of *Married Love* possesses a vaporous sonic quality, an alliterative rhyme that twins two words, even as it nudges their meanings apart: "each winning should necessitate a fresh wooing."[35] The denotative sense here is both plain enough—each act of penetrative sexual intercourse should be preceded by the arousal of the vagina—and difficult to reckon. Was this really news? Yet that denotative meaning obscures the fact that "winning" and "wooing" are, within the genre of sentimental discourse, virtually synonyms, each seeming to indicate a state prior to consummation. The phrase, then, "each winning should necessitate a fresh wooing," twins the two gerunds in two ways (phonic and semantic) while differentiating each as chronological sequence and as logical procedure—in both cases, "wooing" is to precede "winning," even though "winning" is the subject of the clause and has been mentioned first. Syntactically, then, the sentence stretches backwards from "wooing" to "winning," pushing the ideas gently apart, as if performing rhetorically the very touch that is being prescribed. It might sound fanciful to suggest that the phrase "each winning should necessitate a fresh wooing" imitates the digital stimulation of the clitoris and labia, but after all, the sexual vitality of *Married Love* was acknowledged by all its early readers, despite its apparently euphemistic half-silence on the very topic (the exhortation to foreplay) for which it was most widely known and read.

In other words, the so-called technique with which Stopes's name was immediately associated was not exactly a learnable skill, but a wholly new rhetorical construction of sex. If the intimacy of its address was sensed most vividly in these moments of erotic mimicry, its narrative structure was reinforced and reproduced in the text's narrative syntax: sex consists of male labor towards female pleasure, the attainment of which is the enterprise's proper end. Alexander Geppert suggests that the book "created a new pressure, a previously unknown demand to achieve a pleasurable and satisfactory sex life, thus raising standards of performance for men and women."[36] Yet this labor was distributed unevenly: its primary burden was to fall on men, for whom sex was to become a hobby or a skill, a transformation that brought out the tinkering engineer in many of Stopes's male correspondents. One, a husband from

Crewe, wrote to Stopes: "I have generally waited until the 2nd wave time, and then by caresses and love play tried to intensify my wife's longing for connection . . . If I control it by going too slowly, I don't arouse the sensation at all . . . And it is only going moderately quick that she feels her nature aroused."[37] Doan is clearly not wrong to say that some of Stopes's readers, at least, "[assess] female desire in terms of male control."[38] One is left only to contemplate whether the male tinkerer is being created as a fantasy figure for women readers, or actually positioned as the book's ideal reader by the text itself.

It is surely the latter. Though, as mentioned, *Married Love* is sometimes described as a woman's book, it was "dedicated to young husbands and all those who are betrothed in love"; many of the readers with whom Stopes corresponded were men; the preface claims to speak to the "nearly normal"—a phrase which, if it is gendered, suggests a hapless male reader more than a dissatisfied female one.[39] The ironic construction of the various chapters suggests a male addressee: the chapter entitled "Woman's Contrariness," for example, begins with a narrative fable about "the average man who marries, happily and hopefully, a girl well suited to him," presenting with careful, Eliotic precision, his mental state as he observes her queer being: "gnawing at the very roots of his love is a hateful little worm—the sense that she *is contrary*."[40] The chapter's protagonist is himself subject to a certain kind of ironic counterobservation from the narrator's perspective, but the "contrariness" of the woman is simply explained—it is the product, indeed, of her "rhythmic sex-tide," the menstrual cycle which governs her sexual desires more fundamentally than his conduct could. It is difficult to imagine what the narrated "contrary" woman could gain from such a narrative—perhaps simply fodder to share with her husband—but to the male reader, the revelation of the menstrual basis of his wife's sexuality is both morally reassuring and aesthetically satisfying. In other words, despite Stopes's sentimental idiolect, the realist mechanism of *Married Love* depends upon the reader's identification with husband, rather than wife, as the sole protagonist of sexual intimacy. This conclusion is not to undermine the feminist value of a text explicitly concerned to elevate and center female pleasure, but rather to observe that the cost of that centralization is a secondary objectification of women, no longer now as objects of men's will, but as objects of men's *skill*.

We are perhaps so used to reciting Foucault's phrase "putting sex into discourse" that we underestimate how unpredictable were the effects of the late-nineteenth- and early-twentieth-century attempt not merely to describe sexual desire, but to bring something of sex itself into the very rudiments of speech and language. Here, for example, Stopes's construction of a rhetoric of sexual technique depends upon a strange substitution of sexual object for language (as in the "winning"/"wooing" pair), and the creation of a new mythic emplotment of pleasure as a field of ingenuity and endeavor. Stopes's narrative framing of sex as (male) labor towards (female) pleasure recreates heterosex as an ontogenetic recapitulation of the phylogenesis of heterosexuality as such, in the sense that the "climax"—a term sexology draws from narratology, rather than vice versa—of sexual activity corresponds with the social reproduction of what Stopes relentlessly calls the "race."[41] Yet the climax of heterosexuality can hardly, even in Stopes's own terms, be so simple, since one can imagine the plot of heterosexual coupling with anywhere between zero (nobody cums) and two (partners cum sequentially) terminal events. Thus the technique of sexual foreplay discloses its asymptotic motivation: not because foreplay is interminable, but because the singularity of "climax," and therefore the singularity of heterosex, can never be taken for granted.

"it works. it really does."

Though one could hardly say that "alcoholics anonymous" is a misnomer, the title of the "big book" after which the groups and movement are named will mislead some people encountering it for the first time, since the consumption of alcohol—while it occupies an important *narrative* place in AA's discourse—has nothing whatsoever to do with the technique, or indeed the final purpose, of the "twelve steps." The author of *Alcoholics Anonymous*, Bill Wilson, imparts those steps early on in the text, the main part of which is a patient, although uneven, exegesis of them—uneven, because Step 2 is granted a whole chapter, while Steps 6 and 7 share a paragraph. The steps work not to prevent the initiate from drinking, but to synthesize a quasi-mystical experience through the cultivation of a daily spiritual practice; *that experience* is then endowed with the power to keep the alcoholic sober, but sobriety is a secondary effect of spiritual enlightenment, and one only obtained in the late stages of the steps, after Step 10, by which time "we will seldom be interested in liquor. If tempted, we recoil from it as from a hot flame," where "it" could refer either to the liquor or to the temptation.[42] If AA works, then, it does so through a complex mode of address in which the presumptively anonymous authors of a book—in reality one person, Wilson—speak as a "we" that hails and eventually absorbs the reader, who thereby acquires the "solution" to her problems by virtue of joining an imaginatively introjected discourse community, a "we," that has already solved them.

Scholars have long connected the hydraulics of sympathy upon which such a mechanism depends with those of nineteenth-century realism: Robyn Warhol, in particular, has linked the 1939 text of *Alcoholics Anonymous* with George Eliot's early story "Janet's Repentance," which Warhol persuasively frames as the first modern recovery narrative, albeit that "modern" in this sense has the slightly unusual meaning of treating alcoholism, as does *AA*, as the hinge between spiritual and medical maladies, treatable only by mystical overwhelm.[43] As Susan Zieger argues, Eliot's story coincided with the medicalization of alcoholism, after which, like Foucault's homosexual, the alcoholic "was now a species."[44] Bill Wilson delivers "Bill's Story" as the first chapter of the Big Book.[45] Prior to introducing the twelve steps in the fifth chapter, "How It Works"—the "it" as the theological intermediary of the "we" and the "you," where "it" can mean either God, or the steps, or the God-who-is-immanent-to-the-steps—Wilson offers an account of the structural purpose of the narrative parts of the book: "Our stories disclose in a general way what we are like, what happened, and what we are like now."[46] Disclosure in a general way: such, too, is the paradoxical condition of realist characterization, as Catherine Gallagher outlines it in her landmark essay "George Eliot: Immanent Victorian," in which she describes the novelist's conflicted attitude towards indulging the sensuous intimacy of narrative sympathy, and the necessity of making characters precisely interchangeable, diagrammatic, empty.[47] The deployment of narrative sympathy in *Alcoholics Anonymous* moves towards a goal as individualistically transformative as the "incalculably diffusive" powers of Eliotic sympathy, but with a twist: instead of founding an ethical relation on the experience of readerly *difference* from character, Wilson's address seeks to dissolve the reader in an experience of readerly *sameness*, in which the reader can understand herself as already represented, her own desires and secrets already disclosed in a general way, by the text of *Alcoholics Anonymous*. The intention of producing readerly sameness is intensified by various forms of discursive paratext, as when (for example) attendees of an AA meeting are invited to "take what you like and leave the rest"—to simply absorb the aspects of a text which already feel like sameness and ignore those that feel alienating or differential.

As *Married Love* mobilized the putatively feminine idiolect of sentimental fiction, "Bill's Story" self-presents as a boy's story from the beginning: "War fever ran high in the New England town to which we new, young officers from

Plattsburg were assigned, and we were flattered when the first citizens took us to their homes, making us feel heroic. Here was love, applause, war; moments sublime with intervals hilarious."[48] The first sentence begins in "war" and ends with "heroic," a picaresque narrative of roguish pleasures, capacitated perhaps by the invisible reproductive labor of those "citizens" who "took us to their homes," and delivered in entirely vague asyndeton, a generalizable recipe of masculine glory—"love, applause, war." The *Gatsby*-esque retrospective inflects, inevitably, "in October 1929," when Wilson, having made a pile as a stockbroker, now loses it and turns to alcohol as solace, narrating the objective events and their subjective ramifications in the same sparse prose: "I was finished and so were many friends. The papers reported men jumping to death from the towers of High Finance. That disgusted me. I would not jump. I went back to the bar. My friends had dropped several million since ten o'clock—so what? Tomorrow was another day. As I drank, the old fierce determination to win came back."[49] The pizzicato rhythm of these sentences echoes the ticker tape, beating out its mechanical and minimal messaging of financial ruin—and just as the self-aggrandizing alcoholic blurs his cognitive process into the rhythm of history itself, so the reader allows herself to be given up into the widening slipstream of sympathy.

AA's many defenders often argue that the emphasis on interchangeability—in narrative terms, on the substitution of the reader for the narrator—differentiates the group from other self-help movements, because its destination is not an empowered ego but a "we" connected only by "powerlessness." Mariana Valverde suggests that "to this extent, AA indirectly subverts the neoliberal discourse of personal entrepreneurship and perpetual improvement," and Warhol adds that "no one profits from AA's activities, and no wealth can accumulate within the groups."[50] I am not so sure that the refusal to avow ego-restoration as the goal of a spiritual procedure "subverts" the logic of capital, which after all depends upon the escalating ontologization of compulsion as a basis of market rationality, but it is notable that, unlike Stopes, Wilson never sold gadgets or doohickeys, and he declined offers of capital investment from, among others, Nelson Rockefeller, when fearing that AA's expansion would compromise its independence.[51] What is remarkable, however, is the degree to which AA's work is effectuated by a psycho-theological power named "it," whose force is indeed governed by the physics of immanence, a desire for which Gallagher attributed to Eliot.[52] In the chapter introducing the steps, "How It Works," "it" seems to refer to "a program of recovery," but the phrase "it worked" or "it works" has already come up in "Bill's Story," where it is passed on by the anonymous man, whom we know to have been Ebby Thatcher, who has tried out a "practical program of action" as the result of a revivalist Christian outreach, and "the result was self-evident. It worked!"[53] (By the time the text of *Alcoholics Anonymous* was published, Ebby's sobriety had already lapsed, but he died sober, cared for by Wilson, in 1966.)[54] Later, however, what "works" is not the program, but prayer: "We shouldn't be shy on the matter of prayer. Better men than we are using it constantly. It works."[55] And then later, after elaborating the psychically easing consequences of prayer and meditation, in a paragraph all on its own, "It works—it really does."[56]

Like "every winning necessitates a fresh wooing," "it works" is both euphemistic and performative in the illocutionary sense—the phrase does something, immanently, that is more than hortative. "It works" closes the gap between attempt and outcome, such that the "it" that works becomes none other than the "we" that is working. The point of prayer, after all, is to acclimate the one praying to the gap between desire and experience, so that "we are careful to make no request for ourselves only," and "we are careful never to pray for our own selfish ends. Many of us have wasted a lot of time doing that and it doesn't work. You can easily see why." What works is a purposive dampening of the psychic drive towards efficacy: technique as mere practice, without expectation of reward. In that sense, Eliot's position as forerunner of the genre of AA-style recovery narrative depends less on "Janet's Repentance," then, and more on the more mature Eliot's experiments with animism (in *Mill on the Floss*, where the collision of active and passive modes of desire radiates disastrously between characters and landscape) and empathy (in *Romola*, whose antihero, Tito, bears a certain degree of resemblance to one of Wilson's self-exculpating clones, pre-bottom).[57] One of the major plots of *Middlemarch*, indeed, depends upon another one of Eliot's introspective and self-deluding men, in this case Nicholas Bulstrode, making a judgment over whether allowing an alcoholic access to alcohol constitutes an act of murder—an ambiguity that depends upon whether one thinks that an alcoholic's compulsion to drink is a law of nature, or that the alcoholic's no doubt attenuated capacity for self-control could still, in principle, keep him from poisoning himself.[58] George Eliot's mother, Christiana Evans, several biographers have speculated, may have been an alcoholic; others have pointed out that the prevalence of drunk and stoned characters in Eliot's fiction allows the novelist to explore states of partial volition and to narrate compromised but not vitiated freedom of will, like those of John Raffles and, differently, Bulstrode himself.[59]

Beyond the odd "Poor Janet!," by contrast, "Janet's Repentance," the last-printed of Eliot's three *Scenes of Clerical Life*, makes no especial play for its reader's sympathies, casting a rather Dickensian mixture of satire and sentiment upon the Trollopian plot of Janet Dempster, her violently and drunkenly abusive husband Robert, and her eventual confessor and pastor, Mr. Tryan.[60] Yet the dramaturgy is pure AA. The husband's drinking catalyzes the wife's, until she flees, in terror for her life—one is left wondering what "repentance" the narrator will deem necessary or even possible—and Tryan is brought before her as "a fellow-sinner" to express the hopelessness of her alcoholism: "I feel sure that demon will always be urging me to satisfy the craving that comes upon me, and the days will go on. . . . I shall always be doing wrong, and hating myself after—sinking lower and lower, and knowing that I am sinking."[61] Mr. Tryan, as Ebby Thatcher, replies, "Yes, dear Mrs. Dempster . . . there *is* comfort, there *is* hope for you. Believe me there is, for I speak of my own deep and hard experience. . . . Ten years ago, I felt as wretched as you do. I think my wretchedness was even worse than yours, for I had a heavier sin on my conscience." From there on, her "repentance" practically complete, Janet returns to her alcoholic husband, who is deranged on his deathbed, having been run over by a horse and gig. After which, things are polished off expeditiously: Robert dies; Mr. Tryan moves in and then dies; Janet lives a life of sober contemplation, unshackled by any kind of husband.

Eliot's depiction of the scene of alcoholic conversion includes two complications absent from Bill Wilson's more macho version: first, Janet's addiction seems to have derived from Robert's in some sense, and second, the sins for which she must repent are not self-evidently moral harms at all. The problem, from Janet's perspective, is that the admission of "powerlessness over alcohol" that begins Wilson's journey into grace, and which he treats as the icon of a broader, indeed absolutely primary, powerlessness, means something different to a swaggering male Wall Street broker than it means to a violently threatened female survivor of spousal battery—that is to say, to a subject whose powerlessness is an introjected spur to spiritual reflection, and one whose all-too-familiar powerlessness is socially reproduced. Yet by virtue of Eliot's awareness of that very complication, one can detect in the concluding passages of "Janet's Repentance" the distant imagining of sexual transposition, of a male alcoholic becoming, by virtue of his having been made powerless by alcoholism, a kind of psychic woman; or, more teasingly, the specter of a female alcoholic becoming, by virtue of her recovery, a kind of psychic man. Robert Dempster's deathbed scene is one of the most lexically and syntactically imaginative sequences in Eliot's oeuvre: a series of paratactical ejaculations in which he rages at his ecclesiastical rivals ("I'll make them say the Lord's Prayer backwards . . .

I'll pepper them so that the devil shall eat them raw . . .") and, consistently, animated and animalistic hallucinations concerning his wife's transformation into various figures of horrific, cross-sexed and cross-species, menaces: "stop her . . . she wants to drag me away into the cold black water . . . her bosom is black . . . it is all serpents . . . they are getting longer . . . the great white serpents are getting longer . . ."[62] The vision of his wife's black bosom transforming itself into a long white serpent does more than manifest to a dying man the transsexual metamorphosis he cannot produce in his own body. It also, and more satisfactorily, provides evidence to the wife—who, in fact, sits by his side unnoticed by the deranged man—that her transgender metamorphosis, from economic dependent to soon-to-be-heir-to-a-fortune, has left her unrecognizable to the man she has fled.

. . . unself unhelp

Neither Stopes's activism for sexual satisfaction nor Wilson's organizing towards collective reprieve from alcoholism explicitly concerns transition in the sense in which I used it at the start of this introduction. It is striking, though, how imaginatively proximate the idea of a sex change feels, at least to Stopes and to Eliot, to those attempting to lay down protocols for achieving the impossible and for making those protocols practicable and verifiable. Nor is either strictly engaged in "self-help": in neither case does self-empowerment occupy an important role in the techniques being imparted; in no case is a "bootstrap narrative" deployed to celebrate the strength and power of those who survive despite their disadvantages. Neither Stopes nor Wilson *was* especially disadvantaged—both members of a wealthy, white professional class whose bootstraps were hardly worth pulling. AA is more usually classified as a "mutual aid" organization; Stopes's endeavors were part of the wider eugenics movement, articulated with the imperial state rather than as an organ of it, with some commercial endeavors of her own. I offer these caveats because I have found that people have sometimes tended to suppose that the work I've been researching falls into the broad category of self-help literature—in the mold of Samuel Smiles, perhaps—which strikes me as a fundamentally different class of enterprise.[63] In the sense that these books attempt to guide a reader to lead a more fulfilling, or happier, life, one might agree—but so broad a definition would end up including much, perhaps everything, not usually thought of as "self-help." The point is not merely that, if the goal of a spiritual program is ego-annihilation, then the "self" that is helped is profoundly different to the self seeking help (indeed, the "help" in question requires a complete surrender of the "self"). Rather, the point is that while Smiles, and much else in the mainstream of self-help literature, imagines redirecting the unproductive or wayward body back towards productivity, labor, and social harmonization, the techniques I am following here pull those who follow them out of the bourgeois labor market entirely and into new, queerer forms of social organization—cults, for example, or communes, or polycules. This is a history of techniques of transition, rather than techniques of advancement. Whether or not they produce salable goods (as in Stopes's case) or remain wholly nonprofitable (as in Wilson's), the techniques of transformation I have been discussing are not, in general, interested in active accounts of discipline—that is, the attainment of pleasure by ever-intensifying exertion. Rather, one of the characteristic features of the rhetoric of technique is its insistence that one work *less,* that working smarter rather than harder will get results—that, indeed, the intensification of mere effort may be a defining characteristic of the problem one is trying to solve. One can then object to Paul Peppis's observation that "[Stopes] sexes middle-class women, marriage, and love by marrying a 'feminine' literary language to a 'masculine' technical language."[64] If technique in Stopes has a gender, it is feminine.

"Dermatologists Hate Her" is sometimes claimed to be the origin of the "one weird trick" model of online advertising. Of course it isn't; the origins of that genre of sales pitch must at least predate Christina Rossetti's poem "Goblin-Market," and are likely traceable to the origins of the word "commodity," whose etymon means "commodious"—easy, or *too* easy. Sianne Ngai traces a connection between literary device and the commodity form in *Theory of the Gimmick,* developing an account of the gimmick as "a form we marvel at *and* distrust, admire and disdain, whose affective intensity for us increases precisely because of this ambivalence."[65] Yet the weird trick is unlike the gimmick in one important particular: one never sees it or learns the first thing about it beyond its hypothetical existence. Clicking the link attached to this image, for example, would lead one to a series of interminable click-through pop-ups, after which one would (perhaps) land on a twenty-minute embedded video, in which the rhetorical gas would be pumped up, with (again, only perhaps) finally a sales pitch for a new book, or cream, or investment opportunity. The image presented as evidence of the one weird trick is self-evidently impossible, a mythic dream of transformation without obvious participation in the sale or trade of circulating goods. What is being mimicked in this image,

FIG. 1. *Dermatologists HATE HER // For Discovering // $5 WRINKLE TRICK // From Home.* Online banner ad, c. 2009

indeed, is not finally the use of a commodity, but the transformation of the body *as the horizon of historical becoming itself.* The image depicts transition as not merely possible, but inevitable—as inevitable as the shedding of one's epidermic cells.

One might, in that sense, place "Dermatologists Hate Her" in the tradition of bodily practice formalized by the queer choreographer Merce Cunningham. The cells collaborate to form tissue; the tissues collaborate to form organs. The organs, acting relatively independently, allow themselves to be organized into a body, which now exists in order to harmonize itself with its spatial, visual, and sonic environment. The body also organizes itself into love relationships, which (typically for Merce Cunningham) consist of games of pushing and leaning. Moving up the scale from the very simple organism (the cell) to the very complex (the relationship of love), the organism's freedom increases, as does the intensity of its relatedness to other organisms. The habits of speech that one might usually use to describe such a project are, palpably, inadequate to the task: to say "at the heart of Merce Cunningham's aesthetics is a new way of thinking collaboratively," for example, would be to locate that new way of thinking in a singular body, and therefore to treat collaboration as one man's idea. Which would not be collaboration, but the nonrelation Melanie Klein calls "projective identification," according to which the unconscious forces another person to bear, perhaps unknowingly, the condition of being oneself.[66]

FIG. 2. Meg Harper (right) in Merce Cunningham's *RainForest* (1968)

There are parts of myself that I love but cannot bear to believe are my own, so I transfer them onto you, that I might love myself *in* you, rather than know you. No relation. *Variations V* (1966): in the playroom, we take turns leaning on each other. In *RainForest* (1968), I shall lift my arms and you run under, but who then is tricking whom? A power to push becomes a need to lean; resistance to force becomes a clay-like passivity, "each central to itself."[67]

A love relationship? But there is no affect; there is only technique, "a place where rigor and freedom can exist in common time."[68] Nonetheless, under the conditions of a meditative practice common to John Cage and Merce Cunningham, I choose to believe that the relation of collaborative bodies is called love, and I then adopt for myself the task of learning what love is by observing that relation. Love as theory of relation; love, therefore, as technique—a theory that stretches back past Cunningham to Charles Darwin, whose *Descent of Man* proposed a perfectible theory of sexual selection and thus subordinated love to technique. And past Darwin to Friedrich Schiller, whose operative metaphor for the play of freedom and rigor, play and form, was always choreographic: "the disordered leaps of joy become the dance, the formless gesture is changed into an amiable and harmonious pantomime."[69] Schiller on grace:

> Grace is a kind of movable beauty; I mean a beauty which does not belong essentially to its subject, but which may be produced accidentally in it, as it may also disappear from it. It is in this that grace is distinguished from beauty properly so called, or *fixed* beauty, which is necessarily inherent in the subject itself. Venus can no doubt take off her girdle and give it up for the moment to Juno, but she could only give up her beauty with her very person. Venus, without a girdle, is no longer the charming Venus; without beauty she is no longer Venus.[70]

Ontologies of dance; foundations of love.[71]

PLEASURE AND EFFICACY

PART ONE

How to Change Sex Like a Pragmatist

It must be seen that the ordinary definition of the personal pronouns as containing the three terms, *I*, *you*, and *he*, simply destroys the notion of "person."

—ÉMILE BENVENISTE, "THE NATURE OF PRONOUNS" (1956)

I

Trans Realism and Its Referents

"Woman's genital organs arouse an inseparable blend of horror and pleasure; they at once awaken and appease castration anxiety."

—SARAH KOFMAN, *THE ENIGMA OF WOMAN: WOMAN IN FREUD'S WRITINGS*

WHATEVER ELSE LITERARY REALISM has in common with psychoanalysis, they share at least this: they are too often assessed purely on the basis of their depictions of objects and too rarely understood as practices of self-care.[1] Within realism, the objects that detain readers consist of individual characters or character types, historical situations or themes, and poignant little details. Within psychoanalysis, they can include luridly contrived pathologies, theories of psychological development, and vivid symptoms. Yet for their creators, realism and psychoanalysis were both also techniques to be evaluated not just on the basis of their elegance, but on the basis of their efficacy. George Eliot and Sigmund Freud both claimed for their writing a therapeutic power that could help readers and patients lead happier and more fulfilling lives. These descriptive and normative goals sometimes conflicted.[2] But the therapeutic impulse was never fully subordinated to the abstract in either Freud's or Eliot's career, so that as late as his "New Introductory Lectures on Psycho-Analysis" in 1932, Freud could privilege the "practical" task of psychoanalysis (which called for a "technique") over the "theoretical task," which "can only be a theory."[3] Likewise, it was not merely the young Eliot of *Adam Bede* (1859) that extolled the power fiction holds to moderate unrealistic expectations; the narrator of Middlemarch laid down a truth for all of that novel's grateful readers when concluding that "things are not so ill with you and me as they might have been."[4] These techniques, of realism and psychoanalysis, work to deprive readers and patients of the pleasure that beautiful but damaging fantasies provide and to supplant that pleasure with the deeper sense of well-being that comes from having grown into the ugly world. That, in short, is the premise for this essay, which attempts to describe the rhetoric of "realness," that Eliot and Freud, perhaps surprisingly, share: an address designed to persuade their patients and readers to relinquish a beautiful fantasy and face a discomforting truth about the inadequacy of their own material existence. Against the Romantics' attempt to make the desirable possible, realism and psychoanalysis persuaded their addressees that the possible was, after all, desirable.

Of course, as soon as we have accepted that premise, we realize it cannot possibly be so simple—that the relation of self to self encompasses the regime of objects in crucial ways. Our problem derives from the complexity of the word *real*, which means a number of different (and contradictory) things, including: theoretically plausible (realistic); mimetically reproductive of the material world (naively realist); actually existing; praiseworthy on the basis of honesty or authenticity. To take an important recent addition to this sequence: in *Redefining Realness*, Janet Mock reframes the transgender coming-out narrative to place realness not as a type of socialization (that is, realness as passing) but as a theory of subjectivation (that is, realness as accepting an apparently impossible truth about oneself).[5] The titular definition that Mock contests derives from the vocabulary of the documentary *Paris Is Burning* (dir. Jennie Livingston, 1991) and specifically from the film's "sage" (Mock's term), who defines realness as, again in Mock's words, "the ability to be seen as heteronormative, to assimilate, to not be read as other or deviate from the norm."[6] Yet although it is an "ability," or a complex of abilities, Mock argues that trans women and femmes do not understand realness as a kind of performance but as a kind of embodiment: "a trans woman or femme queen embodies 'realness' and femininity beyond performance by existing in the daylight."[7] This realness is not ratified by the outside world—"a world that told me daily that who I was would never be 'real' or compare to the 'real' thing"—so, accordingly, it is felt as a relinquishing of both social interpellation and egoistic control of a trans woman's personhood; it is felt as surrender.[8] The last sentence of *Redefining Realness* is: "Eventually, I emerged, and surrendered to the brilliance, discovering truth, beauty, and peace that was already mine."[9]

In literary historical terms, we might say that Mock's account of realness dislodges the term from the domain of romantic irony and reconstructs it as a realist psychology. Defending *Paris Is Burning* against the antitrans feminists for whom mtf trans expression is necessarily "an imitation based on ridicule and degradation," Judith Butler argues that "identification is always an ambivalent process . . . [that] involves identifying with a set of norms that are and are not realizable, and whose power and status precede the identifications by which they are insistently approximated."[10] Not so for Mock, whose narrative indicates that the very instability of social regimes of identification and introjection necessitates the grounding of the sexed subject in a psychic terrain reducible neither to socialization nor embodiment. What Mock calls here "the brilliance" is often casually referred to in medical terms as gender dysphoria, and I shall refer to it here as *trans realism*. By using this term, I mean to introduce into trans theoretical writing a term responsive to the ontologies of trans life absent the categories of parody and drag and to orient us away from the descriptions of trans as instability, fuckery, or interstitiality that reduce such ontologies to intellectual or aesthetic patterns. The realism on which Mock's redefinition turns may be characterized as the overwhelming feeling that one's body is not sexed adequately and that one's claim on the world depends on a self-shattering acknowledgment of that fact; the method by which it is accessed is not experimentation but submission, not appropriation but surrender.[11]

The notion that realness, the only realness worth the name, derives from a rejection of the social coding of the sexed body is, I will argue, surprisingly consistent with the realist rhetoric of Eliot and Freud, both of whom took the reversal of an apparently unassailable premise about the sexed body as the most real aspect of their projects. Indeed, I will argue that our understanding of Eliot's literary realism and Freud's psychoanalysis is merely hypothetical and formal until we have reckoned with the account of transsexuality that underpins both these projects. Trans realism appears in Eliot as the ethical injunction to re-sex the body, an injunction that, in startlingly literal terms, the author formerly known as Mary Ann Evans materialized in the masculine figure of Eliot, a figure for whom the term "masculine pseudonym" has never proven persuasive. In Freud, it appears as the bedrock fact of sexed subjectivity, but a subjectivity only partially or tentatively grafted onto the biological matter of the body and returning to consciousness as the two perennial truths of neurotic experience—penis envy and castration complex—whose literally fundamental presence within proprioceptive consciousness proves to the neurotic subject that, at any moment, sex can be and is subject to change. The second step of this essay's argument, then, is to demonstrate not merely that realism operates as a technique for these two writers, but that they both, somewhere near to the center of their intellectual projects, sought to reorient through technique the subject's relation to the sexed body. For Eliot, realism will not have been achieved before the reader has fully grasped the clumsy, ugly truth of the human body that therefore he or she is, a truth that must be imparted through novelistic craftwork, and indeed comes to define the novelist's craft in such moments as Eliot reaches to account for it. For Freud, castration complex and penis envy form, on the one hand, the ontological ground of neurosis and therefore the asymptote that psychoanalytic psychotherapy continually approaches; on the other hand (or rather, by virtue of that asymptotic relation), the utopian possibility of overcoming or thwarting penis envy or the castration complex suffuses Freud's writing on technique, an apparently inert metadiscourse by which the physician can prove the practical utility of the psychoanalytic method. The type of realism that comes into view when one foregrounds the question of technique, then, is not necessarily mimetic; nor does it in any necessary sense enjoy a privileged relation to history, as György Lukács argues.[12] On the contrary, a negation of the actually existing world's conventional pieties is the foundational gesture of both Eliotic and Freudian rhetoric. But this is not to deny that the normative element of realism is intimately connected with the descriptive or aesthetic element. The *Oxford English Dictionary* (*OED*) treats these meanings of realism separately, as "characterized by faithfulness of representation" (which it dates to 1829) and "concerned with, or characterized by, a practical view of life" (which it dates to 1869),[13] but as Raymond Williams points out in his genealogy of realism, the two are hardly so separate. The "practical view of life" is, after all, the view from the boardroom, and accordingly, "realistic" is "an immensely popular word among businessmen and politicians."[14] That realist novels have plots, and that the success in those plots is usually figured simply as commercial gain or heterosexual world-building, might incline us to think that realism has established the contract of self-care in what Fredric Jameson describes as "bad faith": it simply wished, after all, to hollow out some desires that might have been troubling to the bourgeois class that produced and circulated novels and, using a complex network of stylistic trickery, rewire their husks with less ambitious fantasies.[15] Nonetheless, the realness of Eliot's realism does not depend on any judgment about the ontology of the worlds it calls into being. "Better knowledge is ultimately hidden knowledge," the psychoanalytic critic Jacqueline Rose observes of *Middlemarch*: true and hidden within the subject supposed to know.[16]

Consider the following passage of the novel, which has some claim on being the single realest moment in the whole novel and whose "awful fidelity" was picked up by Eliot's reviewer in the *Edinburgh Review*.[17] Nicholas Bulstrode, publicly shamed and ruined for his financial misdeeds and his part in the death of the alcoholic, Raffles, sits awaiting his wife, Harriet, to return, not knowing how she will respond to his disgrace:

> It was eight o'clock in the evening before the door opened and his wife entered. He dared not look up at her. He sat with his eyes bent down, and as she went towards him she thought he looked smaller—he seemed so withered and shrunken. A movement of new compassion and old tenderness went through her like a great wave, and putting one hand on his which rested on the arm of the chair, and the other on his shoulder, she said, solemnly but kindly, "Look up, Nicholas." He raised his eyes with a little start and looked at her half amazed for a moment: her pale face, her changed, mourning dress, the trembling about her mouth, all said, "I know"; and her hands and eyes rested gently on him. He burst out crying and they cried together, she sitting at his side. They could not yet speak to each other of the shame which she was bearing with him or of the acts which had brought it down on them. His confession was silent, and her promise of faithfulness was silent. Open-minded as she was, she nevertheless shrank from the words which would have expressed their mutual consciousness as she would have shrunk from flakes of fire. She could not say, "How much is only slander and false suspicion?" And he did not say, "I am innocent."[18]

The goal of this passage is to make even the experience of being shamed desirable, and that goal is achieved with brutal efficiency: the recitation of oddly zeugmatic phrases ("his eyes bent down"; "her changed, mourning dress") disorients the reader enough to find the conspicuous plainspokenness profoundly reassuring, as though we were ourselves undergoing the experience of grace Harriet confers upon Nicholas. Especially the pacifying repetitions, which resonate with an almost maternal sleepiness: "was silent . . . was silent"; "she could not say . . . he did not say." The passage risks a kind of pedantic literalism—"putting one hand on his which rested on the arm of the chair, and the other on his shoulder"—in order to produce a powerful aesthetic of straightforwardness. Although the novel's narrator articulates this climactic state of intimate incapacitation between spouses, for the most part, as a series of negatives, nonetheless the "mutual consciousness" that obtains between the two characters is tender and even utopian; Harriet's "promise of faithfulness," after all, indicates to the reader (though not, explicitly, to Nicholas) that the condition that exists between them at this moment has some chance of enduring. But nonetheless, the encounter between the Bulstrodes is not epiphanic, if that word implies discovery and heroic breakthrough. Nobody learns anything, and Harriet's "new compassion" is tempered by an "old tenderness." Rather, in this powerful moment, *Middlemarch* demarcates an aesthetic realness predicated on acceptance of a shared condition; of two people beginning to recover from their despair, to heal the shame of one and the suspicion of the other. To describe this moment as realism is to ascribe that aesthetic not to objective, but to subjective phenomena and, in this sense, is one of any number of moments in the novel where the same happens: when Dorothea finally confronts her feelings about Casaubon, and when she and Will are finally honest with each other.

Nor, obviously, does psychoanalysis primarily represent objective phenomena; just as the vehicle for Eliot's realism was fiction, Freud's stock-in-trade mostly consisted of fantasy on both sides of the ledger: his patients' dreams and stories for his own grand mythopoetic narratives. The name Freud gives to the cognitive experience of the real world—the reality principle—is one of the richest and most contradictory ideas in his oeuvre: the reality principle entails an exchange of fantasy for reality, where what one loses (fantasy) is both present and false; what one gains (reality) is both absent and true. The psychical difficulties of that implied quadratic detain Jean Laplanche and Jean-Bertrand Pontalis in their brief gloss on Freud's reality principle, in which from multiple angles they strive to demonstrate that the mental experience of reality does not supersede but in fact precedes fantasy, just as the instinct to self-preservation must have preceded the sexual instinct.[19] So readjusted, reality within psychoanalysis is not the sole authority against which instincts and desires are tested, but a felt dimension of psychic life itself. Not merely one fantasy among many, but not the singular antithesis of fantasy either, reality can only enter into psychic space, as it were, obliquely.

In short, it was the remit of both Eliotic realism and Freudian psychoanalysis, then, to subsume both the realm of objects and the entire business of getting to know them and talk about them, within the domain of what Michel Foucault calls the "*epimeleia heautou*,"or the care of the self; glossing Marcus Aurelius, Foucault describes self-care as "a sustained effort in which general principles are reactivated and arguments are adduced that persuade one not to let oneself become angry at others, at providence, or at things."[20] As Foucault's mixture of passive construction ("are adduced") and middle voice ("persuade one not to let oneself become") suggests, however, self-care is not as simple as it sounds and involves a nuanced rhetorical positioning in which the analyst/novelist's task is to persuade the patient/analysand to give up a satisfying hallucination in favor of a less satisfying, but *realer*, self-relation.[21] In this sense, the rhetoric of ugliness is an attempt to answer the most serious objection to a self-relation of realism, which Freud himself articulates in his 1917 paper "Mourning and Melancholia":

> It is a matter of general observation that people never willingly abandon a libidinal position, not even, indeed, when a substitute is already beckoning to them. This opposition can be so intense that a turning away from reality takes place and a clinging to the object through the medium of a hallucinatory wishful psychosis.[22]

Not only does Freud appear to contradict the possibility of realism in the sense outlined above, he does so in a pair of sentences that could almost, were it not for the words "libidinal" and "psychosis," be taken for Eliotic—ascribing a hard truth to "general observation" before illustrating it with the authority of personal experience.[23] And this problem concerning the relation between the pedagogical and erotic dimensions of the realist project has been at the center of a number of recent major essays on Eliot. Gallagher's essay concludes with the claim that Eliot "is the greatest English realist because she not only makes us curious about the quotidian, not only convinces us that knowing its particularity is our ultimate ethical duty, but also, and supremely, makes us want it."[24] David Kurnick, perceiving in Gallagher's formulation an echo of a nineteenth-century debate over "whether the novel reader was (erotically) entranced or (intellectually) edified," answers: "always both . . . implicit in Eliot's method of making characters is the idea that novel reading offers access to a kind of insight through submission."[25] And a formulation similar to Gallagher's opens a recent essay by Mary Ann O'Farrell: the admission that "George Eliot makes me want to be bad."[26] Though Gallagher and O'Farrell surely have different objects in mind, yet how suggestive their common formulation "to make [one] to want," a formulation that resolves Freud's doubt regarding the abandonment of a libidinal position by synthesizing an external injunction (exhorting the patient to accept an ethical norm) with an internal decompression (permitting the patient to acknowledge what they already want)—what psychoanalysts might call a therapeutic decathexis, or unblocking.

We can already see that self-care is a complex procedure, glimpsed only intermittently throughout these two oeuvres, one that must to some degree efface their technique. James Strachey, the editor of the English translation, remarks that "the relative paucity of Freud's writings on technique, as well as his hesitations and delays over their production, suggests that there was some feeling of reluctance on his part to publishing this kind of material," attributing that reluctance to Freud's dislike of "the notion of future patients knowing too much about his technique" as well as his insistence that "a proper mastery of the subject [of psychoanalysis] could only be acquired from clinical experience and not from books."[27] Moreover, in the *Papers on Technique* itself, Freud expresses his awareness that his understandable anxiety that patients' access to psychoanalytic technique would ruin the magic (specifically, would drive the patient's resistance to treatment further into the unconscious and distort their dreams) was, profoundly, a question concerning the elegance of any psychoanalysis requiring vocabulary drawn from the discourse of aesthetics:

> I submit, therefore, that dream-interpretation should not be pursued in analytic treatment as an art for its own sake, but that its handling should be subject to those technical rules that govern the conduct of the treatment as a whole. Occasionally, of course, one can act otherwise and allow a little free play to one's theoretical interest; but one should always be aware of what one is doing.[28]

The rhetoric of psychoanalytic technique therefore accomplishes two quite divergent ends: first, it protects the patient from knowledge that will inhibit their progress; second, it protects the analyst from the embarrassment of having been caught up in their own aesthetic experience. If one therapeutic purpose of psychoanalysis is the strategic disenchantment of aesthetic phenomena—the draining of the fantasy of the beautiful—then the rhetoric of technique appears both as a pure discursivity deprived of any aesthetic illusion and as capturing the rhetoric of aesthetics ("art for its own sake"; "a little free play") and ascribing it to the analyst's experience of the treatment.[29] In order to maintain the ruse, however, Freud notoriously foreclosed that very aesthetic (and erotic) dimension of the analyst's own experience in the same *Papers*, offering nothing more than a "warning against any tendency to a counter-transference which may be present in [the analyst's] own mind."[30]

The repudiation of countertransferential expression comports, clearly enough, with Freud's general injunction in the *Papers on Technique* that "the doctor should be opaque to his patients and, like a mirror, should show them nothing but what is shown to him."[31] The impassive word "doctor," moreover, replaces references to the more labile young and eager psychoanalysts, whose understandable but callow impulses towards individualizing themselves for their patients Freud seeks to redress. On the other hand, the *Papers on Technique* offer an account of psychoanalytic practice notable for its flexibility and frank emphasis on the analyst's spontaneity. There is only, Freud announces, "a single precept" to be borne in mind, which is that "the doctor must put himself in a position to make use of everything he is told for the purposes of interpretation."[32] This rule is merely the "counterpart to the 'fundamental rule of psychoanalysis' which is laid down for the patient," that is, to the principle of letting one's speech be governed by free association that Freud outlines in "On Beginning the Treatment": "you must say [the unimportant or nonsensical thing] precisely because you feel an aversion to doing so. Later on you will find out and learn to understand the reason for this injunction, which is really the only one you have to follow."[33] Lest the new analyst suspect Freud of overstating the case, he also clarifies his position that technique is useful to the extent that it enables the free play of the interpretive faculty (which alone will ensure the success of the treatment) and unhelpful to the extent that it displaces the metapsychological research merely to become another metadiscourse constricting the flow of language and interpretation between patient and doctor:

> One of the claims of psychoanalysis to distinction is, no doubt, that in its execution research and treatment coincide; nevertheless, after a certain point, the technique required for the one opposes that required for the other. It is not a good thing to work on a case scientifically while treatment is still proceeding—to piece together its structure, to try to foretell its further progress, and to get a picture from time to time of the current state of affairs, as scientific interest would demand. Cases which are devoted from the first to scientific purposes and are treated accordingly suffer in their outcome; while the most successful cases are those in which one proceeds, as it were, without any purpose in view, allows oneself to be taken by surprise by any new turn in them, and always meets them with an open mind, free from any presuppositions.[34]

The desire for an iterable protocol by which symptoms might reliably be alleviated encounters its formal opposite: the free play of the faculties in an aesthetic state of contemplation. The result is a technique of zero technique—or, rather, a technique that subtends the discourse only as rhetoric, as the insistence that doing nothing, "without any purpose in view," is the most technically astute technique of all.

When the first idea came to Freud in 1909 for the text that became the *Papers on Technique* was "'a little memorandum of maxims and rules of technique,'" supposed to circulate among a very limited readership of practicing analysts.[35]

The six papers themselves were written and published separately between 1911 and 1913, and, despite the sequence of their publication being interrupted by other papers—crucially, for these purposes, by "Formulations on the Two Principles of Mental Functioning" (1911), the first major articulation of the "reality principle"—they were republished together in 1918 and are still treated as a single text in the *Standard Edition*. The *Papers on Technique*, that is to say, exist in an unusual relation to the rest of Freud's oeuvre; we read them in a breach of professional protocol quite unlike the breach of privacy in which we read, for example, the dreams of Freud's unnamed patients or the detailed diagnoses of the more celebrated ones. A similar breach, or "pause" is the precondition for the self-theorizing of realism in Eliot's first novel proper, *Adam Bede*, which breaks off a third of the way through for "Chapter XVII: In Which the Story Pauses a Little."[36] Or rather, the narrative is interrupted by a voice ascribed to the reader:

> "This Rector of Broxton is little better than a pagan!" I hear one of my readers exclaim. "How much more edifying it would have been if you had made him give Arthur some truly spiritual advice. You might have put into his mouth the most beautiful things—quite as good as reading a sermon."[37]

This chapter has been examined in more or less every theoretical framing of Eliot's realist aesthetics to date—understandably, since it is so uniquely positioned as an argument for realism and therefore invitingly orthogonal to realism. Readers of novels were, and are, of course, used to being addressed. Indeed, Eliot has already done so by the second sentence of *Adam Bede*, in a tone closer to a contract than an intimate disclosure: "This is what I undertake to do for you, reader."[38] But to be the object of a narrator's prosopopoeia is an altogether more unusual affair—no less because, introduced now as "one of my readers" rather than the singular "you," any intimacy conveyed by narrative apostrophe has been decisively violated. Rather than a confidant or even a co-negotiator, the reader is cast as merely one among a mob of dullards—indeed, put in the curious position of not being the addressed reader, but another reader over whose shoulder somebody else is heckling the narrator, who responds:

> Certainly I could, if I held it the highest vocation of the novelist to represent things as they never have been and never will be. Then, of course, I might refashion life and character entirely after my own liking; I might select the most unexceptionable type of clergyman, and put my own admirable

> opinions into his mouth on all occasions. But it happens, on the contrary, that my strongest effort is to avoid any such arbitrary picture, and to give a faithful account of men and things as they have mirrored themselves in my mind. The mirror is doubtless defective; the outlines will sometimes be disturbed, the reflection faint or confused; but I feel as much bound to tell you as precisely as I can what that reflection is, as if I were in the witness-box, narrating my experience on oath.[39]

The narrator's response revises one model for realist narration, the mirror, and replaces it with another, the "oath." As we have seen with Freud's injunction that analysts behave like mirrors, the mirror metaphor was not as simple as he, or indeed Eliot, might have wanted. In *Adam Bede*'s first sentence, the narrator had conjured an image of mimetic reproduction supervened not only by an Orientalist idiolect, but by an image contrived to conjoin opacity with reflectiveness: "With a single drop of ink for a mirror, the Egyptian sorcerer undertakes to reveal to any chance comer far-reaching visions of the past."[40] J. Hillis Miller has synthesized this image elegantly: "The mirror mirrors itself, not an external world which corresponds point for point to the sequence of the narrative."[41] But the "as if" clause conjoining narrative art to legal testimony is surely no less complicated in the context of a novel whose narrative resolution depends on a religious confessor's capacity to obtain a truth that the witness-box had been unable to supply. Such witnesses who appeared in the trial of Hetty Sorrel for infanticide are not depicted but described to Adam (who waits outside the courtroom) by Bartle Massey in gently cynical terms: "the counsel they've got for her puts a spoke in the wheel whenever he can, and makes a deal to do with cross-examining the witness, and quarrelling with the other lawyers. That's all he can do for the money they give him."[42] When the novel's central event (Hetty's murder of her child) is finally narrated, it is not in the witness-box but "In the Prison" (the name of the chapter)—and not to a courtroom weighing evidence, and therefore sensitive to rhetorical construction, but to the confessor Dinah Morris, whose only role is "to be with you, Hetty—not to leave you—to stay with you—to be your sister to the last."[43] Indeed, the realness that Hetty's confession approaches, like the realness of the encounter between the Bulstrodes, is conditioned upon the verdict already having been passed—a species of honesty not positioned as an alternative to the witness-box, but as a type of narrative dependent on the functioning, and then departure, of the social apparatus of judgment. The difference between the style of Hetty's confession and that of the narrator of *Adam Bede* is more than that the character's speech is spoken ("subsumed to her own story as orally remembered and renewed," as Garrett Stewart puts it) and the narrator's written.[44] Rather, the prison scene captures a version of realism whose telos is purgative, not persuasive, the effect being a story that is both profoundly inconsistent ("'I did do it, Dinah'"; "'I didn't kill it'"; "'I didn't kill it myself'"; "I couldn't kill it any other way"; "I put it down there and covered it up"; "I couldn't cover it quite up") and, obviously, true.[45]

To return to chapter 17: the mirror and the witness-box having been raised and, the first explicitly and the second ironically, complicated as defenses of realism, the narrator sets up a third possibility, that of readerly self-interest. The reader's objection describes a first-order pleasure that might be obtained from the broad-brush caricatures Eliot is eschewing—or at least claiming to eschew:

> Perhaps you will say, "Do improve the facts a little, then; make them more accordant with those correct views which it is our privilege to possess. The world is not just what we like; do touch it up with a tasteful pencil, and make believe it is not quite such a mixed entangled affair. Let all people who hold unexceptionable opinions act unexceptionably. Let your most faulty characters always be on the wrong side, and your virtuous ones on the right. Then we shall see at a glance whom we are to condemn, and whom we are to approve. Then we shall be able to admire, without the slightest disturbance of our prepossessions: we shall hate and despise with that true ruminant relish which belongs to undoubting confidence."[46]

Before describing the narrator's response, let me note in passing that the first interlocutor—"one of my readers"—appears to have been swapped out for another character, "perhaps you." The styles of the passages are a little different too: the first, the reader that was, so to speak, addressing the narrator from over your shoulder, was impetuous and enthusiastic; "perhaps you" is pompous, cruel, and very clearly a satirical personification. The narrator's response, however, does not register that switch, and turns instead to appeal to the reader's self-interest:

> But, my good friend, what will you do then with your fellow-parishioner who opposes your husband in the vestry?—with your newly-appointed vicar, whose style of preaching you find painfully below that of his regretted predecessor?—with the honest servant who worries your soul with her one failing?—with your neighbour, Mrs. Green, who was really kind to you in

> your last illness, but has said several ill-natured things about you since your convalescence?—nay, with your excellent husband himself, who has other irritating habits besides that of not wiping his shoes? These fellow-mortals, every one, must be accepted as they are: you can neither straighten their noses, nor brighten their wit, nor rectify their dispositions; and it is these people—amongst whom your life is passed—that it is needful you should tolerate, pity, and love: it is these more or less ugly, stupid, inconsistent people, whose movements of goodness you should be able to admire—for whom you should cherish all possible hopes, all possible patience.[47]

This second, more satirically constructed interlocutor is now possessed of an ostentatious set of predicates, whose conspicuous features the reader is, paradoxically, invited to adopt for herself: you have been sick but have recovered; you are a propertied and married woman whose husband holds some ecclesiastical position; you have no realistic hope of escaping a living situation that, evidently, brings you little joy. This is the same procedure in reverse, I think, as the characterization of Mary Garth that Gallagher details. There, a rhetorical construction ostensibly designed to render Mary representative of a type ("ten to one you will see a face like hers in the crowded street tomorrow") proceeds instead by superadding characterizing details such as "perfect little teeth" that render Mary less of a type, but more of a character. Leading, Gallagher observes, to this remarkable effect: "the progression the reader is asked to follow from sighting a Mary to tasting one, from distanced viewing to more intimate sensation, figures the movement from type to fictional particularity as, paradoxically, a process of increasing embodiment."[48] Here, that fictional embodiment is, even more paradoxically, the reader's own: if, stuck in romantic fantasies about human beings, we find ourselves unable to accept the necessary problems of everyday life, the proposed solution is to cultivate a love for the "ugly, stupid, inconsistent" people that, implicitly, we have allowed ourselves to become.

Over a few more paragraphs, Eliot's narrator illustrates the proposition that ugly people are to be not merely accepted, but desired, in order that readers learn to accept the inevitable disenchantment of the world. The bodies in question are always sexed and exhibited with sadistic, satirical precision.[49] The major theme that emerges from their descriptions is erotic desire, the type of which is introduced through "an awkward bridegroom" and "a high-shouldered, broad-faced bride" surrounded by "elderly and middle-aged friends . . . with very irregular noses and lips"—an entire social confection of heterosexual defectiveness, which the author attaches to other stock characters as well: a "friend or two" of the narrator, on whom "the Apollo curl . . . would be decidedly trying," and the "motherly lips" of the women who admire them; the "young heroes of middle stature and feeble beards" and the "wife who waddles," with whom they permit themselves to be "happily settled."[50] What might feel like an oversupply of examples of the same thing drives towards a payoff whose effect is likewise dependent on the quantitative difference between beautiful and ugly people: "There are few prophets in the world; few sublimely beautiful women; few heroes. I can't afford to give all my love and reverence to such rarities: I want a great deal of those feelings for my everyday fellow-men."[51] That is to say, although "ugly" here is the underprivileged side of a binary construction, that construction is not merely reversed—this is not merely "an inverted romance," as Ian Watt calls the mistaken view of realism as simply "life from the seamy side."[52] Rather, the ubiquity of bodily dysphoria works to break a primal link between beauty and desire, and, like Bulstrode, who is erotically drawn to his own moral failings, we are drawn to confront our physical inadequacies without euphemism—our fatness, our unevenness, the inadequacy of our facial hair—and to encounter ourselves as degraded, and desiring, bodies.

So, this "perhaps you" is no less ugly than the others. But why must "you" be endowed with that especially demeaning characteristic, an attribute that, after all, belongs firmly within the domain of aesthetics, rather than ethics? Some readers have been tempted by a peculiarly tenacious (and, it need hardly be said, deeply misogynist) biographeme that has resurfaced recently in, for example, Rebecca Mead's *New Yorker* article "George Eliot's Ugly Beauty" and by Lena Dunham's 2013 tweet offering the "thesis" that Eliot was "ugly AND horny!"[53] In thrall to a barely disguised (and fairly Eliotic) eroticization of the ugly, Henry James panted that she was "magnificently ugly, deliciously hideous"; in a more maudlin mood, Eliot's early twentieth-century biographer Anne Fremantle reflected that "it must be a terrible sorrow to be young and unattractive: to look in the mirror and see a sallow unhealthy face, with a yellowish skin, straight nose, and mouse-colored hair."[54] Yet, though Eliot's letters and personal writings disclose some self-consciousness when it came to looks, one finds nothing to justify either James's panting or Fremantle's concern-trolling. Eliot self-describes as an "anxious, fidgety wretch" and rues that "I had never been good and attractive enough to win any little share of the honest, disinterested friendship there is in the world."[55]

One word with which Eliot never self-describes, however, is the word that the narrator of *Adam Bede* is especially eager to foist upon the novel's reader and the world at large: *ugly*. That word—which does indeed occur frequently in Eliot's correspondence—is reserved primarily for architecture—and, more specifically, for the type of Continental European buildings that smack of Catholicism: the streets around the Trinità di Monte in Rome; St. Peter's Cathedral in Rome; Rome itself; Prague Castle; the theater in Dresden; the effect of marble statues on the otherwise splendid chapel in San Lorenzo; the leaning towers of Bologna; the Council Chamber in Florence; closer to home, the Welsh seaside town of Llandudno; and, most puzzlingly and ambiguously of all, the effect on a view of the Alps of one's needing to look at them sideways because the sun is in one's eyes.[56] In other words, Eliot reserves for fiction this particular phenomenology of physical displeasure; in the letters, ugliness is not merely unfleshed; it is associated with the very tropes—ornamentation, fashionableness, filigree—against which it is euphemistically contrasted in *Adam Bede*.

some pronouns for the author of *Middlemarch*

Middlemarch's pronouns are important, and the novel *knows* they are important. I won't pretend that they are the "key" to *Middlemarch*, a word, in any case, Eliot teaches us to mistrust—to substitute with "tomb." In one sense, pronouns are important because (like many things Eliot valorizes) they are unremarkable, pragmatic, and nearly invisible. Neither our eyes nor our minds savor them as they do the novel's spicier words: "*Parerga*," "*morbidezza*," "squirrel." (Though "squirrel" actually occurs twice.) They are words to which *Middlemarch*'s narrator occasionally draws our attention, because they cannot draw attention to themselves. But more to the point, pronouns have come to interest me as I've been beginning to write about the rhetoric of realness, because they refer to people and things that they don't represent—that are "elsewhere in the discourse," as the *OED* has it. Their unique capacity to specify particular objects ("him"; "me"; "that") without representing them directly might additionally strike a reader as especially important in the context of realism, a literary mode that also depends on the play of abstraction and particularity, ontogeny and phylogeny, individual and type, among whose recurring themes are the paired questions "how will I be referred to?" and "how should I refer to others?" Pronouns in English possess an additional unique and bizarre characteristic: that, despite the obvious fact that we can group objects in any number of ways—some are evangelical lay preachers, some are merely hamlets, some are wealthy, some have just knocked over the water pitcher, etcetera—only one such taxonomic scheme exerts a grammatical effect upon the English language: gender. But it is plain weird, if one is prepared to unlearn the fact in a conspicuously naïve way, that the English language uses gendered pronouns at all, as though we required different prepositions to describe all the ways in which objects can be in contact with a tea table rather than a writing table.

Since the notion of a "trans Eliot" has become controversial in recent years—partly, I should admit, because of my own publications on this topic—some clarification on this point might be prudent, though I will suggest that such wariness is occasioned not by any ambiguity in the terms I'm using, but by the extraordinary lengths that scholarship has gone to neutralize, arrest, and curtail gender nonconformity in Eliot's novels. These might sound like strong words, but they are sometimes used quite self-consciously. For Gillian Beer, for example, Eliot was a writer who "sought to slough off the contextuality of her own name and enter a neutral space for her writing."[57] Henry Alley prefers "the quest for anonymity" as a name for Eliot's vibe, and associates the novelist's labor with the "hidden life" and "unvisited tombs" of *Middlemarch*'s unhistoric number. I realize of course that Beer does not think Eliot completes this "escape from gender," or believe such an escape possible, but even as a description of fantasy her account only tells the less important half of the story: the fantasized liberation of a self from a disenchanted (and gendered) body into a data stream of liquid indexicality, apparently as free of gendered particularity as "reality" itself. But a trans Eliot would subordinate that (negative) notion of writing as the erasure of gender to its converse, the (positive) proliferation and conspicuous manifestation of genders, against and apart from those with which we conventionally work.

A second discrimination: "George Eliot," I contend, was something less than an identity but more than a name for the person whose first given name was "Mary Ann Evans." As readers of Eliot's work we are asked, for whatever reasons and with whatever degree of subjective investment, to treat that work as produced by a masculine author-function, an invitation that a large majority of Eliot's readers have chosen to decline. We have done so for a variety of reasons, some of which (it goes without saying) are very good. Some have limited their speculations to the field of the literary text and choose their gendered pronoun based on an interpretive claim about the narrator (to take two of the best examples of either choice: Robyn Warhol uses "she" for the narrator; D. A. Miller uses "he"), others (Kathryn Bond Stockton is particularly self-conscious about this) problematize their own references to Eliot as *her* in the name of a feminist politics, and many have concluded that Eliot's masculine self-presentation was merely a tactical disguise designed to fox her publisher, William Blackwood, requiring no particular deference from a readership that considers itself in the know. Even if so, however, the implied distinction between an "authentic" and a "tactical" deployment of masculine or feminine pronouns strikes me as pretty shaky, insofar as no expression of selfhood could, entirely, divest itself of social interest, especially in relation to gender; nor could an attempt to access social or institutional space ever fail, entirely, to symptomatize an interior condition. That problematic provides the setting for what I take to be an antitransphobic approach to Eliot. I ask us, then, to forget the familiar premises with which we are accustomed to approaching this question: centrally the premise that, generally or always, female authors have published under male names in order to obtain social recognition under the conditions of patriarchal oppression—a premise that, while obviously true in many cases, always obscures as much as it reveals (why do we refer to "George Eliot" but not "Currer Bell"?) and, more importantly in the case of Eliot, will tend vastly to oversimplify the psychic motivations for and consequences of such survival strategies.

In the middle of *Middlemarch*, towards the end of the final chapter of the fourth book, Dorothea Brooke rages, for the first time, at a man's "unresponsive hardness."[58] Her rage takes the form of an interior monologue thick with pronouns: "What have I done–what am I–that he should treat me so? He never knows what is in my mind–he never cares. What is the use of anything I do? He wishes he had never married me."[59] These *he*'s refer, obviously, to Dorothea's husband, Edward Casaubon, but Dorothea has not spoken the name "Edward" yet in the novel—she will not do so, indeed, until fifty pages later when she begins their *final* conversation with the question "Are you ill, Edward?"[60] Literally speaking, then, this masculine pronoun does not replace a proper noun ("Edward" or "Mr. Casaubon" or even "my husband"), but substitute for one. It could only be Edward, but the reader is left to infer this fact because we understand that Edward is the salient *him* in Dorothea's life; the biographical particularity ascribed to Casaubon retreats to make room for a vivid formulation of the symbolic relation between *him* and *me*; "Now she said bitterly, 'It is his fault, not mine.'"[61] If this moment is consequential, for Dorothea or for the novel, it is because she has successfully unlearned the content of her relationship with her husband and grasped it in its purest form, stripped of equivocation and euphemism. Eliot elevates Casaubon's pronoun, in other words, *above* his proper noun, both in the aesthetic sense that the word "he" *means* more here than would Edward's name, and in the psychological sense that the "he" enables Dorothea to work through a cathexis that, the novel has taken pains to tell us, has been inhibiting her spiritual and intellectual growth, no less than her erotic development. Later, in another interior monologue, Rosamond Lydgate comes to a similar conclusion about her own marriage, but her use of her husband's proper name—"it was Lydgate whose intention was inexcusable"[62]—makes clear how little she has grasped about their real symbolic relation, how estranged from him and from herself she has allowed herself to become.

Taken as a discourse on the relationship between character and type, the above analysis might seem merely to contradict, in pedantically linguistic terms, a famous observation of Gallagher's about *Middlemarch*, that the novel's tension between typical signification (that signified by the *he* and *she*) and fictive particularity (that identified by the *Edward* and *Dorothea*) is generally resolved in favor of the latter. Yet, as I have been thinking about this problem, I have been increasingly returning to the French structural linguist Émile Benveniste. In the essays collected in *Problems in General Linguistics*, Benveniste developed a powerful and persuasive theory of language as a vehicle for the communication of subjective experience. At the root of this explanation is an account of the personal pronoun as the logical and psychic foundation of linguistic communication, an avatar exported from consciousness into the world, where it both speaks for interiority and, somehow, reports back to it: "Language is possible only because each speaker sets himself up as a *subject* by referring to himself as *I* in his discourse. Because of this, *I* posits another person, the one who, being, as he is, completely exterior to 'me,' becomes my echo to whom I say *you* and who says *you* to me."[63] Communicative language exists in the crevice between the *I* emitted by one person and the *you* by which it is met; on the other side of that *you* is a person untouchable by language, and on the other side of this *I* is a soul that will never find its way *into* language. This set of conditions demarcates the discursive limits of the branch of linguistics Benveniste calls "pragmatism"—a usage quite distinct from the Peircean mode I discussed above.[64]

Middlemarch indeed draws its readers' attention to many such utterances of *I*. Met by the unwelcome news that her husband is in debt to the tune of three hundred and eighty pounds, Rosamond Lydgate asks, "What can *I* do, Tertius?" to which the narrator appends the observation:

> That little speech of four words, like so many others in all languages, is capable by varied vocal inflexions of expressing all states of mind from

> helpless dimness to exhaustive, argumentative perception, from the completest self-devoting fellowship to the most neutral aloofness. Rosamond's thin utterance threw into the words "What can *I* do!" as much neutrality as they could hold.[65]

Here, "neutrality" means inert, spiteful coldness. Rosamond's *I* is sent into the world to delimit her sphere of responsibility, stipulate her dissent from her husband's affective condition, and protect her own subjectivity from contamination by whatever radiation that condition is transmitting back at her. The pronoun as ambassador; the pronoun as prophylaxis. For Benveniste, this entire universe of subjective expression can only exist in the space between two words—the *I* and the *you*. And, like Benveniste, Eliot distinguishes between the rhetorical work of the first- and second-person pronouns and the work of the third-, but reverses the values. When Dorothea comes to her husband to begin what will be their last conversation, we again encounter a discourse thickly populated with pronouns—in this case, *I* and *you*. (In a novel possessed of such lexical largesse as *Middlemarch*, our attention is drawn the more keenly to the passages of simplicity.) Yet where "it is his fault, not mine" enabled Dorothea, however contingently, to surpass a blockage and find a way out of her claustrophobic state, the *I* and *you* that pass between husband and wife stultify, ossify, and fix the two participants in the discourse in their unhappy places.

> "Are you ill, Edward?" she said, rising immediately.
>
> "I felt some uneasiness in a reclining posture. I will sit here for a time." She threw wood on the fire, wrapped herself up, and said, "You would like me to read to you?"
>
> "You would oblige me greatly by doing so, Dorothea," said Mr. Casaubon with a shade more meekness than usual in his polite manner. "I am wakeful; my mind is remarkably lucid."
>
> "I fear that the excitement may be too great for you," said Dorothea, remembering Lydgate's cautions.
>
> "No, I am not conscious of undue excitement. Thought is easy."[66]

As though resentfully following the letter, but not the spirit, of advice from a marriage guidance counselor—"use *I*-statements!"—the Casaubons address each other lovelessly through the intermediaries of *I* and *you*. If the passage entails anything like hope, it is administered by a third-person narrator that can say "she" and describe what Dorothea did, "threw wood on the fire," without requiring the deadening self-positioning that the dialogue so excruciatingly ekes out. But that is hypothetical: what is punishingly clear is that the ballet of *I* and *you* fails even to achieve the respect for the alterity and personhood of the other that, the imaginary marriage counselor thinks, it has been choreographed to secure. It is precisely through pronouns that Edward Casaubon launches his most outrageous assault on the autonomy of his wife, in the form of his last wish: "It is that you will let me know, deliberately, whether, in case of my death, you will carry out my wishes, whether you will avoid doing what I should deprecate and apply yourself to do what I should desire" (449). In *Middlemarch,* as the *I* seeks to expand its dominion over the *you,* the *he* retains the capacity to function independently.

We have been watching a debate take place over how Dorothea should absorb an object—Casaubon—into the world of her own consciousness, not as a mere auxiliary to her ego, but as a constituent and determining *component* of that ego itself. In psychoanalysis, this absorption is called "introjection," and although best known now through the hyperbolic idea of "incorporation" that Freud describes in *Mourning and Melancholia* and *Instincts,* introjection was first theorized by Sandor Ferenczi in 1909 as a name for the "growing onto" objects that enables people to feel anything about anybody else at all.[67] Indeed, for Maria Torok, the logic of introjection runs quite counter to that of incorporation, since while the latter idea induces a mode of relation organized around the consumption of a taboo object, an "eminently illegal act," the former works to unleash repressed libidos that are inaccessible to the ego.[68] "Thus," Torok writes, "it is not at all a matter of 'introjecting' the object, as is all too commonly stated, but of introjecting the sum total of the drives, and their vicissitudes as occasioned and mediated by the object."[69] The *unconscious drive* and the *regime of objects* are far more alike to each other than either resembles the cognizing ego.

Which is not to say such moments are always felt as mourning. When, later, Dorothea bids Will Ladislaw goodbye for the second and final time, the narrator remarks: "It was in her nature to be proud that he was blameless, and through all her feelings there ran this vein—'I was right to defend him.'"[70] Here the "him" that serves as a proxy for Dorothea's "nature" is a positively, rather than negatively, invested object, but again the narrator makes clear that the vitality of the psychic relation depends on the transference of a certain portion of selfhood onto an object relation. The consequence, at this point, is that Dorothea is exhibited to the reader in one of her more aloof, priggish aspects, yet what might appear as one symptom of secondary narcissism (the treatment of other subjects as mere objects) is in fact, Eliot has taken pains to show us, a symptom of something like its inverse: Dorothea's increasing equanimity concerning her own objectlikeness, her burgeoning capacity to forego her self-righteousness in favor of the erotically, ethically neutralizing condition of being—in this moment at least—relatively free from her more self-examining instinctual neurosis.

A subjective condition becoming referential, ceding authority over its selfhood to lines of social relation: such is the porous condition that, in its more optimistic modes, we are used to thinking of as Eliotic sympathy. But there are much more menacing modes of address too, including a nightmarish version of the same idea as the threat of *rumor* that attaches at different points to Ladislaw (over his parentage), Casaubon (over his putative cuckoldry), Rosamond (over her faithfulness—the cheeky twist being that Dorothea, whose moral narcissism thrives on feeling misunderstood, becomes the mistaken *observer* of a scandal), and chiefly to the two brothers in ruin, Bulstrode and Lydgate. Despite the general anxiety over reputation and, therefore, reference that suffuses the mental lives of each of our focal characters and governs most of their choices, for good and ill, Eliot delays until chapter 71 a full representation of actual gossiping, in the form of a chorus of minor characters divided into the gendered spaces of the Green Dragon and Dollop's to pore over the fortunes of the professional class. It has been observed that *Middlemarch* is at its most Dickensian when it thematizes rumor most directly—critics have detected something fishy in the naming of Mrs. Dollop, Raffles, Joshua Rigg, etc.—as though the bringing into discourse of a *vox populi* could not be achieved without doing the voices of "Mr. Popular Sentiment" himself.[71] Yet while these parabasic stagings of reference extort from Eliot a performance of genre not entirely the novelist's own, the interior monologues of characters anticipating being talked about incorporate far more smoothly the generic tropes of Eliot's trashier contemporaries. The first and perhaps most dramatic of such occurs in the tale of Mme. Laure, Lydgate's murderous French paramour whose very theatricality appears itself metadiscursive, the tale oscillating between diegetic and metadiegetic spaces like an echo: "Paris rang with the story of this death: was it a murder?"[72]

The novel's smooth absorption of an otherwise squalid tale from far beyond the provincial life of the Midlands attests to one of the genre's most celebrated features—its rough, patchwork polyphony. Yet where Dickens delights in such polyphony as its own aesthetic and political end, in *Middlemarch* it is one of a number of techniques for querying relationships between experiencing subjects (in this case, Lydgate) and the referencing social world (in this case, not merely Paris but the melodramatic genre). So, it is not precisely that

Middlemarch is preoccupied with rumor, but that the novel repeatedly rehearses the ambivalent excitement and dread entailed by the fantasy that one is going to be talked about. Perhaps inevitably, the aftermath of that ambivalence, when it is represented at all, turns out to be quite different from the fantasies that preceded it. At the end of chapter 70, Lydgate nervously plots a new beginning after having been helped out of a tight spot by Bulstrode: "I shall set up a surgery . . . if Rosamond will not mind, I shall take an apprentice."[73] Yet as well-founded as are Lydgate's doubts about his professional prospects, and about his wife, within a couple of pages he has been drawn into a scandal involving murder and grand larceny on a scale previously unimaginable; he is no longer being referred to as a callow neophyte with a maniacal taste for cadavers, but as a paid accomplice in the murder of John Raffles. Bulstrode, too, expedites Raffles's death in order to suppress rumor ("the judgement of his neighbours and the mournful perception of his wife"[74]), and having catalyzed the alcoholic's demise by brandy, believes himself free of rumor: "his conscience was soothed by the enfolding wings of secrecy."[75] The law of genre dictates, as no reader of *Middlemarch* will have failed to predict, that Bulstrode will be denuded of these wings: what is striking though is how *quickly* he is plucked from them, and how little direct representation Bulstrode is able to make in his defense, whether at the town meeting where he is challenged, or in the profoundly moving encounter with his wife that passes largely in silence. Despite its reputation for loquacity, *Middlemarch* has no taste for litigation: if you're explaining, you're losing.

Which is surely the lesson to draw from Casaubon's unfortunate, if comical, self- cuckolding-by-proxy—"one of his freaks," Mr. Brooke calls it, being, Sir James Chettam chimes in, to have "framed" a "codicil . . . so as to make everyone believe that [Dorothea wanted to marry Ladislaw]."[76] Somehow through Casaubon's bungling, even the word "codicil" acquires a pronominal quality, as though it were not merely both a rhyme and a synecdoche for "Will," but additionally an echo for "Ladislaw": he whom Casaubon would have designated the "lad I slew," made, rather, the symbolic beneficiary of his "lady's law." The profusion of alveolar laterals in Ladislaw's "slippery name," as Raffles calls it to himself when trying to retrieve a word "almost all *L*'s" a few chapters later,[77] may or may not have been among the aspects of his characterization that Henry James saw as glitchy: "[Ladislaw] is, we may say, the one figure which a masculine intellect of the same power as George Eliot's would not have conceived with the same complacency; he is, in short, roughly speaking, a woman's man."[78] But the narrator of *Middlemarch* (or perhaps George *El*iot) deploys Ladislaw as a self-surrogate in sometimes surprising ways. Shortly after the details of Casaubon's will have generated gossipy rumors about his cousin, Will, among the Middlemarchers, the narrator generates one of the novel's most stereoscopic constructions of free indirect discourse: stereoscopic because, unless one is following the pronouns quite carefully, it isn't easy to subordinate the various consciousnesses being represented. Lydgate has unknowingly mentioned Ladislaw to Dorothea as "a sort of Daphnis in coat and waistcoat," not knowing the rumor concerning the codicil and having forgotten his wife's tattling about Will's crush on Mrs. Casaubon:

> Happily Dorothea was in her private sitting-room when this conversation occurred, and there was no one present to make Lydgate's innocent introduction of Ladislaw painful to her. As was usual with him in matters of personal gossip, Lydgate had quite forgotten Rosamond's remark that she thought Will adored Mrs. Casaubon. At that moment he was only caring for what would recommend the Farebrother family, and he had purposely given emphasis to the worst that could be said about the vicar in order to forestall objections. In the weeks since Mr. Casaubon's death he had hardly seen Ladislaw, and he had heard no rumour to warn him that Mr. Brooke's confidential secretary was a dangerous subject with Mrs. Casaubon. When he was gone, his picture of Ladislaw lingered in her mind and disputed the ground with that question of the Lowick living. What was Will Ladislaw thinking about her? Would he hear of that fact which made her cheeks burn as they never used to do? And how would he feel when he heard it? But she could see as well as possible how he smiled down at the little old maid. An Italian with white mice! On the contrary, he was a creature who entered into everyone's feelings and could take the pressure of their thought instead of urging his own with iron resistance.[79]

Clearly the first sentence locates Dorothea and describes, if not her state of mind directly, at least the conditions of possibility for her state of mind. The following two sentences, with only a shade more ambiguity at that initial "him," draw us into Lydgate's thoughts. From there on it gets trickier, since while "he had hardly seen Ladislaw" feels defensive in a characteristically Lydgatean manner, "he had heard no rumour to warn him" could not, being a negative formulation, refer to anything happening within the doctor's head. We become more aware of the breathlessness of the narrator's alliterative aspirations, too; what Eve Marie Stwertka writes about as the "oral tradition" dimension of the narrator's voice.[80] Lydgate's *H*'s are supplanted, then, by a set of *L*'s, the narrator gallantly passing the conch from one character to the next with phonic as well as semantic cues, "when he was gone, his picture of Ladislaw lingered . . . that question of the Lowick living." Note, too, that in order for that transition to take place, we need to emphasize the "her" in "lingered in her mind" more than initially feels intuitive, since "Mrs. Casaubon" had appeared in the previous sentence merely as a prepositional object and is now, via a pronominal reference, elevated into the syntactical position of subject. The passage's coup de grace, however, is to associate this very facility of consciousness-hopping with Will Ladislaw himself: "he was a creature who entered into everyone's feelings, and could take the pressure of their thought instead of urging his own with iron resistance." Ladislaw's low-key sexy passivity merges with the novel's own structure of reference; a structure Eliot constructs not merely from themes, but through a complex psychic syntax that takes in both pronominal reference and, weirdly, the letter *L*.

Now, nobody likes Will Ladislaw, from Sir James Chettam through Henry James to any number of contemporary readers for whom the little Daphnis's brittle charisma withers into dry vapidity in the stately shade of the grand widow Casaubon.[81] It would probably be cheap—and, in any case, kind of obvious—to remark that his very inadequacies as the hero of a marriage plot are precisely the qualities that make him a powerful surrogate for a trans masculine author figure: his capacity to "enter into everyone's feelings" without tarrying inside them for long; his effeminate, playful creativity that neither fully hardens into a *künstlerroman* plot nor gets negated by a professionalization narrative; the familial history compiled piecemeal from various accounts.[82] But it might be worth briefly reflecting on Ladislaw's unique position in the composition history of the novel. *Middlemarch*, as we know, was the result of a synthesis and expansion of two stories on which Eliot had been working in 1869 and 1870: "Miss Brooke" (the Dorothea plotline) and "Middlemarch" (the Lydgate/Bulstrode plotline). Since Ladislaw is the only character in the novel that plays a major role in both stories, there circulates around his emplotment a somewhat irritatingly magical air: as Jerome Beaty puts it, "that Will Ladislaw, his first wife's grandson, should appear in [the Midland town where Bulstrode remarried] is coincidence enough. That Bulstrode's second wife (née Vincy) should have a relation (Peter Featherstone) whose illegitimate son (Joshua Rigg) had a stepfather (Raffles) who had been an associate of Bulstrode's in London and had indeed helped Bulstrode keep Will's mother from her rightful inheritance, is surely an incredible multiplication of coincidence which operates on a level of reality quite different from that of the rest of the novel."[83] Beaty observes, reasonably enough, that "the complicated plot contrivance is an attempt to tie the two stories together"[84]—and goes on to treat Ladislaw, again credibly, as a prototype for Daniel Deronda. But not only is the rumor of Ladislaw's Jewishness not, in fact, instantiated by what we know of his ancestry, what Beaty's explanation undersells is the gendered work that Ladislaw does for the novel as he shuffles between the masculine plot of professional ambition and its tragic collapse, and the feminine plot of marriage and remarriage, belonging comfortably to neither and playing the role of spoiler in both. Will Ladislaw: *Middlemarch*'s trans hero/ine.

"the may-beetle dream"

> She called to mind that she had two may-beetles in a box and that she must set them free or they would suffocate. She opened the box and the may-beetles were in an exhausted state. One of them flew out of the open window; but the other was crushed by the casement while she was shutting it at someone's request.[85]

This dream is one of the three with which Freud illustrates "the work of condensation," perhaps the most important technique by which, he held, the mind transforms fantasies beyond the reach of consciousness into the content of dreams.[86] It is the most important because, as many of Freud's readers have emphasized, the condensation of multiple elements of fantasy into a single image—that a beetle may simultaneously represent disgust, compassion, and sexual desire—is a procedure without fixed limits. Condensation respects no economy of scarcity; more and more meanings may always be discovered to have been condensed within a single image, and consequently not merely is the interpretation of a dream an interminable procedure, as Freud has acknowledged from the start, but even the interpretation of any particular element of a dream is inexhaustible. This account of interpretation showcases Freud at his most broadminded and the project of psychoanalysis at its most utopian: the unconscious mind he depicts is limitless in its resources and capacity for creativity. A claustrophobic narrative about two fragile junebugs, meanwhile, has violated the no less fragile sense of infinite possibility even before one of them has been killed. Indeed, the stupefied cruelty of the may-beetle dream possesses a bathetic force that seems to push Freud onto the defensive; uncharacteristically, he remarks that he will offer only "part of the analysis" of this particular dream; that he will "not be able to pursue the interpretation of the dream to the end" and that consequently "its material will appear to fall into several groups without any visible connection."[87]

So it does. In most respects, the thematics of the dream turn out to be epiphenomena of bourgeois heterosexuality's stock repertoire, as the concern for an animal derives from two sources: (1) the dreamer's having read a book in which "some boys had thrown a cat into boiling water, and had described the animal's convulsions";[88] and (2) the action of her fourteen- year-old daughter, with whom she was in bed and who had observed, but not remedied, a moth having fallen into her glass of water just as they were falling asleep, so both dreamer and, perhaps, daughter lay in guilty anticipation of a bug's death. Her unhappy marriage had taken place in May and was beset in a tedious sort of way by her husband's "aerophobic" sleeping habits, which chafed with her own "aerophilic," which tension appears in her dream as the ambivalent outcome of closing the window.[89] The closest thing Freud offers to an explanation of the whole, however—"the wishful thought concealed by her present dream"—is rather strange, since it interprets the slamming window as a peculiar presentation of penis envy.[90] Crushed beetles, like that mechanically produced by the slamming of the casement (in line with her husband's aerophobia), are the primary ingredient of the aphrodisiac known as Spanish fly, and so what might otherwise have appeared as a castration image has been transformed into its formal opposite: "the wish for an erection."[91] Strachey retains the German construction "may beetle" as a translation of *Maikäfer* in order to maintain the connection to the diurnal rhythms of the dream; nonetheless, the Anglophone reader learns from his footnote that the "commoner English equivalent . . . is 'cockchafer.'"[92] A footnote of Freud's own, meanwhile, refers to Heinrich von Kleist's play *Penthesilea,* about the sexually insatiable Amazon queen who devours her discarded lovers—the only moment in the entire *Interpretation of Dreams,* according to Didier Anzieu, where the association between oral sadism (biting) and castration anxiety converges on a woman, rather than a man.[93]

The interchangeability of fear (of castration) and desire (for a penis) is a well-worn psychoanalytic theme; indeed, in Sarah Kofman's influential reading of these phenomena, the female patient's desire for a penis serves the theoretical purpose of assuaging or deferring the fear of castration. Reading between Freud's papers on fetishism and Medusa, Kofman observes: "Woman's penis envy thus . . . provides man with reassurance against his castration anxiety; the horror inspired by Medusa's head is always accompanied by a sudden stiffening (*Starrwerden*), which signifies erection."[94] Yet the possibility of literally switching one of these complexes for another, a possibility latent in Freud's interpretation of the may-beetle dream, is unusual, not just in Freud's own work, but among the many trenchant critiques of psychoanalysis that have focused on penis envy as mere male wishful thinking. This idea returns forcefully, however, as a rhetorical pairing of castration complex and penis envy in the final paragraphs of Freud's final technical paper, "Analysis Terminable and Interminable," published in 1937, many years after the *Papers on Technique* were first assembled and published: "At no other point in one's own analytic work does one suffer more from an oppressive feeling that all one's repeated efforts have been . . . 'preaching to the winds,' than when one is trying to persuade a woman to abandon her wish for a penis on the ground of its being unrealizable or when one is seeking to convince a man that a passive attitude to men does not always signify castration and that it is indispensable in many relationships in life."[95]

"These two themes," Freud holds, comprise "some general principle"; accordingly, "in spite of the dissimilarity of their content, there is an obvious correspondence between the two. Something which both sexes have in common has been forced, by the difference between them, into different forms of expression" ("A," 250). Sure that the fear of castration and penis envy constitute the "bedrock . . . the rock-bottom" of the analytic, Freud morbidly concludes that the bedrock is, after all, natural and occluded from the ambit of technique and that consequently "the repudiation of femininity can be nothing else than a biological fact, a part of the great riddle of sex."[96] It is not that these particular mythopoetic framings (castration complex and penis envy) are, exactly, true; rather, they have become names for the asymptote of sexual difference towards which analysis of both men and women grinds interminably on.

Yet Freud's explicitly melancholic assessment obscures a complexity in his response; the admission of a sense of defeat in the face of sexual difference ("the oppressive feeling" that one is "talking to the winds") was in one sense remarkably performative, specifically in his decision to adopt Alfred Adler's term "masculine protest" to describe men's "struggle against [their] passive or feminine attitude towards [an]other [male]."[97] Adler had developed that term in 1910 to describe the "ramified feminine traits carefully hidden by hypertrophied masculine wishes and efforts" that he had observed among male neurotic patients.[98] Since which time, Freud loathed Adler and this "reactionary and retrograde" theory: "one has the impression that somehow repression is concealed under 'masculine protest.'"[99] Adler died in the same month that "Analysis Terminable and Interminable" was published, prompting Freud to write cruelly to Arnold Zweig: "For a Jewish boy from a Viennese suburb . . .

a death in Aberdeen, Scotland is an unprecedented career and a proof of how far he had come. Truly, his contemporaries have richly rewarded him for his service in having contradicted psychoanalysis."[100] In the paper itself, Freud had allowed himself to produce a more evenhanded assessment of both the value and the limitation of his old colleague's nomenclature: "It fits the case of males perfectly; but I think that, from the first, 'repudiation of femininity' would have been the correct description of this remarkable feature in the psychical life of human beings."[101]

Freud wrote *The Interpretation of Dreams,* of course, before the castration complex and penis envy were fully articulated theories, although after rearranging the manuscript of *The Interpretation of Dreams* into the chronological order of its composition. Anzieu is able to date the discovery of castration anxiety to autumn 1898, "almost certainly" the period in which Freud heard about the may-beetle dream.[102] And in one sense, the dream does seem to precipitate the fuller articulation of the theory in the *Essays on the Theory of Sexuality* (1905) and the *Analysis of a Case of Phobia in a Five-Year-Old Boy* (1909); the image of the window crushing the bug subsumes both the desire for a penis and the fear of losing one, in a cycle as infinite as, though far less cheerful than, condensation itself. To be possessed of a penis is to be permanently in fear of losing it, which (if it happened) would assuage the fear but create anew the unquenchable desire to possess one. To lack a penis, likewise, is to organize one's desire around gaining a penis, which if achieved would immediately create the urgent problem of defending it against the threat of castration. We are accustomed to seeing the system of sexual difference that structures Freud's thinking about fear/desire, as a binary division demarcated by a firm line. But the line in the may-beetle dream—the window—is an agential object possessed of its own force. The dream analysis stumbles into the queer polysyndeton of sexual difference, imagining a fear of castration stemming from the nonpossession of a penis, or a desire for the penis of which one is already possessed.

So much for the crushed beetle: both sloughed-off penis and germ of an erection to come. But what of the beetle that escapes? It is surely the relation between the two ostensibly like objects (beetle and beetle) that prompts the irruption into the analytic scene of, who else but, the Victorian novelist George Eliot. It is difficult to track exactly how that irruption takes place:

> The patient reflected over this contradiction. It reminded her of another contradiction, between appearance and character, as George Eliot displays it in *Adam Bede*: one girl who was pretty, but vain and stupid, and another

> who was ugly, but of high character; a nobleman who seduced the silly girl, and a working man who felt and acted with true nobility. How impossible it was, she remarked, to recognize that sort of thing in people! Who would have guessed, to look at her, that she was tormented by sensual desires?[103]

The patient is struck by the "contradiction between appearance and character." But is the *Adam Bede* association the dreamer's or Freud's? That is, it isn't clear whether the dreamer has herself associated that second contradiction with Eliot's novel or whether Freud is riffing on or glossing her initial association, either for the reader's benefit or for the dreamer's. The same ambiguity exists in the German: "*Er erinnert an einen anderen Widerspruch, den zwishchen Aussehen und Gesinnung, wie er in* Adam Bede *von der Elliot dargestellt ist*"[104]—in which Anglophone readers encounter another complexity, the parapractical interpolation of an additional *L*, about which there is no reason not to observe that the interpolated letter sounds the same as the principle syllable, "El[l]," nor that it is formed by a single, straight stroke of the pen, endowing thereby a name, already notoriously unstable with respect to the phallus, with an additional, albeit ornamental, appendage. Freud, we know from his correspondence with Martha Bernays, did read two of Eliot's other novels and took both to heart: *Middlemarch* as a guide to their developing romance, and *Daniel Deronda* as a strange and possibly suspicious repository of knowledge about the things Jewish people "speak of only among ourselves."[105]

I can put off no longer the inevitable admission that I have been trying to bring out, or at least to imagine worlds in which have been brought out, two authors: one, an Austrian doctor obsessed with the psychic ramifications of castration; the other, a Victorian novelist whose masculine pseudonym has, unlike "Currer Bell," stuck around—though nobody really bothers to explain the difference.[106] There is perhaps no need to do so.[107] Eve Sedgwick describes the queer theoretical position as oscillating between the poles of universalism and minoritization; trans criticism seems likewise to find itself pulled between a claim about interior identity ("this is who I am, underneath") and a theatrical negation of gendered convention ("I want to be irreferable, for language to slip off me as rain off a window"). Yet there is, I think, a certain pleasure one senses in Eliot, especially, contemplating the incognito of pseudonomized authorship, albeit a pleasure that Eliot sought to regulate among readers of the book who believed they could identify the author of *Scenes of Clerical Life*. To one such, Charles Bray, Eliot wrote, "There is no undertaking more fruitful of absurd mistakes than that of 'guessing' at authorship; and as I have never communicated to any one so much as an intention of a literary kind there can be none but imaginary data for such guesses."[108] Yet Eliot annotated such guesses, both general ("a clergy-man, a Cambridge man," a party at Helps's) and specific ("Eliot Warburton's brother," William Blackwood) in detailed journals, in which it is impossible not to sense a livelier feeling when Eliot had been thought to be a man than when thought to be a woman:

> [Blackwood] came on the following Friday and chatted very pleasantly—told us that Thackeray spoke highly of the "Scenes," and said they were not written by a woman. Mrs. Blackwood is sure they are not written by a woman. Mrs. Oliphant, the novelist, too, is confident on the same side, but both have detected the woman. Mrs. Owen Jones and her husband—two very different people—are equally enthusiastic about the book. But both have detected the woman.[109]

Eliot's glee when passing, and mild concern when not, have countless pragmatic explanations: the fear that a conservative publisher would jettison a writer living in sin; the impropriety of women writing about clerical matters; that patriarchy, in all places and at all times, organizes itself to the benefit of the creatures it designates as men. One might respond that Eliot simply did not like female authors and did not want to be associated with them. That would be a reasonable assessment of the author of an essay entitled "Silly Novels by Lady Novelists," which, while it elicits a good degree of delight in what it calls "feminine fatuity," is nonetheless steeped in antifemme contempt—or, indeed, of the author of an essay on Madame de Sablé that takes biological difference between the sexes as the root of differences between masculine and feminine literary styles.[110] On the feminine side of that equation are more or less the same femmy qualities that in "Silly Novels" comprise "the most trashy and rotten kind of feminine literature."[111] But there is also the pleasure and the radical encounter with the dysphorically sexed body that underpins their formulation of their aesthetics. By way of concluding, I will simply observe that it is unusual to align a literary writer with an analyst; psychoanalytic literary criticism invariably places itself in that position and the author (or, in the poststructuralist visions of psychoanalysis, the text) as the patient.[112] My decision to do so here does not derive from, or gesture towards, a new theory of psychoanalytic criticism. It simply extends from my own acceptance, after a couple of decades of reading, teaching, and trying to write about Eliot, of a truth that I cannot put any less vulgarly than this: one cannot top Eliot any more than one can fail to top James.

II

The King's Two Anuses

> It is distressing that someone entering the ranks of the professoriate—particularly someone who claims the credentials to teach about issues of free speech—should be unfamiliar with, or indifferent to, these foundational principles [of academic freedom]. Distressing, but perhaps not surprising, given how the pose of youthful outrage requires certain kinds of strategic ignorance concerning the accomplishments of earlier generations of activists. This is as true for those who would renounce commitments to academic freedom and free speech as for those who set themselves up self-righteously to "correct"—and when that doesn't work, to censor—gay, lesbian, and queer scholars who dare to question the litanies of your brand of trans-correctness. Is this demand to suppress voices that questions [*sic*] perhaps because you have no answers to our queries, starting with this one: what does it mean to claim to be "in fact" a woman?
>
> —CASTIGLIA AND REED

prelude

Desire is an ending. Identity, one would think, ends certain things. It ends, for example, the polysemy that precedes it; it is felt as an imposition, especially when it must be avowed. But it isn't a strong ending in the same way. It allows for play, secondary revision, fuckery, negotiation. Not so desire. Once desire lands, it's all over. So, my ending was this: at some point, I realized that I wanted to transform my body into a woman's body, that I had wanted to do that for a very long time, and that I wanted to do that more than I wanted almost anything else. Additionally, I wanted to transform the story of my body into the story of a woman's body, an even more unstable and asymptotic procedure. I think of my femme sister Elizabeth Freeman, who writes, "Erotohistoriography admits that contact with historical materials can be precipitated by particular bodily dispositions, and that these connections may elicit bodily responses, even pleasurable ones, that are themselves a form of understanding."[1] I know, and I know that she knows, that the history in question may be the history of the very body that is doing the experiencing. Beth talks of the butch dyke's dick not as a replacement for a penis, but as a commemorative object that stands in for the penis that the butch has always had. In such temporalities, one's body, in the present, now apprehends the past that perhaps it once merely inhabited, and grasps that body's knowledge of its past as its own to cherish. Pleasurable knowledge, but not just pleasure, and not just knowledge. So I think of Julie Andrews's beautiful voice, sounding clearer than the clearest thing:

> Perhaps I had a wicked childhood.
> Perhaps I had a miserable youth.
> But somewhere in my wicked, miserable past,
> There must have a moment of truth.
> For here you are, standing there, loving me,
> Whether or not you should,
> So somewhere in my youth or childhood,
> I must have done something good.[2]

Next to the voice, which is flawless, the most beautiful aspect of this song is the willingness to believe that grace existed in one's life, even when it cannot be remembered or retrieved—and not merely the kindness of strangers, but one's own grace. To interpret the world as though there had been something good in one's miserable past; to perceive that one is loved, as a woman is loved, and to allow that to be the proof that one was lovable.

What I am describing perhaps rather too airily is the phenomenon sometimes referred to as autogynephilia—the love of oneself as a woman.[3] It is a term derived from the work of Ray Blanchard, a highly controversial medical specialist in trans medicine, whose appointment as chair of the American Psychiatric Association's "paraphilia subworking group," in which role he helped to draft the *Diagnostic and Statistical Manual of Mental Disorders, Fifth Edition* (DSM-5)'s entry for "gender dysphoria," was widely criticized.[4] Blanchard's protest that his advocacy of ex-trans conversion therapy for teenagers was not inconsistent with support for adult trans people has been more difficult for his defenders to argue in recent years—at least since he became the kind of doctor who publicly describes trans identification as a kind of "demonic possession."[5] *Autogynephilia* is the term Blanchard and his "gender critical" supporters use to name those transsexuals whose sexual object choices are frequently women; the term therefore works to (1) deny the "realness" of a subset of trans women and (2) resurrect and project onto trans women the image of the untamable lesbian rapist whose very presence in public women's toilets, or any other female-centered environment, arouses uncontrollable sexual urges. I do not, by using the term *autogynephilia* here, then, concede Blanchard's hierarchizing of real and fake transsexuals; rather my goal is to align trans women with other queer women, both on the grounds of our arousing the same kind of sex panic and on the grounds that autogynephilic desire—a love of women that entails the fantasy that one is a woman—does not distinguish trans women from nontrans lesbians. On the contrary, the structures of desire and of fantasy are psychoanalytically indistinguishable.

Like narcissism, autogynephilia is both a species of auto-affection and an object choice. It is an attachment to the idea of "women" that presents itself as a desire to become one and often entails a female sexual object choice as well. Under conditions in which womanhood is associated with humiliation, this kind of desire finds itself caught in a paradox. It is a wish to be a thing that nobody would wish to be—indeed, a thing defined in some ways and by some people (including feminists) by its wish to be something else. In an essay concerning the impossibility of endings, Freud wrote that "the repudiation of femininity must surely be a biological fact, part of the great riddle of sex."[6] What kind of desire could occupy such a space, except either a masochistic one or a fetishistic one? It is the former diagnosis that has historically administered the connections between trans women and the affective dispositions of poignancy, faded glamor, and bittersweetness; the latter likewise connects trans women with the serial killer and his associated regime of body-horror nightmares.[7] These figurations depend on the shared premise that under conditions of patriarchy, transsexual desire must be transgressive and edgy, a premise that it has suited many, although not all, trans women's interests to affirm. For many of us, being trans is a gift. It is something good.

the one who speaks is another

The sigil by which ideology discloses the existence of trans people to the world is the discourse of free speech. Some historical justification for that claim will be necessary, since it will not appear self-evident to anyone unfamiliar with the state of the "trans issue" as it appears in public discourse.[8] But at the outset I wish to be clear that I am not going to argue—nor am I going to deny—that an entity, called variously "the media" or "social media," has manipulated the lives of trans people and misrepresented them in order to push an ideological debate about an abstraction. It is not obvious to me that "free speech" is any more or less abstract than "transness." Both of these terms describe an implicit theory of mind, and these theories of mind have a certain amount in common. For example, both are, in the terms proposed by Rei Terada, essentially "expressive" theories of consciousness that depend on the notion of an interior subject that is externalized and accommodated through the expression of emotion. In the opinion of the so-called free speaker, whether the figure one rotates into that position is Thomas Paine or Pepe the Frog, language is an unproblematic medium that communicates the free workings of free minds unless and until it is interdicted by power—which, when it happens, merely indicates the justness of the opinion that has been censored. For trans people, the fact of having transitioned is submitted as evidence that one should have transitioned—is does not so much imply "ought" as define it. In both cases the presumed efficacy of an action taken (speech or transition) constitutes retroactive proof of the viability of the expression, yet the reasoning is, in both cases, conspicuously circular. As Terada puts it, "The purpose of expression tropes is to extrapolate a human subject circularly from the phenomenon of emotion. The claim that emotion requires a subject—thus we can see we're subjects, since we have emotions—creates the illusion of subjectivity, rather than showing evidence of it."[9]

Consider, for example, the conventional—albeit, in many cases, entirely fictitious—framing of a trans life as that of "a woman in a man's body," an account that is only legitimized once a confession has been extracted of the type "I knew since I was a child." Meanwhile, the trans child who knows, and who says what she knows, is the very figure by which trans people are, in general, discredited. Nobody knows anything when she is a child; or, more directly, the episteme against which the knowledge of children is formulated is perpetually subject to secondary revision and reinscription through the interventions of parents, teachers, professors, johns, men, and the prison industrial complex. At some point between childhood and adulthood, trans people are required to have become people who always knew, to have interposed not merely a postulated subject capable of expressing, but a subject incapable of not expressing. Hence, the overexpressive and "extra" trans woman, too effusive and barely holding herself together, does not merely instantiate the expressive theory of subjectivity on which a claim for her civil rights would have to be based; she also embodies the stereotype by reference to which trans women can be deprived of those rights. Here, what we might characterize as a "liberal" account of trans life works to deprive trans women of the rewards that, in general, political liberalism exhibits as its greatest gifts.

At stake in these scenarios is precisely the question of a trans woman's capacity to speak and the governmental limitations on what trans women may say. These, however, are not the real problems that trans women face. To take a contrary example: it is well known that, in order to be prescribed the hormone replacement therapy, usually estradiol and spironolactone, by which trans women initiate their transitions, they must first be diagnosed with "gender dysphoria," as outlined in the DSM-5. Of course, neither doctor nor patient generally believes that trans identification is, or should be, a diagnosable pathology, and, generally speaking, neither party minds too much if the contract is agreed on the basis of a little white lie. The trans writer Dean Spade includes examples of many such tactical responses to the medicalization of transness in his essay "Mutilating Gender," and one is struck less by the force of the imposition of the lie than the ease with which lying seems to solve all of the problems it addresses. Trans people pretend to conform to the dominant identitarian narratives about transition in order to obtain their treatments.

So, to the promised historical evidence that transness is made visible under the sign of free speech, I will offer two quick examples, almost at random, the quality they share being that they have been published in major media outlets in the last two weeks. I have chosen them to give some sense of the rapidity with which trans controversies are confected at the present time. The first concerns an op-ed in the online periodical *Quillette* by the writer Meghan Murphy, who had founded an award-winning blog titled *Feminist Current*. Murphy's essay is written in defense of an asserted right to refer to trans women by their pretransition names and of using masculine pronouns. These practices she describes in the following terms: "'Misgendering' refers to the practice of identifying a biologically male individual as 'him' or 'he' if the individual identifies as a transwoman (or vice versa in the case of self-identified transmen). 'Deadnaming' refers to the practice of using the real name that a (now) trans-identified person used prior to deciding they wanted a new gender identity and the associated pronouns."[10] The argument that Murphy implies with these definitions is unambiguous: the category of person that we call a *trans woman* is a "biologically male individual" who at some point "decid[ed] they wanted a new gender identity," on the basis of which caprice the person now "identifies as" a woman and uses threats of legal and disciplinary action to enforce the suppression of a "real name." Once the phenomenon of trans life has been introduced in those terms, as an implied violation of the First Amendment rights of feminists, Murphy goes on to explain that "various governments in North America and Europe have passed laws that allow people to determine their own sex in a way that grants them unfettered access to women's facilities, such as change rooms, transition houses, shelters, bathrooms, and even jails." The reason why these laws are not more widely known, Murphy implies, is because of the gag order that prevents "the simple reporting of facts," which of course in this context includes—indeed derives from—the central "fact" that trans women are men.

Already at this early stage in the argument, a dialectical reversal seems all but inevitable. The speech act "I identify as a woman" has been, it will be remembered, extracted (sometimes violently) from the trans woman as a condition of transition; it was not, so to speak, spoken freely, even though it was chosen freely. It was a speech act that we might characterize as felicitous but faithless: in context, it works perfectly and is understood by all, but it is, nonetheless, extorted from trans people as a condition of medicalization. Now, Murphy argues, that extortion has been turned against a third party—"millions of ordinary, perfectly tolerant people who are deeply troubled by the way these sweeping new measures are being implemented"—who are forced to play along. The dialectical turn would be something like: demedicalize transition, on the one hand, and, on the other, confess the truth of Murphy's assessment of trans women as either pathological or perverted men. Versions of this position indeed seem to be growing in popularity among trans activists and writers for whom repetitive litigation of the statement "trans women are women" has become simply too draining to pursue.[11] Perhaps "dialectical" is the wrong term for a response on the part of some trans women that seems, rather, to accept that we've lost. In any case, the concession would not have been made without the framing of the issue around the question of freedom of expression, and particularly the freedom to express the idea "trans women are men." Murphy makes no attempt to defend or even to explain that proposition, but merely claims that it has been censored and that this is obvious. Neither the title nor the subhead of Murphy's article mentions trans people: it is called simply "Why I'm Suing Twitter," and below that Quillette posted a picture of the company's Tenderloin headquarters. There is no need to specify, because there is only one thing she would sue Twitter for: excessive deference to trans people.

The startling rapidity with which controversies surrounding trans people regenerate and supplant each other, along with the perpetual sense that trans discourse exists precisely as discourse to stifle and suppress speech, sustains a sense of crisis around trans issues while making individual outrages difficult to contest. The second quick example: on February 17, 2019, the lesbian tennis champion and gay activist Martina Navratilova published an op-ed in the *Sunday Times* purporting to explain why trans women should not be able to compete in women's sporting competitions but in fact once again turning to the theme of free speech in order to make the case.[12] Navratilova's editorial begins, "Shortly before Christmas I inadvertently stumbled into the mother and father of a spat about gender and fair play in sport. It began with an instinctive reaction and a tweet that I wrote on a serious forum dealing with the subject.... Perhaps I could have phrased it more delicately and less dogmatically, but I was not prepared for the onslaught that followed from a Canadian academic." When Navratilova finally articulates the argument that she claims has been censored, it resembles the plot of an Ealing comedy:

> To put the argument at its most basic: a man can decide to be female, take hormones if required by whatever sporting organization is concerned, win everything in sight and perhaps a small fortune, and then reverse his decision and go back to making babies if he so desires. It's insane and it's cheating. I am happy to address a transgender woman in whatever form she prefers, but I would not be happy to compete against her. It would not be fair.

Has this ever happened? Of course not. Does Navratilova seriously think it might? I doubt it. But the framing of trans lives as case studies in an ongoing conversation about free speech does not merely license, but in fact necessitates, ever more lurid and surreal speculations.

Eventually, the theme of free speech mutates into a performance of freedom that no longer needs to name itself as such. Reporting on Navratilova's dismissal from her position as spokesperson for Athlete Ally, an LGBT sports advocacy organization, a columnist in the conservative British newspaper the *Spectator* assessed the current state of women's sport in the following terms: "And meanwhile, blokes keep winning everything. Sometimes they are blokes who have had some becoming breasts appended to them and a bit of lippy, sometimes they are blokes who seemingly make no effort at all to disguise the fact that they are blokes."[13] Navratilova's intervention explicitly thematized the importance of speech and the sense that, in the presence of trans people, it was being stifled. In the *Spectator* editorial, that theme has been sublimated entirely into a principle of tone. In *Ugly Feelings*, Sianne Ngai problematizes that category by drawing an analogy between the tone of a literary or cultural work and aesthetic judgment in a more general sense. For Ngai, tone belongs neither to the object that one observes nor the observing subject, but is rather "the dialectic of objective and subjective feeling that our aesthetic encounters inevitably produce" (30). To name the tonal effect of the *Spectator* piece—induced by its signature technique of repeating *blokes* in a comically informal register—as "triggering" would not require evidence that anyone had been triggered, but would rather suppose that the general disposition toward the world in which the *Spectator* finds itself depends on the possibility of the suffering of trans women. An argumentative trope that began as a claim about the proper governance of the public sphere mutates by degrees into an ambient cruelty, felt in every domain but never precisely spoken. Hence the socialization of trans women, our emergence as political subjects, depends not merely upon insult in a general sense but on a specific theory of insult. Judith Butler's analysis of the insult—that "by being called a name, one is also, paradoxically, given a certain possibility for social existence, initiated into a temporal life of language, that exceeds the prior purposes that animate that call"—depends on a number of limitations on the effectiveness of the insult: on infelicity, on the semiotic shifting that may occur between its illocutionary and perlocutionary effects; on the possibility of the insult's being reclaimed or *détourné*.[14] It is by no means clear, however, that an analytic claim like "trans women are women" could survive any of these slips, either.

As I've already suggested, the "transgender rage" on which trans studies was founded may simply be too high-intensity an affect to survive an environment in which the dignity, personhood, and finally "social existence" of trans women is enabled, when it is, by an apparently intolerable affront to the speech of others.[15] Which is not to say that such rage would not be ethically necessary, or a precondition for any meaningful political response to these escalations, but rather, that the grounds on which rage might have arisen are populated otherwise with sadness and gallows humor. And, of course, suicide. The overall rate of suicide attempts among adolescents is 14 percent; for ftm, nonbinary, and mtf teenagers, it is 51 percent, 42 percent, and 30 percent, respectively.[16] These affective dispositions emanate from the meme cultures of online trans communities, in which suicidal ideation is both a theme and a method. This Luigi meme, for example, depicts a laconic desire that, according to its caption, "speaks for all of us" (see fig. 3). Yet speaking for all of us in this context is confusing: If the "us" in question were trans femmes (who do not, presumably,

FIG. 3. Trans_Memes_for_SadBeings, "I Might Look Like a Guy but I Want to Die." Instagram, Sept. 8, 2018.

want to look like guys), then why the "but"? If the presumed speaker is trans masc, then the implication is that looking like a guy is inadequate treatment for the suicidal ideation. Perhaps the joke is that guys aren't supposed to want to die; one thing trans boys and trans girls have in common, after all, is that they are both conspicuously different from nontrans men. The meme has been caught up in its own self-delighting and infantile performance of free speaking.

To juxtapose those figures with the hypothesis that an unscrupulous man might take advantage of excessive tolerance of trans people in order to win the French Open would be to risk being accused of bathos. And indeed, trans bathos, like that of the present chapter's title, may turn out to be a critical resource after all. But first, a brief personal interlude concerning Supreme Court Justice Brett Kavanaugh.

A BRIEF PERSONAL INTERLUDE CONCERNING SUPREME COURT JUSTICE BRETT KAVANAUGH

As is the nature of these things, I must now contradict the account of myself I gave at the start of this chapter. I must, truly; this is not a matter of choice. On September 27, 2018, a psychology professor named Christine Blasey Ford gave evidence to the Judiciary Committee of the United States Senate, evidence that would be weighed as the Senate decided whether or not to confirm Brett Kavanaugh to the Supreme Court. Ford's evidence, the credibility of which was initially agreed upon by all sides, including (at first) the president, consisted of a narrative of having been sexually assaulted by Kavanaugh and a young friend of his in high school. I shall refrain from recounting the rest of this history, except to say that in the days after Kavanaugh's confirmation on October 6, I became aware for the first time of the subtle, microbial gestures and glances by which terror (and its antibody, which perhaps should just be called "sisterhood," though it's an embarrassing enough term in some ways) circulates between women in public spaces. I felt a profound need for it, a need I had never quite allowed myself to notice before.

On the train as I headed into the city, I saw J., the ASL interpreter for the lecture class on Victorian literature I was teaching at the time. We'd never spoken, but now she asked me how I was doing, and I said I was feeling shaken. She said that she felt the same way. She drew an analogy between the Kavanaugh confirmation and other natural and political disasters. It feels like an enormous earthquake, she said, but one that only women seem to have noticed. I had noticed, and I knew that as she formulated those words she was thinking of me and drawing me into the zone of shared grief.

I was already there. I reached out my arm to her and she touched it, inside the commuter train. I cannot now remember whether I was still on the train or whether this happened later, but eventually my body became gripped by a logical proposition that was tested in the flesh and proven and has now become something I know about myself. It was: the brett kavanaughs of my life knew i was a woman before i did. But what was there to know? As everyone who has not transitioned thinks when they hear that someone else has, there are after all many ways to be a boy, and many concupiscences that feminine boys can arouse in generally heterosexual men. I have experienced such impulses from straight men; they are not what I am talking about. I am talking about a second body, a Grace that was there even before the doctors made me. This, I suppose, is the mystery of what Freud has taught us to call "latency." I embarked on this journey because I wanted to become a woman, not because I believed I had always been one. And yet I have discovered that in certain ways, at certain moments, for certain people, I have always been one. Latency presents as the discovery of an identity in the other end of desire—the identity that marks me as one who desires; the desire whose object is to be identified as desiring—dedramatized for me the statement "trans women are women," whose rather fragile realism I had, myself, felt a little too tired to bother with. I now suppose it to be a descriptive statement, rather than a petition. The phrase "trans women are women" means: we are already women.

All of the subtle questions one might wish to ask along the lines of "what does it mean to be, 'in fact,' a woman?"—and there are versions of that question more pressing than the one I have cited in my epigraph above (however aggressively I was put to it)—must ultimately test themselves not against Monique Wittig or Judith Butler, but against a fact that remained as conspicuous during the Ford and Kavanaugh hearings as in the "Open Letter" to me: if they could extinguish every one of us, at once, and get away with it, they would do so in a heartbeat.

I returned again to the witty defenses with which Butler opens *Bodies That Matter*, batting away the scandalized responses to *Gender Trouble* with a delightful and endearing little bit of memoir: "Actually, in the recent past, the question was repeatedly formulated to me this way: 'What about the materiality of the body, Judy?'"[17] Butler objectifies her experience quickly and formally, assigning to the speech "a certain patronizing quality which (re)constituted me as an unruly child," without registering much any of her own responses to being patronized. But the tone of the memoirist endures through the next few paragraphs in the form of free indirect discourse. As the rhetorical questions pile up, and climax in "Couldn't someone simply take me aside?," Butler's prose seems to learn that bad-faith performances of projective empathy tend to reveal more about the speaker than intended. Eventually, to dispel the rude pedants, Butler unveils the following reductio ad absurdum:

> Matters have been made even worse, if not more remote, by the questions raised by the notion of gender performativity introduced in *Gender Trouble*. For if I were to argue that genders are performative, that could mean that I thought that one woke in the morning, perused the closet or some more open space for the gender of choice, donned that garment for the day, and then restored the garment to its place at night. Such a willful and instrumental subject, one who decides on its gender, is clearly not its gender from the start and fails to realize that its existence is already decided by gender. Certainly, such a theory would restore a choosing subject—humanist—at the center of a project whose emphasis on construction seems to be quite opposed to such a notion.[18]

What chumps we all are! And Butler, too: it might be worth inquiring into which of this passage's various closets and costumes has disappeared the autobiographical "Judy" of the preceding passage. Is Butler mimicking her own fantasy morning routine, as though in the opening scenes of *The Truman Show*? Perhaps. The characterization of the "willful subject," after all, recapitulates the trope of the "unruly child" as whom she has been cast. Butler's auto-chumpification, if one might put it that way, opens up an unexpected identification in her text. Such a subject assumes, willfully, and as either an "unruly child" or an "adolescent" (to use a word from a different context), that she will decide who she will be today. But then, the psychic and political protocol according to which she devises her own willfulness is eventually exposed as an irresistible principle that she merely believed herself to have been manipulating. In this cartoon form, Butler's bowdlerized account of gender performativity strikes me as a viable description of the social position of trans women.

the king's two anuses

Regarding the hole in the middle of the facial plane of the forty-fifth President. Whether or not we allow ourselves the obviously merely compensatory pleasure of psychoanalyzing this particular hole, a choice that entails not merely a question of professional competence (the so-called Goldwater Rule) but also political strategy, I contend we can perceive, empirically, in the flesh itself as it is percussed by power, trauma, and disgust, an unmistakably excremental quality. I do not mean merely that this hole—like the one whose rhythms are mimicked in these very inky splotches on paper—enjoys both talking shit and shit-talking, and the rest of that kind of thing. Rather I observe, distinctive to this hole, a relation to language that works to dispense with it as quickly as possible, to slough words out of this slack anus mouth—an anus political—as though they were pig slurry. Speech is not articulated, or even properly speaking "symptomatized," from an interior onto an exterior, but ritualistically shed in a spirit of mortification; this mouth speaks in confident anticipation that the loathed flesh itself can and will be flayed from the body politic. (Loathed insofar as flesh, the substance of embodiment, is always feminizing if not, as Andrea Chu has suggested, always already female.)[19]

By treating this mouth as an "anus political," which does on behalf of a sovereign body the work that the backside does for a human body, I invoke Ernst Kantorowicz's 1957 history of the "the king's two bodies," a theory of medieval and early modern kingship that attributes to sovereign power both a body natural and a body political, which inhabit the world in very different ways. The differences between these versions of personhood are well known: the body natural ages, decays, and shits, whereas the body politic, in the words of Edward VI's lawyers, "is utterly void of Infancy, and old Age, and other natural Defects and Imbecilities, which the Body natural is subject to, and for this Cause, what the king does in his Body politic, cannot be invalidated or frustrated by a Disability in his natural Body."[20] This latter, figural body is thereby exempted from the exigencies of natural embodiment. The sovereign can't shit. There is, according to Michel Foucault, something else—perhaps more surprising—that the sovereign can't do: the sovereign cannot speak freely, cannot engage in the practice called *parrhesia*.[21] That term designates the rhetorical self-positioning (also and supremely an affective posture: the word means "boldness") that underpins not just the civil rights of citizens in Athenian democracy but, thereby, the rights discourse of "free speech" as it passes into the liberal rhetoric of the Enlightenment. And, for the Athenians Foucault describes, a man's choice to engage in free speech entailed a necessary relation to risk "since the tyrant may become angry, may punish him, may exile him, may kill him."[22] Accordingly, "it is because the parrhesiastes [the free speaker] must take a risk in speaking the truth that the king or tyrant generally cannot use parrhesia; for he risks nothing."

Speech and shit: a predictable enough association. But this was more than a mere historical oddity. It is a logical necessity that founds both the State and the University as interlocking but distinct institutions: by indexing the relative freedom of a speech act to its ability to, as the cliché has it, "tell truth to power," we thereby position the free speaker at some distance from the seat of power. Of course, we recognize that the parrhesiastes was a relatively privileged participant in a democracy: to engage in parrhesia, one must have been a free, natural-born male citizen of voting age. So the class was already limited. Nonetheless, the free speaker was not the king, and the king was not a free speaker—a contradiction that occasions what Foucault calls, throughout, a "crisis of democratic institutions."

In our present moment, the most visible sign of such a crisis is the spectacle of a sovereign power demanding access both to parrhesia and to the shit closet. We know, for example, that sovereignty presents itself not as power, but as powerlessness, the absolute anus of male victimhood, spectacularly harassed equally by the form of embodiment it has learned to call trans and the anonymized body that we, also learning, have begun to call "the deep state." Once, this power called that body "Sergeant Dobias":

DT: I'm standing there at the military academy and this guy comes out, he's like a bulldog, too, rough guy. He was a drill sergeant. Now they call him "Major Dobias," but he was a sergeant. When I first knew him, he was "Sergeant Dobias," right out of the Army. And he was a rough guy, physically rough and mentally rough. He was also my baseball coach. He said things like, "Stand up!" and I went, "Give me a fucking break." And this guy came at me, you would never believe it. I mean, it was really fantastic.

MICHAEL D'ANTONIO: Did he rough you up?

DT: Oh yeah, absolutely.

MD: Grabbed you by the shirt . . .

DT: It doesn't matter, it was not like what happens today. And you had to learn to survive. It was tough. It wasn't today. Those were rougher times. . . . These guys, you go back to some of those old drill sergeants, they can't even understand what's going on with this country.[23]

The speaker enjoys reciting the name "Sergeant Dobias" and feeling it in the cavity of his mouth as much as he enjoys reliving an historical memory of male intimacy—the brutal male violence specific to military intimacy—that, sadly, has been smoothed out with the times: "It was not like what happens today." Quite: the roughness of male bodies has been smoothed, and the speaker's persecutors are no longer "rough guys" whose violent love kindled the embers of an abusive paternal relation ("he was also my baseball coach"), but smoothly sexed bodies like that of the deep state, whose brutality lacks the bristly texture that renders male violence aesthetically and ethically justifiable. (Violence as antonym of and reagent to "flesh," ergo "male violence" as pleonasm.). A delight that emerged from a memory of pain—spontaneous and fragile—has been absorbed back into the shame that both animates and delimits every exterior cell of the traumatized body of Donald J. Trump. Here emerges again the specter of a male masochism that cannot be avowed and so is displaced in time ("not like what happens today"). In other words, the smoothening that has made this kind of pleasure impossible (whether by abolishing it or, more subtly, simply by refusing to ignore it) has produced for this body the desire to speak freely: to tell it like it is, to speak truth to power, to complain about "what's going on with this country," to reclaim the right to be rough.

A sovereign performative speech act that does not produce policy, but roughness, is the phantasmatic occasion, too, for the contemporary defense of free speech. It is a desire whose apparent sadism (the desire to punish, discipline, flay, abolish, mutilate, imprison, and chastise) merely inverts, as the Dobias anecdote makes clear, the primary masochism of this rough man (the desire to be beaten, cared for, roughed up, forgiven, let off, and loved). Thus, whenever we hear that a present-day "free speech advocate" such as the fascist provocateur Milo Yiannopoulos has some individual in mind for harassment and victimization, we hear shortly thereafter that he can take it as well as dish it out, that he loves to be teased, and that finally, "I'm grateful for Father Michael. I wouldn't give nearly such good head if it wasn't for him."[24] That speaker's default to the language of traumatic symptom—"I did joke about giving better head as a result of clerical sexual abuse committed against me when I was a teen. If I choose to deal in an edgy way on an internet livestream with a crime I was the victim of that's my prerogative"—no doubt secured the sympathy and care it has been contrived to extract, but nonetheless the defense of gallows humor once more fails to recapture the utopian possibility of masochism as it had been initially articulated, in all its unpardonable and dubious glory. If that particular speaker's "fall" was a tragedy, it was not so merely because a gay man had underestimated the homophobia of the institution into which he was seeking admission, but because, by publicly neutralizing his pleasure, he allowed himself to become retroactively cajoled into an older, more inert species of homophobia than that which had held him in place up until then. The one man who had seemed poised to take advantage of the moment came to a rather preneoliberal end: he became a spokesperson for the wrong kind of homophobia, the kind that loathes sexual pleasure as such.

Lest this resemble a psychological reductionism, I want to suggest that this overfamiliar dialectical stratagem—punish that one can be punished in turn—is neither an individual pathology of two men who both happen to be fascists, nor, obviously, a necessary or even especially common feature of fascism. Rather, it is an intimately scaled ramification of the crisis of democratic institutions occasioned by the collapse of parrhesia as an institutionalizable practice, by its forced entry into the place of sovereign power rather than (mere) privilege. In order to explore this idea, I turn to *The Fundamental Issue*, a book Kantorowicz had printed privately and considered circulating in 1950 but was persuaded not to by his concerned colleagues. Not only was the University of California, Berkeley, the international focus for the problematization of the discourse of "free speech" by an insurgent white ethnonationalist movement in 2016–2018, it was also the location at which Foucault delivered the lectures on free speech that were initially given as a fall 1983 seminar titled Discourse and Truth and eventually published as *Fearless Speech* in 1986. The public university, almost by definition, is the site at which free speech is tested most aggressively.

On April 21, 1950, the Board of Regents of the University of California voted by a margin of twenty-one to one to require all employees of the university to take the following oath:

> Having taken the constitutional oath of the office required of public officials of the State of California, I hereby formally acknowledge my acceptance of the position and salary named, and also state that I am not a member of the Communist Party or any other organization which advocates the overthrow of the Government by force or violence, and that I have no commitments in conflict with my responsibilities with respect to impartial scholarship and free pursuit of truth. I understand that the foregoing statement is a condition of my employment and a consideration of payment of my salary.[25]

By the time that Kantorowicz compiled his book, *The Fundamental Issue*, 157 workers altogether (academic and nonacademic staff) had been fired, and hundreds of faculty members who had initially refused to sign had reversed their decision under pressure of termination. The nonsigners had sued for reinstatement in *Tolman v. Underhill*, but that case had not yet been decided—which it was, by the California Supreme Court on October 17, 1952, in favor of the plaintiffs, leading to an order to reinstate all fired workers. Kantorowicz, who refused to sign the oath, accepted an offer of employment from the Institute for Advanced Study (an offer, incidentally, secured on Kantorowicz's behalf by Erwin Panofsky and tendered by J. Robert Oppenheimer, the military engineer, who was the institute's director).

The oath itself is replete with such contradictions that it is now unclear that it could possibly have been signed in good faith. It made Cretan liars of all who signed it. First, and most obviously, the acknowledgment that one is "not a member of the Communist Party or any other organization that advocates the overthrow of the Government by force or violence" is plainly contradicted by the following clause attesting that one has made "no commitments in conflict with my responsibilities with respect to impartial scholarship." Only slightly less obvious, and more puzzling, is the strange chronology that the oath produces: it is an oath to be taken after having taken the "oath of office" and as a gesture "hereby" accepting the position that has been offered, but nonetheless "the foregoing statement is a condition of my employment," a phrase that elides the implied verb ("[making] the foregoing statement is a condition of my employment") presumably because, in fact, the employment has been offered prior to the oath's being uttered and accepted in the act of uttering it. The syntax of the oath implies an infinite regression whereby one's having a job depends on having taken the oath that, because it presumes that the "oath of office" has already been taken, can only take place when one already has a job. In his notes on the affair, Kantorowicz similarly concludes that the oath could not have been signed in good faith but suggests that that was indeed part of the point: that the real enemy of the Regents was not Communists, but the idea of scholarly exception—that is, the idea of *parrhesia* itself. Persuade the scholar to "buy and sell [his] academic position and scholarly dignity at the price of [his] conviction and conscience" and you have degraded the privileged position of the parrhesiastes to such an extent that he will no longer defend himself or his institution against whichever crisis the Regents were trying to accelerate (21). Which might even have included—one of Kantorowicz's more paranoid theories—Communism itself.

It would be a mistake, then, to attribute Kantorowicz's belief in the exceptionality of the academic to liberalism—"I am genuinely conservative," he says on the first page of *The Fundamental Issue*, "and have never been taken for anything else." Indeed, his argument depends entirely on the idea that professors, unlike "janitors" (a comparison to which he relentlessly returns), are irreplaceable and therefore should not be subject to employment regulations of any kind. The freedom that professors enjoy, he argues, means, too, that their (our?) labor is entirely unalienated, and the difference between him and the office of which he is a part falls to nothing: "In short, it is entirely up to him how much of his life, of his private life, he is willing to dedicate to the University to which he belongs and which he, too, constitutes. The exact amount of time he invests is bound by no regulations. It is purely a matter of Love, and of Conscience" (20). Yet here, as in the oath, syntax reveals what semiosis disguises: that subordinated phrase "of his private life" can of course be read either as an appositive gloss on "his life" or as a contradiction of it. Does the professor indeed have two lives, as the king has two bodies?

This, I think, is the "fundamental issue" that Kantorowicz has in mind. It is, in its way, a question of the anus as well: "fundamental," of course, meaning "referring to a bottom," and Kantorowicz's purpose being, therefore, to get the bottom of things, to reframe the matter of the oath, so to speak, from the bottom. Here is the first page in more detail:

> Why I did not sign the oath—although, or because, I am not and never have been a Communist, and although, or because, I am genuinely conservative and have never been taken for anything else—I shall indicate in the

> following pages. This is not intended to be "The Year of the Oath." This subject has been admirably dealt with by Professor George R. Stewart. I merely wish to illustrate, by a few documents and a few marginal notes, some aspects of the oath controversy and its fundamental problems.
>
> What the fundamental issue is has been obvious to me from the minute the controversy started. Perhaps I have been sensitive because both my professional experience as an historian and my personal experience in Nazi Germany have conditioned me to be alert when I hear again certain familiar tones sounded. Rather than renounce this experience, which is indeed synonymous with my "life," I shall place it, for what it is worth, at the disposal of my colleagues who are fighting the battle for the dignity of their profession and their university.[26]

One point is worth clarifying: by "my personal experience in Nazi Germany," Kantorowicz does not refer simply to his having been exiled from Germany fleeing ethnonationalist genocide but also to the far more ambivalent experience of having a part in the emergence of that ethnonationalism. As he writes in a letter to President Sproul, "My political record will stand the test of every investigation. I have twice volunteered to fight actively, with rifle and gun, the left-wing radicals in Germany; but I also know that by joining the white battalions I have prepared, if indirectly and against my intention, the road leading to National Socialism and its rise to power."[27] It is a most unusual kind of life that can proudly assert that one's political record will "stand the test of every investigation" in one sentence and then take responsibility for the rise of Hitler in the following two. But then, what is the fundamental "life" of this subject? Its synonym is "this experience," where "this" deictically affirms "both my professional experience as an historian and my personal experience in Nazi Germany." Here the reader encounters another infinite regression problem, unless one takes the thing-that-is-the-synonym-for-life to mean the synthesis of intellectual and material experiences, the work one does by thinking with that which is done to one. Yet even there, following the syntax back to the bottom (that is, the bottom that is the top), we notice another kind of split at the origin, a rupture or fissure in the fundament, between "genuine conservative" and "have never been taken for anything else," an identity that is both active and passive, one that is originally embodied and referred to, both a conservative natural and a conservative political.

The professor's two fundaments. To translate Kantorowicz's startling disclosure into a more recognizable scholarly framework, we might say that his refusal to sign the loyalty oath constituted an assertion of the rights of free speech on a contradictory basis: on the one hand, a claim about identity ("I am a genuine conservative") and, on the other, a claim about referentiality ("I have never been taken for anything else"). We see, then, in Kantorowicz's thinking about his own history, an echo of the thought of the Victorian historian F. W. Maitland, whose engagement with the theory of the king's two bodies occasioned Kantorowicz's own.[28] The difference between the two thinkers was less analytical than dispositional: Maitland was wont to think of the idea of a king possessing two bodies as "metaphysical—or we might say metaphysiological—non-sense," whereas Kantorowicz accords the idea the dignity not of accuracy, but of "man-made irreality," or, even more suggestively, "important heuristic fiction."[29] Yet even this hardly holds the regression problem at bay, because a question emerges as to whether the fiction is the existence of the second body (the body politic) or the difference between the two bodies. In any case, and to summarize Kantorowicz, what his writing on the loyalty oath demonstrated was that there could be no performance of free speech without being entrapped by the paradox of the sovereign subject: that in order to assume a right to speak, one must postulate a sovereign political body capable of speaking, but that once such a body has been postulated, one has lost forever the implied subjective unity in whose name that sovereign political body would speak.

a worksheet

To trans people, the notion of a sovereign speaker possessed of two bodies is likely to resonate in a few ways. Rather than explore each of them in detail, I offer a list as a prompt to further contemplation:

- the difference between the body I have vs. the body that I believe I should have (gender dysphoria)
- the difference between the voice of authoritative and complete transness that I feel forced to adopt in public vs. the voice I allow myself to use once alone
- the difference between the pre- and post-transition bodies, or pre- and post-transition experiences of embodiment
- the two bodies that exist, if only momentarily, once the body has been cleaved in two by a surgeon
- the body I inhabit and the embodiment I perform

- the embodiment I perform and the body whose performance I am consciously or unconsciously mimicking
- the two breasts that emerge from the body of a trans woman undergoing hormonal transition, whose rise supplants the singular embodiment of the phallus (itself a fiction and, moreover, a fiction that entails the same infinite regression problem)
- the body as it is accounted for in the work of French feminist writers like Hélène Cixous and Luce Irigaray, so often wrongly counted as an essentialist (and therefore putatively antitrans) account of embodiment, rather than a materialism of a body in flux that produces meanings in its own specificities
- the body as mediated through penis and neo-vagina: "When I pay my surgeon to cut my penis into a neo-vagina, I am moving toward myself through myself"[30]
- the body in the moment of being misgendered, or shocked by being hailed, cracked into an interior and an exterior

the dupe

The "I" that began with the desire to speak everything did so nonetheless in these unlivable conditions of totality, about which, said Freud, "nothing is known," although nonetheless "it seems certain that the newborn child brings with it the germs of sexual feelings which continue to develop for some time and then succumb to a progressive suppression, which is in turn broken through by the proper advances of the sexual development and which can be checked by individual idiosyncrasies."[31] Freud's accounts of the "latency period" describe the paradoxical state of a condition of desire before object choice, of meaning before the speech act, of semiosis before significance. Latency is also a theory of two bodies: the developmental body and the potential body; the body I have been and the body as I might allow it to have been. It's superficially strange that Freud uses versions of the same word, *Latenzzeit* and *latenter Inhalt*, to refer to both a stage of infantile sexual development and a theory of interpretation, specifically the interpretation of dreams. This latter version of latency, the "latent content" of a dream (or, Laplanche and Pontalis clarify, "in a broad sense a designation for everything that analysis gradually uncovers"[32]), is precisely not a period in the history of a subject, but a kind of material that is constantly available to a subject at any stage in which that subject is entered into analysis. In the first case, latency is a historical meaning that passes into history and is sublimated by the phallus; in the second, latency is the meaning that subordinates the historical into the position of mere "manifest content" over which and under which latency holds sway. For the Lacanian critic Joan Copjec, it is this alignment of the latent with the ahistorical that proves, finally, that the (psychoanalytic) subject's sexuation is not a matter of cultural reproduction, but a matter of something like human essence. More specifically, sex belongs, for Copjec, on the "terrain of the drives." In "Sex and the Euthanasia of Reason," she argues:

> Freud . . . accuses Jung of evacuating the libido of all sexual content by associating it exclusively with cultural processes. It is this association that leads Jung to stress the essential plasticity or malleability of the libido: sex dances to a cultural tune. Freud argues, on the contrary, that sex is to be grasped not on the terrain of culture but on the terrain of the drives, which—despite the fact that they have no existence outside culture—are not cultural. They are, instead, the other of culture and, as such, are not susceptible to its manipulations.[33]

It is clear, in the context of Copjec's polemic against "gender theory," to which she assigns the invidious goal of "the elimination of sexual difference," that this particular strand of Lacanian thinking will not easily lend itself to an explanation of trans phenomena. Yet to take it on its own terms for a moment, what is clear is that an object called sex is being moved from one part of the psyche ("the terrain of culture") to another ("the terrain of the drives"). What are the consequences of that kind of shift?

I should say that I don't think this move is strictly justified by the Freud. In "Analysis Terminable and Interminable," Freud describes sex difference as the "bedrock" and the "rock-bottom" of the psychic field, but he does so on the grounds of "the biological factor": it is in the domain of biology that, as I quoted at the start of this chapter, "the repudiation of femininity must surely be a biological fact, part of the great riddle of sex."[34] It has been objected, in response to this reading of mine, that by characterizing this "biological factor" as a "riddle" Freud thereby relegates biology to a realm beyond significance, outside his proper problematic. This seems to me contradicted by the plain sense of Freud's words, but on the other hand it is true that when the sexual subject speaks in Freud, it is not from the position of biology, but from that of a subject translating the biological "riddle" into language. Or, more concisely, when a subject speaks sex, that subject does so as one interpreting a latent condition. This interpretation of the latently sexed body encompasses two gestures, entails two bodies. First, the subject interprets a felt body as though it possessed natural sex; second, the subject interprets the body on the grounds of that phantasmatic assignment, as though it could form a natural ground for this entirely unnatural type of meaning. Neither of these movements need be described as "gender" in any of the usual senses of that word. Here, I am merely glossing Freud's use of the word "riddle," but the model of interpretation that emerges is isomorphic, I think, with the account of dream interpretation in Freud's landmark study. First, the dreamer translates dream into language; then, the analyst interprets the linguistic sign of the dream back into latency.

In other words, Freud has installed another category—biology—into the position that Copjec, along with many of Freud's readers, reserves solely for the drive.[35] Indeed, it is difficult not to associate Freud's pair of geological images, "bedrock" and "rock-bottom," with the similar cluster of geological images in *Beyond the Pleasure Principle* with which Freud introduces the death drive. The origin of the drive to die, Freud famously argues, is the moment at which "the properties of life were awakened in lifeless matter," when "inanimate matter" first became biological microorganisms, a process that "by some operation of force which still completely baffles conjecture" engrafted upon the first living cells its "first instinct . . . to return to lifelessness."[36] The death drive is the name we give to the trace of this lifeless matter retained, in each evolutionary ontogenetic recapitulation, as a fantasy of inanimacy, of rude unshaped stuff, into which the subject plots to transform. Like the "great riddle" of "Analysis Terminable and Interminable," then, the "inanimate matter" marks the material limit of the psychoanalytic subject's domain—and, clearly, Copjec's decision to treat the two as identical makes sense on those grounds. Yet it is worth underlining that, for Freud, they are not the same: there is nothing to suggest that any limit encountered or proposed by the death drive in *Beyond the Pleasure Principle* characterizes sex, nor anything to suggest that the "bedrock" "great riddle" of "Analysis Terminable and Interminable" possesses anything like the tropic or motivating force of the drive. The felt conditions of the "bedrock" in the latter are derived, clearly, from something irrelevant to the former: the anatomical shape and function of the sexual organs.

The conflation of these two, then, proves to have profound political consequences. Trans people are very used to being told that there just *is* a difference between men and women and that that difference is unbreachable, albeit difficult to locate. In particular, we are keenly attuned to a timely switch between genitals and chromosomes, where "chromosomes" are taken to refer to an immanent condition of sexuation that is self-evidently available to each subject, and "genitals" can be disguised or (deceptively) misrepresented but are essentially a plastic, anatomical accident. This notion remains remarkably popular within Lacanian psychoanalytic theory, which, with a couple of partial exceptions, treats trans women either as dupes or cowards, as men who have either made the mistake of believing that changing our biology will have any effect on the fundamentals of our consciousness or who are refusing to grapple with castration anxiety by simply dodging the question.[37] What these positions share is the certainty that sexual difference is destiny because it is drive; consequently, none of the means that trans women use to enact something like castration (ranging from neo-invagination to hormonal transition) have actually got anything to do with something of such sublime theological importance as the castration complex. For Slavoj Žižek, indeed, transfeminizing bottom surgery is merely another failed attempt to circumvent the castration complex in the Symbolic domain where it truly belongs: "One can well guess that transgenderism is ultimately an attempt to avoid (the anxiety of) castration: thanks to it, a flat space is created in which the multiple choices that I can make do not bear the mark of castration."[38]

Žižek's position, nestled within one of his typically fell evasions, is not repudiated but amplified and fleshed out by his Lacanian colleagues. In his recent book on Lacan and God, for example, Lorenzo Chiesa claims that "there is no overlapping between anatomy and symbolic sexuation" and that the latter is belatedly grafted on to the body "only through the phallic function."[39] Exploring the issue further in a footnote, he explains:

> Transsexuals do not refute this. On the contrary, transsexuals exacerbate such a "common error" . . . . What the transsexual really wants to get rid of by changing sex/organ is not, as he claims, his being positioned on the "wrong" side of anatomical difference, but the phallic signifier that decrees castration on both sides of sexuation. He mistakes the absence of the sexual relationship in language for an error of nature. Or, better, he psychotically mistakes the "common error" of transposing sexual difference onto the natural possession or lack of an organ for an error in the very order of nature that affects his body.[40]

The "psychosis" in question is not, as it might appear, the delusional belief that one is in the wrong body—a belief that, as I have already explained, trans people tend to use opportunistically when at all—but, for Chiesa's transsexual, the belief that "his" body is a site at which "the order of nature" can be contested.

His source for this account of transsexual desire as psychosis is Geneviève Morel, herself a practicing Lacanian analyst. In her book *Sexual Ambiguities* (*Ambiguïtés sexuelles*), Morel considers the proper treatment of trans women, acknowledging that "it is love for a woman that is the determining factor" across the range of interviews and clinical treatments she conducts for her book. Nonetheless, the goal of the analytical treatment of transsexuals is, for Morel, stunningly clear: "In analysis, a transsexual subject may find solutions to the problem of sexuation other than the mutilation of surgery (e.g., transvestism, or a 'classifying' identification)."[41] Psychoanalysis as ex-trans conversion therapy. In Alenka Zupančič 's recent book *What Is Sex?,* a related criticism of "the contemporary psychotherapeutic take on sexuality" takes the form of a reduction of psychoanalysis to the idea of the "impossibility of full sexual satisfaction . . . as an integral part of unconscious sexuality as such."[42] The real lesson of Freud's writing on sexuality, Zupančič argues, is the impossibility of fully exteriorizing any desire entailing sexuality, and she summarizes that writing as: "Sexual meanings were revealed ['behind' symptoms], connections leading to [sexual meaning] established and reconstructed; yet the problem/symptom persisted."[43] Psychoanalysis as the abolition of sexual therapy altogether.

At the heart of these theoretical figurations of the transsexual is a certain pacifying delight in "his" play with gender, his wanton gender-fuckery. It is a sadistic delight that casts "him" as a fool useful for demonstrating the generally contradictory nature of sexuation. The transsexual exemplifies the Lacanian dupe, a blessed fool who has avoided the psychic traps of maturity, correctness, and other forms of anality. It is indeed in the first session of Seminar 21, a session titled "Les non-dupes errent" ("the nondupes are wrong"), that Lacan expresses, with his characteristic geniality, "I have to find a point of departure, which is a . . . mere supposition, the supposition that there is a male or female subject. It is a supposition which experience shows us to be quite obviously untenable." It is easy to see how this playful liberality might be taken as an indirect endorsement of the civil rights of trans people, but in fact it is precisely this form of indeterminacy whose authority is denied by the transsexual who does not present himself for consideration as a peculiar kind of travesty, but asserts her personhood as a rights-bearing subject. Of course, no Lacanian theory could concern itself with the psychic viability of a sex change; the entire realm of activity that constitutes transsexual desire as such is cast not even as a symptom, but as a perhaps revelatory but never efficacious failure to symptomatize—as a trivial evasion of the problem of sexuation.

Freud's understanding of the "bedrock" of sexual latency, meanwhile, circumvents all such hyperbolic summaries. Returning to "Analysis Terminable and Interminable," we can sense not merely the possibility of a universal trans femininity, but a subject required to seek redress for her transness in the terrain of biology. What if we allowed ourselves to take these apparently most embarrassing aspects of psychoanalytic theory—its willingness to take embodiment as an object of discourse and to endow it with profound power—literally? What if the castration complex were precisely what it sounds like: an obsessive relation to castration that draws in both fear and desire? What if we took penis envy, that most execrated dimension of Freud's thinking, as an attempt to formulate the possibility of trans masculine desire? Not only might we be able to imagine trans feminism within the domain of theory, but we might be able to get analytical purchase on the disturbing, and one might say transsexual, fact that biology certainly now exists on the terrain of culture—or rather, of history, if it did not always; that biology can be changed and indeed is continually being assigned new meanings; and that it is indeed infinitely negotiable by any number of regimes of bodily modification, chosen and unchosen. These topics all look very different from the perspective of someone who used to, but no longer does, possess a penis or to someone who has acquired one in adulthood through the expenditure of labor, time, and money. For such a subject, the plasticity of the sexual organs—of the "bedrock" of sexual difference—is no mere fantasy, but a quotidian reality, a premise on which life has taken place. It is a truth such subjects acquire from our bodies, which bear the traces (including traumatic traces) of our developmental histories and respond as we exert our will (or as our doctors exert theirs) to transfigure what is merely manifest into what might, finally, count as latent.

The fantasy of a sovereign subject who can say *I am a woman* is, of course, as "man-made" an "irreality" as the self-congratulation of the parrhesiastes. Further, both are relativized as relational psychic positions that only make sense within certain historical frameworks—broadly, a democratic institution, especially one in a phase of crisis, and the psychic and institutional nexus of patriarchal oppression. This would not mean that these two subjects are "equal," however, nor that the "expressions" of "free speech" and "trans identification" are in themselves formally identical. This argument will have done its job, rather, if it has been able to discriminate between trans identifications as a certain psychic and political action, something one *does* rather than something one simply *is*, and free speech petitions as a certain kind of psychic entitlement, a compensatory fantasy designed to restore faith in a theory of expression that is, at least within the framework of a democratic institution, impossible to hold in good faith. Reflecting one last time on Eva Hayward's image of a body pulled through itself in the act of invagination, we might imagine the language to which we could ascribe the property of freedom as similarly pulled through itself, similarly invaginated in the act of articulation, and similarly at war with the bedrock of its own psychic field. I don't believe that we either have or require a better name for the subject of such language than "woman."

do the hustle

"Making it look easy," one might think, is the privilege of the managerial class. But what is the "ease" that appears when labor is sublimed into pure ideology? The question fringes much of the mainstream culture of neoliberal accelerationism. In the work of Aaron Sorkin, for example, the bureaucrat's office figures as a place of absolute political efficacy, where the mind of the male genius works as a shred of platinum to transform sweat into history. Sam Seaborn makes it look easy; Josh Lyman makes it look *fun*. That *The West Wing*'s fantasies of political efficacy had entirely swallowed and reconstituted the "political" ideological state apparatus was obvious as early as 2006, when the UK Conservative Party copied the plot of an episode in order to defeat the first reading of the government's "Racial and Religious Hatred Act."[44] They had good hustle! Ease as the whiteness of, for example, the collar.

This feels a long way from the question of autobiographical criticism, no doubt. Yet perhaps our profession's oft-remarked method-manifesto fatigue would look a little easier if we understood it as Aaron Sorkin might, as a set of disagreements about how managerial-class workers should approach the question of professionalism. In the heyday of de Manian deconstruction, John Guillory described such theory (and its signature strategy, "rhetorical reading") as an essentially managerial metadiscourse whose purpose was to subordinate the social field, in which literature and criticism might have otherwise had a stake, to its own unreal form of political analysis, whose phantasmatic causality follows from the claim that, in Guillory's words, "political questions are derivative of linguistic ones."[45] Although the most spectacularly visible effect of that subordination was the election (and promotion, etc.) of a new class of suited-and-booted metamanagers, its most historically significant effect was the sublimation of the object, in this case "literature," into a *merely* discursive object wheeled out to confirm the emerging class's necessity. Whether or not Guillory was right about deconstruction (I'm not sure), it seems notable that the age of metadata, which figures both markets and labor forces as microbundled identity segments, has so far overlapped entirely with the age in which "the way we read now" has somehow appeared a salient topic of conversation, despite the erosion of the "we," the multiplicity of "ways," and the world-ending obliteration of the "now." Do we debate "the way we read now" to persuade ourselves that, even if nobody else does, *we* (still) read (now), much as Elaine Stritch, or whomever, reassures herself that "I'm Still Here"?[46]

So this is all bullshit, but on the other hand if "calling bullshit" were enough to end this parade of vanities, or if merely *noting* that these debates are pointless denuded them of their capacity to titillate and self-replicate, we wouldn't have gotten into this problem in the first place.[47] And one might even wonder whether "this is bullshit" isn't one of the methods by which contemporary pseudoproblems manifest(o) themselves. So rather than say that autobiographical criticism is good (a meaningless statement) or bad (equally), that it is new (potentially meaningful, but not true) or old (self-evident and politically ambiguous), that it is "reactionary" or "radical," "politicizing" or "dehistoricizing," let me say instead that none of these pairs is remotely contradictory, any more than "depth" contradicts "surface," "form" contradicts "history," or "distant" contradicts "close." Antonymy is not the same as contradiction. This point is vital if we are to understand the ways in which methodological metadiscourse serves to obscure the conditions of alienated labor under the neoliberal phase of capitalist relations, which is neither "subjective" nor "objective," but irreducibly both.

Irony seems too futile a word to append to what the *New York Times* called "the case of Paul de Man" (christened "Paul Deman"), as oedipalized an Oedipus as has been yielded by the Complex and its decedents.[48] It was de Man, writing in 1979, who argued that the will to narrate governs the choices one makes, such that "the autobiographical project may itself produce and determine the life."[49] He illustrates the point by reference to Gérard Genette's reading of the closet scene in Proust, "of which it is impossible to say whether it is fact or fiction."[50] Conventionally, we fudge this problem with the bland phrase "semi-autobiographical," to designate a partial fictionalization delivered in such a manner as to leave partly exposed the author's life, or let's say, as Barthes does, her "thing."[51] But de Man was right to observe that autobiography isn't a matter of *degree*—a titillating "semi"—but a matter of quantum ontology, where the autographical signature is either effaced or exposed. So the phenomenon called "autobiography" is neither real or unreal, but a way of thinking about the signature, that may appear or disappear at any given moment depending on the angle of one's approach.

Given which, it would appear at best foolish, and at worst dishonest, to take an ethical position on autobiography as such. To claim, for example, that the autobiographical impulse of a given strand of critical writing closes itself off from public engagement by locating its field of evidence solely within the critic's sensorium would be no more than to enclose one's own solipsism with an isomorphic, but merely different, truism. What we are really talking about is power. Or more specifically, about *brand*. Everyone knows which critics have brands and that it isn't just those whose work avows the quantum autobiography. It would be interesting, though perhaps a little unkind, to name a couple of blue-chip scholarly brands and unfurl a theory of marketing; we could argue, along the lines Sharon Marcus recently laid out, that the celebrity scholar's brand results from more or less conscious labor, albeit labor exchanged for only a fraction of its value under exploitative conditions.[52] (Although, is a brand also a form of capital? Value compounded from the value earned on unearned value . . .) There may be, indeed there self-evidently are, academic brands whose character derives from an apparent negation of branding. Consider figure 4, for example.

Easy enough, of course, to notice the neatly self-annihilating visual logic of the page: the brand derives not so much from the logo-that-is-no-logo, but from the pleasing self-distancing effect that the cover enables, flattering the viewer into the position of the one who can see both a logo and no logo, and move between the two positions at will.[53] Yet the stranger part is the incursion of negation into the author's own signature: the red "NO" that becomes "N[a]O[mi]." We can read that migration as a diminishment (it gets smaller), as a viral contamination, as a descent down the page, or perhaps as a mutation, of quantum logo (or logos) into quantum author function. We clearly cannot read it as merely the absence of a logo!

In the vocabulary of the moment, *brand* implies *hustle*, just as in another register "autobiography" implies "fabrication." If *brand* is the ethically dubious sign of labor, then *hustle* is its nobler complement: indiscriminately sexualized, racialized, and retro, the hustle can be done ("do the hustle!"), can be American, can take place at midnight, can be kung-fu—can be, in some way, the social strategy of queens, divas, sex workers, and all those who can "use their sexuality," as the phrase goes.[54] The hustle, like the grift (with which it is, in any case, intimately connected in online patter), may entail its own quantum autobiography: it may involve telling a story about oneself, creating and maintaining a persona with the right mixture of thrilling indomitability and seductive vulnerability. Such seduction, it hardly bears saying, depends

FIG. 4. Front cover of Naomi Klein, *No Logo: Taking Aim at the Brand Bullies.* Oslo: Forlaget Oktober, 2002.

upon an audience's capacity to understand that the vulnerability is bogus, and that the stooge tripping over his dick for it is doing the opposite of "using his sexuality."

The true hustler is the one whose physical endowments should exclude her from the heterosexualizing markets to which she petitions for access: Anne Hathaway stands behind Rebel Wilson.[55] To the true hustler, pretty privilege is cheating: she presents also as *trade,* also as *trap,* as both hook and hooker.[56] The displacement of the entity called "the economy" into the sector called "service" culminates with the ontologization of the hustle as the organizing condition of embodied labor. The erotic contours of such service, its rules and entitlements, remain a matter of profound uncertainty. Indeed, it isn't always clear who is servicing whom.

FIG. 5. Still from *Hustlers,* directed by Lorene Scafaria. STX Entertainment, 2019.

The transformation of the university into a consumer experience serves neoliberal capital in two ways. First, it introduces commercial incentives into all aspects of university life and thus monetizes sectors hitherto relatively sheltered from exploitation; second, it obscures (as is consumerism's primary goal) the productive labor of workers—primarily, of course, that of immiserated service workers whose bodies are displayed as signs of diversity while their labor is criminally undercompensated, working conditions rendered ever more dangerous (especially in the present era of accelerationist biopolitics), and job security gutted. But instructional labor too: as commercial service, teaching can be severed from research support—additionally, and not incidentally, depriving the public university of its sole remaining *raison d'être,* the quaint notion that students might deserve to be educated by scholars receiving meaningful research support. Scholarship, as a productive force, must be obscured and transformed into mere commercial service, lest capital incur avoidable (albeit minimal) costs associated with *reproduction*—which in this context might resemble, for example, tolerable research support for all instructors. Meanwhile, *doing the hustle* entails the transformation of productive labor into style—into "making it look good." None of which is to deny that the productive forces of the university are themselves extracted from workers under oppressive conditions, nor that (obviously) such workers would ever be entitled to more than the fractional value of those forces in the form of a wage. But one strategy of neoliberalism is to cause the worker to disappear entirely from the scene of her own labor.

To which end, the phenomenal subject of the humanities poses a problem. It is not difficult to see how the charismatic critic might become, himself, a motive force in the transformation of the discipline into an *experience*; Franco Moretti, rather unfairly, might serve as an example of both.[57] The captivating scholar becomes a mind-blowing teacher; the mind, once blown, disgorges itself first and most joyfully onto RateMyProfessors.com and, later, in a more ambivalent key, against a #metoo hashtag on Twitter. "Queer," if it designates anything in such a setting, would only mean those bodies and teachers scapegoated for the effects of transforming education into entertainment. I write a couple of days after a syllabus of my own, which includes W. H. Auden's erotic gay poem "The Platonic Blow," was described by the cloud of unknowing antitrans agitators who follow me around as "rapey," "predatory," "traumatizing," and "disgusting."[58] The Avital Ronell case is an interesting outlier, in fact, because the predator's many defenders labeled her "queer" on the grounds that she was being scapegoated in such a way, despite the demonstrable fact that she was receiving no more criticism than, for example, Moretti or Jay Fliegelman.[59]

But there was a similarity, too: Ronell, Moretti, Fliegelman—these were scholars whose thought pushed hard against the tendency de Man might have called "autobiographical." These were expert metadiscoursers, and in Ronell's case especially, power exerted itself not primarily in the mode of present embodiment (although clearly it did that too), but in the fantasy of bodily withdrawal. Ronell falsely claimed to Nimrod Reitman that, on the basis of her academic *brand*, she could get him a job with a phone call. That abusive fantasy of disembodied omnipotence—a fantasy that might have appealed to the author of *The Telephone Book*, even—was then, startlingly, affirmed even by those who believed themselves to be criticizing Ronell.[60] The notion that Avital Ronell was merely a worker, deserving equitable but not preferential treatment by Title IX as such, seemed unthinkable on all sides. "Autobiography," then: not so much the name of charismatic self-presencing as that which is suppressed or displaced in order that such presencing might be possible.

If, as I've been suggesting, "autobiography" is a way of understanding the parrhesiastes, rather than a genre of criticism, that split would engender an "allobiography" by which the critic points at a "not me," and thus paradoxically expands the limits of her remit. *Allo* and *auto* are merely the consequences of a psychic splitting engendered by the necessarily catastrophic act of self-narration Freud calls the "reality principle." So I'm more self-conscious than usual about introducing such a point of distinction in this chapter, especially since, conspicuously, there is nothing in this not-me that is not also-me.

But at the risk of allobiographizing the antinomy of such effacement, one might take a moment to observe the trails of disclosure and effacement in a popular recent denunciation of the "subjective" school of literary criticism.[61] Many of Anna Kornbluh's recent essays have diagnosed our present scene as plagued by a memoiristic tendency, a "methodological subjectivism"—whose practitioners are rarely named but metonymically associated with certain social media platforms, especially Instagram, and perhaps with "Instant Messages," which phrase is ominously capitalized.[62] Ranged against the dominance of "the sympathy industrial complex," Kornbluh suggests, is the promise of an "objective" criticism, where the word is taken to mean "a capacity for conceptuality, a faculty for synthesis, which runs perpendicular to, but also parallels, the quantitative or the empirical, the phenomenal and the embodied."[63] The object-world, then, consists of "capacity" and "faculty," while the subject-world comprises "elaborations of the author's intent, of the specific refraction of specific social context, of the unparaphrasable, of the singularity of the literary event, of the resistance to theory, of the right to represent, of negligible sample size," but also "reader response, affect theory, the right to recognition, MRIs, the passion of the critic," and plenty of other forces.[64] The lists seem to produce a parallelism along the following lines:

OBJECTIVISM	*SUBJECTIVISM*
capacity	intention
faculty	unparaphrasability
quantity	specificity
empiricism	MRIs
phenomenon	passion/resistance
embodiment	affect/sympathy

Could we admit that, seeing these lists arranged so, it is difficult to be sure of the exact nature of the structural distinction being asserted? Take, for example, the fate of "singularity." Leaving aside the thorny question of whether, as Kornbluh appears to wish, "singularity" might be completely innocent of quantification, it seems fairly clear that "methodological subjectivism" romances the literary absolute, or at least "the singularity of the literary event." But in the very next paragraph, we learn that methodological subjectivism denies not merely the singularity of literature, but its entire existence: "methodological subjectivism entails of course the frequent thesis that literature itself does not exist."[65]

Is this the harmonization of Jean-Luc Nancy and Michel Foucault?[66] Perhaps not, because as the premises of methodological subjectivism stack up, the ironic position of the critic becomes increasingly difficult to locate. Since the question at stake is whether criticism conceals or exposes the subject who writes, thinks, reads, or conceptualizes, let us try to locate such a subject in the following paragraph:

> Often literary critics connect this emphatic sense of the subjective and the singular to ethical and political positions. Following the lead of our objects, we understand our own knowledge as situated, constructed, and ephemeral. We understand the force of our cumulative knowledge as nuancing, qualifying, hybridizing, and de-reifying, moving against broader socioeconomic forces of abstraction and reification and broader epistemic tendencies of generalization and quantification. The task of the critic, we so frequently argue, is to linger with the fleeting, to cow before the sublime, to host an encounter, to resound imitations. Aesthetic judgment has long ago been forsworn as elitist, so our expertise should not culminate in it. We even undermine the hard-won authority of our own interpretations with constant declarations that literature is inexhaustible and will always court new alternative elaborations.[67]

And let me—subject that I am—acknowledge, then, that I agree with much of this diagnosis; that I have heard some of these words leaving my mouth; that I have heard colleagues I generally like (or at least want to appease) saying these things, and acquiesced to them in passing. I suspect that you—subject that *you* are—may accept this diagnosis too. The question is how to position the "we" that speaks. It is a curious and lovable pronoun, the "we," since it indicates the speaker and others but technically leaves open the question of whether the addressee is included.

The "we" is in that sense itself a quantum allobiography. Here, it substitutes, fittingly enough, for an objective designation—"literary critics"—whose displacement by the pronoun "our" in the following sentence feels, perhaps, a touch unorthodox but hardly outrageous: "We understand the force of our cumulative knowledge as nuancing, etc." Whereas hitherto the reader has encountered literary critics merely in the course of their daily rounds, following their objects, now, a hortative tone begins to predominate, almost like a celebrant articulating a collective grief or grievance. The *we* gains an ethical character by association, like that of "we're here, we're queer" or "yes we can." By the time the sentence has finished, however, that *we* has become purely ironic:

the phrase "we so frequently argue" cannot, of course, refer to *us* as readers and presumably does not refer to the author either, since the purpose of this essay was to try to cajole us out of this position in which we have somnambulated. So who exactly "so frequently" argues that the point of criticism is "to cow before the sublime," who exactly has "forsworn" judgment? Only the hustler that is not one.

My point, of course, is not that there aren't any good reasons to prefer descriptions of objects to disclosures of subjects. And indeed one might understandably feel ticked off with Instagram, or with noodle-minded rhapsodies in Adorno, or whatever happens to be the nearest available scapegoat for "methodological subjectivism." My point is simply that these kinds of conversations are unphilosophical and depoliticizing. Unphilosophical, because the categories at issue simply are not rigorously separable. At the risk of throwing down a gauntlet too rashly, it would be impossible to describe a criticism that was not *both* subjectivist *and* objectivist—the former because the perceptual and cognitive apparatuses of the critic are nothing more than what philosophers since Kant have tended to mean by "subject," and the latter because to designate an act of writing as criticism is to claim that it refers to some *object* in the world. To force some choice between the subjective and the objective, or the autobiographical and the alienated, is like inviting scholars to choose between the letters *a* and *i*. But more importantly, by disguising *clout* as *productivity*, and thereby offloading onto the embodied other the character of the hustler, the gesture depoliticizes not merely thought, but more crucially *work*, by scapegoating the *other* as the (only) hustler. The very same could be said in the other direction: that the consummate stylist, the conspicuous memoirist-critic—oh, let's just say the faggot—is effacing the signs of embodied labor, relinquishing productive force as though merely giving up the spirit. But then there is the dance itself: evanescent, perhaps, but no less real for that.

I dedicate this chapter to Elizabeth Stone Freeman: femme folle, femme fière, femme felle.

III

Picaresque and Pornography in *The Old Curiosity Shop*

LIBERAL DEFENSES OF PORN, it has become something of a cliché to remark, tend to rely more on the theory than the practice: or rather, defenses of porn tend to treat porn as a genre (whose premises are therefore contested), whereas the critique treats porn as either a tone (once introduced, everything ruined) or an industry. The defense does not require the exoneration of all porn, only some; the critique, meanwhile, can claim that some limited exemptions—"queer" porn, where "queer" is used as a synonym for "ethical"; perhaps gay porn in which no women were harmed—aren't really porn. Leo Bersani's remarks in "Is the Rectum a Grave?" appeared to resolve this impasse by ensuring that the "anti-loving" nature of porn reflects the fundamentally anti-loving character of sex, yet here too the assimilation of that negativity into the "queer" mirrored, albeit perhaps undeliberately, the defense of porn with its difference from heterosexual hardcore.[1] (And perhaps not undeliberately: Linda Williams's revisiting of *Hard Core* exhibits remorse that "porn studies" seemed to enable and even encourage the worst excesses of the porn industry.)[2] More recently, Eugenie Brinkema and Kathleen Lubey have examined the formal and political disruptiveness of str8 hardcore, especially as it both instantiates and fails to depict idealized heterosexual relations.[3] Like Bersani, although more subtly, Brinkema and Lubey both accept the antiporn designation of porn as a kind of tone, a moment of palpable meaning which deforms the prevailing condition of its medium and which therefore troubles the differences between medium and message. Though neither engages in what one might call an ethical defense of str8 hardcore, they both treat the most difficult-to-defend aspect of pornography as the one upon which its political effects must finally be assessed.

These theoretical developments, as Lubey shows, can enable readers to discover pornographic methods in texts at some remove from the genre.[4] For example, Charles Dickens's earlyish novel, *The Old Curiosity Shop*, depends, rather surprisingly it must be admitted, upon a reader's capacity to read pornographically.[5] Since the primary object of its fetishistic attention is a girl child and the predatory figures that surround her are all much older men, the ethical stakes could hardly be higher. Some of the novel's readers have examined this dimension of *The Old Curiosity Shop* before. In Catherine Robson's treatment of Little Nell in *Men in Wonderland: The Lost Girlhood of the Victorian Gentleman*, we encounter Dickens holding his heroine's sexual suggestiveness gently and ambivalently—as when the novelist deleted from an early draft a moment when a character asks Nell what she has been doing and she responds, "selling diamonds," a reply that Robson characterizes as "unsettling and potentially equivocal."[6] Robson further observes that Nell's subordination to the schemes of Quilp are less compulsive—because more archly feigned—than her manipulation by the novel's kindly old men, especially her own grandfather. Yet following Brinkema's insistence on the *roughness* of porn, I here suggest that the psychological isolation of Nell in Robson's reading restricts the libidinal economy of a novel whose internal coherence has been detonated, such that the differences between characters can hardly be taken for granted. The first effect of that detonation is the cartoonish and ultimately pornographic rendering of every character as a kind of cipher: *The Old Curiosity Shop* presents a world where everything has been ineluctably, totally, as if in a fairy tale, *miniaturized*. Everything in the novel is small. The central character has become, in the retelling, "Little Nell"; her grandfather's emaciation is described over and again; the villain, Daniel Quilp, is a dwarf; the love interest in the awkwardly tacked-on romance plot is seemingly anorexic. Not just the main characters: Dickens parades past his readers' eyes a sequence of smallened people: a schoolful of children who look like squat adults; a traveling troupe of waxworks of historical personages; a Punch and Judy show—the hero of which, with his cartoonish tendency towards violence and utterly unrestrained pursuit of his own ends, reminds us of Quilp. The novel fully refuses to tell us the difference between a cartoonish violence that is supposed to be taken seriously and one which can be enjoyed as entertainment.

In an unusual and in many ways uncharacteristic essay on Dickens, the Marxist critic Theodor Adorno dwells on the novel's entertainments in much the same way, offering a fascinating explanation for their appearances in *The Old Curiosity Shop*. Adorno writes:

> I would like to talk about [a book] whose title is generally familiar, a book that may still be widely read, especially by children. But in the ninety years since Dickens' *The Old Curiosity Shop* appeared, inserted into another novel, some of the secrets embedded in the work, perhaps without the author knowing clearly that he was doing so, have become discernable. Dickens is currently considered to be one of the founders of the realistic and social novel. Historically, this is correct; but when one examines the form of his work itself, it requires some qualification. For Dickens' fictional work, in which poverty, despair, and death have already been recognized as the fruits of a bourgeois world, a world to which only the traces of human warmth and kindness in individual human relationships can reconcile one—this work also contains the outlines of a completely different sort of view of the world. You may call it prebourgeois; in it the individual has not yet reached full autonomy, nor, therefore, complete isolation, but instead is presented as a bearer of objective factors, of a dark, obscure fate and a starlike consolation that overtake the individual and permeate his life but never follow from the law of the individual, as do, for instance, the fates of the characters in Flaubert's novels. The novels of Dickens contain a fragment of the dispersed baroque that maintains a strange ghostly presence in the nineteenth century. You know it from the plays of Raimund and even Nestroy, but it is also contained, in more hidden form, in the apparently so individualistic philosophy of Kierkegaard.[7]

We can forgive Adorno his rather shallow reading of Flaubert, whose *Bovary* is partly represented here but at the expense of any credible account of *Bouvard et Pécuchet* or even *Salammbô*, because the reading of Dickens is *so* astute.[8] The essence of the Dickensian is a particular kind of remnant of capital's own prehistory, which appears not as romanticism or nostalgia—where it would remain pastoral, as such remnants do for a George Eliot or Anthony Trollope—but as the paradoxically definitive quality of the collective, the urban, the modern. The Dickensian baroque is to capital what the Lyotardian postmodern is to modernism: an effect whose emergence, bizarrely, conditioned the very structure it was supposed to supersede. The postmodern can be found nowhere more fully realized than in the Wildean *fin-de-siècle* (says Lyotard), but the baroque can be found nowhere more fully realized than in the Dickensian novel of modernity (says Adorno).[9]

By way of exploring what Adorno might have meant by "the dispersed baroque" in this context, we might consider one of the novel's many dream sequences, in this case a dream of Nell's after a narrow escape from her pursuer, Quilp, amid the waxworks at Mrs. Jarley's traveling show:

> Notwithstanding these protections, she could get none but broken sleep by fits and starts all night, for fear of Quilp, who throughout her uneasy dreams was somehow connected with the wax-work, or was wax-work himself, or was Mrs. Jarley and wax-work too, or was himself, Mrs. Jarley, wax-work, and a barrel organ all in one, and yet not exactly any of them either. At length, towards break of day, that deep sleep came upon her which succeeds to weariness and over-watching, and which has no consciousness but one of overpowering and irresistible enjoyment.[10]

Clearly, the passage comports with many of the elements of Freudian "dream-work" as he teaches it in 1900: condensation (the Quilp element is saturated by other elements); displacement (the appearance of the barrel organ); and secondary revision (in the sense that Nell's dream creates the conditions of possibility for its own interpretation). The question of scene-setting, that Freud finds so fascinating, hardly occurs in Nell's dream, though perhaps it is the *lack* of a setting that troubles the narrator, who seems aware that the uneasiness of the dream is part of its structure, as well as its content. Yet as startling as may be this foreshadow of Freud, still more so is the realization that the hydraulics of dream possess, for Dickens, the properties of one of their elements: that is, the dream is *waxy*. It waxes; elements wax into each other in it—the dream is almost flesh, but flesh that can merge with other flesh, can become glossy and transmute without denaturing. Moreover, a certain *waxiness* gets glazed onto the bodies of all characters that come into contact with Jarley's exhibition of wax representations of historical figures. "Nell walked down [the canvas], and read aloud, in enormous black letters, the inscription, JARLEY'S WAX-WORK." / 'Read it again,' said the lady, complacently. / 'Jarley's Wax-Work,' repeated Nell. / 'That's me,' said the lady. 'I am Mrs. Jarley.'"[11] Mrs. Jarley later justifies her craft by insisting, "It is not funny at all," and that "I won't go so far as to say, that, as it is, I've seen wax-work quite like life, but I've certainly seen some life that was exactly like wax-work.'"[12] The "dispersed baroque" as the revenge of material against structure, of wax against personhood, against dream.

And against language. Such waxiness drips, or merges, with language itself—which is no surprise, since Dickens also preempts Lacan in his implication that the structure of Nell's dream is formed as a syntax. The Dickensian dream-syntax, however, is prosodic rather than merely semantic. The Jarley

Wax-Work Exhibition advertises itself by deformation and reformation, "in the form of parodies on popular melodies," of which Dickens gives us only one:

If I had a donkey wot wouldn't go
To see Mrs. JARLEY's wax-work show,
Do you think I'd acknowledge him? Oh no no!
Then run to Jarley's—[13]

We are left to imagine the rhyme's closure, which might repeat the second line, but might just as well be "tomorrow" or "bungalow" or such. One modern version of the nursery rhyme suggests that perhaps another couplet is missing from Jarley's version:

If I had a donkey that wouldn't go
Do you think I'd beat him? Oh no no!
I'd put him in a barn, and give him some corn:
The best little donkey that ever was born.[14]

Whereas an American ballad from the same period (published 1840, same year as *The Old Curiosity Shop*, offers a more complex prosodic arrangement:

If I had a donkey wot wouldn't go,
D'ye think I'd wollop him—no, no, no.
But gentle means I try, d'ye see,
Because I hate all cruelty:
If all had been like me, in fact,
There'd ha' been no occasion for Martin's act,
Dumb animals to prevent getting crack'd
    On the head.
For if I had a donkey wot wouldn't go,
I never would wallop him—no, no, no:
I'd give him some hay, and cry, Gee O!
    And come up, Neddy.[15]

The implication here is that beating a donkey teaches the donkey to kick in response, as happens to the villain of the older version, "that cruel chap, Bill Bore."[16] I'm not trying to restore Jarley's jingle into an original version, but rather to observe the curious blend of moralism, violence, and simplicity that can be made to run into each other by this cheerful, mechanical rhyme, which like Nell's dream fails or refuses to make clear what object is what, leaving only the central image—a donkey is being beaten—somewhere out of the range of reference. The dispersed baroque, then, entails a special relationship to violence: since violence cannot be dispersed, and is indeed a mode by which form and matter interact, it poses a particular challenge to Dickens, for whom Punch-and-Judy-like violence is everywhere. Force, terror, impact: these are elements of the jingle and the dream likewise, never absentable and yet never fully representable either. In the dispersed baroque, violence is method.

There is another element of *The Old Curiosity Shop* that demands this kind of attention, and yet Adorno is too polite to mention it: the close affinity between Dickensian waxiness and the Victorian pornography itself. Narrative pornography had already developed a stock of characters, tropes, and devices by 1840—indeed, it had done so primarily through the picaresque, which receded in Dickens's fiction and in that of his imitators but remained from then to the present the dominant mode of pornographic writing (and now, of pornographic video). Yet a question may be asked about whether pornography produces characters, and if so, upon what theory such characterizations depend. One provisional answer nestles in a subordinate clause close to the beginning of Steven Marcus's foundational study of mid-Victorian pornography, *The Other Victorians*, when it is observed in passing that "in pornography no person, object, or idea is incapable of being enlisted in the cause of sexual activity."[17] Character, then, exists only provisionally as a pretext for a more generically primal enlistment, a seduction, a being-sucked-into the whirlpool of sex that pornography sets out, if not to depict, then at least to present. Marcus's point is affirmed at each moment in which porn promises to educate its characters: the moment, for example, when the straight boy removes his blindfold to reveal that it is a man sucking his cock and that he rather likes it; when Justine learns that she can enjoy even the chastisement she receives for her good conduct. Character exists as a mere precondition for an erasure that occurs, both chronologically and formally, at the moment of sexual pleasure. The theory of character would then be something like: there are no characters at the moment of orgasm, and it is the task of pornography to persuade its consumers of this fact. We are all the same underneath our characters—though probably Sade and *BaitBus.com* would entail different conceptualizations of what's underneath.[18]

Pornography turns characteristic particularity into sex, which it must therefore posit as a nonparticularizable field. But character is, as Marcus says, hardly unique in being subjected to such treatment in porn: everything is. On the one side, social organization, medium specificity, the naïve mode of self-differentiation we call "character"; on the other, the shattered sexual subject, an affective intensity whose specificities have been negated, a momentary convergence of fictional and realist epistemologies. Is it possible to talk about pornography without characterizing sex in such absolute terms? Perhaps: Brinkema's work on "Rough Sex" might prompt us to question Marcus's notion of "enlistment" in one particular. What if the sex to which "no person, object, or idea is incapable of being enlisted" lacked the conceptual or institutional unity necessary for such a task? It is not merely, Brinkema might say, that legal and historical authorities cannot agree what pornography is, but that pornography fundamentally disturbs its consumer's sense of what sex is. Not merely in the morally panicked sense of producing "unrealistic expectations." The "roughness" of which Brinkema makes extensive use in her essay associates the violent aesthetics of rough porn with the provisional and chaotic assembly of pornography as a genre, suggesting that, just as the assembly of the archive of pornography is necessarily incomplete, so the constitution of sexual pleasure—that to which Marcus entrusts the responsibility to obliterate character—is founded only haphazardly and contingently. And so it is. Although each number of *The Pearl* contained a few distinct short stories and bawdy poems, each also contained serialized stories in which continuity of character (though not of setting) was reinstantiated. In one such, "Sub-Umbra, or Sport among the She-Noodles," the characters' various sexual encounters hardly climax at all, at least in the narrative sense of the word: each experience of sexual pleasure is itself folded back into the loose narrative framework.[19] Walter (the narrator) and his cousin Annie have sex in the first installment, yet they return to do so again and again in the remaining seven. The relationship between each encounter and its precedents is not precisely accretive—they do not refer to any previous encounters, nor do they seem to learn anything about each other—but, given the continuities and discontinuities of the serial narrative form, we can be sure that these characters have not been simply dissolved in sex either. Though in this particular case the endurance of character is underwritten by the medium of serialized fiction, a similar effect is ensured by video pornography's own "star system": though a particular scene may end predictably, the porn star will return—as actor and as character.

The serial aspect of pornography, therefore appears not merely a vestigial remnant of Victorian print culture, but a condition of possibility for pornographic consumption as such, eludes enlistment into Marcus's quantum singularity of sexual activity. That seriality necessitates some principle of characterology seems important too, insofar as the possibility of sexual particularity remains roundly denied by discussants of pornography on all sides of the question: by antiporn crusaders for whom pornography is a perversion of proper sexuality (or of the ethical treatment of human beings), but also by pro-porn critics for whom the infinite diversity of pornographic fantasy merely reproduces, at a different order, the singularity of fantasy itself. Brinkema's intervention enables a reformulation of the initial question, then, in the following terms: who can survive sex?

In pornography, though, no person, object, or idea is incapable of being enlisted into sexual activity, and one might add, no text either—no text, and certainly not a novel organized around the delicious spectatorship of early adolescent female vulnerability, can immunize itself against pornographic use. Nell's little death in No. 44 (January 30, 1841) occasioned an international outpouring of grief that shattered the border between real-world and phantasmatic epistemologies as decisively as any money shot. That historical event of public tenderness has itself been subject to innumerable cruel recontextualizations: Oscar Wilde may or may not have delivered the words attributed to him by Ada Leverson, that "one must have a heart of stone to read the death of Little Nell without laughing," but they have been attributed to him since.[20] Aldous Huxley certainly did characterize Nell's death as the central example of Dickens's "monstrous emotional vulgarity," adding "there was something rather wrong with a man who could take this lachrymose and tremulous pleasure in adult infantility."[21] The tear-jerking pleasure Huxley assigns to Dickens is patently a symptom of his moral and emotional corruption, contemplation of which stirs in Huxley images of unpleasant liquid emissions: "the overflowing of his heart drowns his head"; "his one and only desire on these occasions is just to overflow"; "a stanchless flux"; "mentally drowned and blinded by the sticky overflowings of his heart"; "whenever he is in his melting mood, Dickens ceases to be able, and probably ceases even to wish, to see reality."[22] For Huxley, at least, *The Old Curiosity Shop* provokes some psychic association between sentimental crying and compulsive masturbation: "He had an overflowing heart; but the trouble was that it overflowed with such curious and even rather repellant secretions."[23]

The novel itself invites such constructions. Serialized in a new periodical, *Master Humphrey's Clock*, established by Dickens in 1840, the first-person narrator upon whom the first chapter alights has generally been referred to as "Master Humphrey," who indeed appears elsewhere in the periodical as a narrator.[24] G. K. Chesterton, who follows this convention with respect to *The Old*

Curiosity Shop, nonetheless admits that it follows "only from moral evidence, which some call reading between the lines."[25] (The evidence appears to be the very proliferation of the subject "I" in the opening chapter: Master Humphrey is a self-involved old cove.) The narrator, in any case, does not introduce himself by name, and when he writes as the novel's opening sentence, "Night is generally my time for walking," Dickens may as well have been talking about himself: he did so, in those terms, twenty years later, in the personal essay "Night Walks" he published in *The Uncommercial Traveler*.[26] An old man who has been walking about at night, reflecting with some vicarious delight on the "unwholesome streams of last night's debauchery" that he encounters in Covent Garden, relates the following:

> One night I had roamed into the City, and was walking slowly on in my usual way, musing upon a great many things, when I was arrested by an inquiry, the purport of which did not reach me, but which seemed to be addressed to myself, and was preferred in a soft sweet voice that struck me very pleasantly. I turned hastily round and found at my elbow a pretty little girl, who begged to be directed to a certain street at a considerable distance, and indeed in quite another quarter of town.
>
> "It is a very long way from here," said I, "my child."
>
> "I know that, sir," she replied, timidly. "I am afraid it is a very long way, for I came from there to-night."
>
> "Alone?" said I, in some surprise.
>
> "Oh, yes, I don't mind that, but I am a little frightened now, for I had lost my road."
>
> "And what made you ask it of me? Suppose I should tell you wrong?"
>
> "I am sure you will not do that," said the little creature, "you are such a very old gentleman, and walk so slow yourself."
>
> I cannot describe how much I was impressed by this appeal and the energy with which it was made, which brought a tear into the child's clear eye, and made her slight figure tremble as she looked up into my face.
>
> "Come," said I, "I'll take you there."
>
> She put her hand in mine as confidingly as if she had known me from her cradle, and we trudged away together, the little creature accommodating her pace to mine, and rather seeming to lead and take care of me than I to be protecting her. I observed that every now and then she stole a curious look at my face, as if to make quite sure that I was not deceiving her, and that these glances (very sharp and keen they were too) seemed to increase her confidence at every repetition.[27]

We have here the materialization of a certain kind of pornographic fantasy, of older male benevolence and pliable female gratitude, replete with details that would fit this scene quite easily into the *Maiden Tribute of Modern Babylon* forty years later—W. T. Stead's anti-prostitution polemic that enabled the passage of the 1885 Criminal Law Amendment Act. As Judith Walkowitz has remarked, Stead's own ferocious prose "replicated, in a moralizing frame, many of the sadistic scenarios that filled pornography's pages."[28] In one such replication, "The Child Prostitute," Stead writes: "It seemed a profanation to touch her, she was so young and so baby-like. There she was, turned over to the first comer that would pay, but still to all appearance so modest, the maiden bloom not altogether having faded off her childish cheeks, and her pathetic eyes, where still lingered the timid glance of a frightened fawn. I felt like one of the damned."[29] The narrator of *The Old Curiosity Shop*, likewise, "felt really ashamed to take advantage of the ingenuousness or grateful feeling of the child for the purpose of gratifying my curiosity," yet he reports with a kind of troubled lasciviousness that she was "more scantily attired than she might have been" and delights in the secretiveness she exhibits about her night's activity: "a great secret–a secret which she did not even know herself."[30]

More pressing than the erotic dramaturgy of the scene—which must have been noticed by more of Dickens's readers than have publicly remarked on it—is the fate of the narrator positioned in the early part of the novel as a surrogate for the reader. He is, as we have seen, initially pulled into the plot by the girl (who will turn out to be Nell); he remains within its ambit purely through his own surreptitious device. When he has returned her to her grandfather—when, that is, he has arrived at the titular "Old Curiosity Shop," by way of a spatial type of metalepsis—the narrator conducts a genial conversation with the old man ("it always grieves me to contemplate the initiation of children into the ways of life") in which some of the exposition is extruded ("has she nobody to care for her but you?"). When his duty has been discharged and it is time to depart, however, the narrator finds himself unable to tear either his body or his thoughts away from the relationship between Nell and her grandfather, which he regards with a Humbert-esque mixture of tenderness, envy, and loathing of his Quilty-esque doppelgänger: "His affection for the child might not be inconsistent with villainy of the worst kind; even that very affection was in itself an extraordinary contradiction, or how could he leave her thus? Disposed as I was to think badly of him, I never doubted that his love for her was real."[31] The narrator lingers, departs, and eventually returns a week later—"yielding" to his desire to return—at which point he is drawn into a sequence which introduces two of the novel's remaining major characters: Dick Swiveller and Daniel Quilp. At which point the narrator declares:

> And now that I have carried this history so far in my own character and introduced these personages to the reader, I shall for the convenience of the narrative detach myself from its further course, and leave those who have prominent and necessary parts in it to speak and act for themselves.[32]

One might expect his final words to indicate that what is to follow will consist of more first-person narrative, perhaps from multiple narrators, but indeed neither this narrator nor any other appears again to speak in the first person. It is a narratological volta with, as far as I am aware, only one analogue, its reverse, in nineteenth-century fiction. In William Morris's *News from Nowhere,* a third person adopts the first: "But, says he, I think it would be better if I told [my adventures] in the first person, as if it were myself who had gone through them."[33]

We might conclude, with Tony Giffone, that *The Old Curiosity Shop* thus stages an early draft of the experiments with "double narrative" associated with the mature Dickens: with the interlocking first- and third-person narrators of *Bleak House,* for example, or the affective retrojection experienced by Pip as he describes his own childhood in *Great Expectations.*[34] But to do so would be to undervalue the two strangest elements of this moment: first, that we have come to understand this character as, first and foremost, a lurker and therefore cannot thereafter console ourselves that he has indeed left these characters alone—perhaps the same unnamed character has merely affected a third-person style of narration in order to lurk more effectively. And second, that his recoil from first-person narration appears to be psychologically motivated—that in fact it seems symptomatically consonant with the ambivalence and shame of his entire encounter with Nell and her grandfather. Although, that is, the narrator proudly finishes himself off at the end of the novel's first number, we can never be sure that we are finished with him; in a novel so concerned with the condition of spectatorship—a condition depicted directly in many of the illustrations by Cattermole and Phiz—we find ourselves in a more than usually paranoid relation to the apparently objective third-person narrator. This unnamed narrator is not therefore merely a pornographic reader himself—one who attributes the basest motives to Nell's grandfather—but an aperture through which pornography suffuses the whole narrative scene. Various characters appear at different moments as resurgences of the nameless narrator: the eavesdropping and malevolent dwarf, Quilp, who reveals his knowledge of the grandfather's gambling habit with the sinister threat "you have no secret from me now"; the urbane literary ventriloquist "of eccentric habits," Dick Swiveller; perhaps above all the mysterious "single gentleman" (named after an ad he answers to let a room), who takes great delight in lurking around Nell and her grandfather after the girl's death: "for a long, long time, it was his chief delight to travel in the steps of the old man and the child (so far as he could trace them from her last narrative)."[35]

In other words, I propose that *The Old Curiosity Shop* understands itself—doubtless paradoxically—as a porn parody of itself. We might understand "porn parody" as a perhaps self-canceling, and perhaps pleonastic, metagenre, by way of a major milestone in the genre, the 1991 movie *Edward Penishands,* in which someone who was not Nikki Sixx of Motley Crüe played a Johnny Depp pastiche, except instead of having spindly blades for hands—a tragedy of overburdened preciousness, of finickiness taken literally—his wrists tapered into bulbous, somewhat repulsive, cocks.[36] In one scene, Edward Penishands attempts to eat a plate of spaghetti with his cock-hands, but finds himself all fingers and thumbs, body switching back and forth between grotesque phallic overcompensation and almost girlish, butterfingered flimsiness. By relocating the phallus from penis to arm, *Edward Penishands* extends and amplifies the problem of phallic embodiment as such: the arms can indeed fuck and fuck hard, but they can't avoid looking stupid while doing so, and if the penis-hands do not connect to the root chakra, one wonders whether the penis-penis ever does either. Is one supposed to laugh or masturbate? Not–Nikki Sixx, with his fiberglass arm-cocks, is dick-fisting two girls, who kneel on the bathroom floor, asses up, moaning the half-defeated, half-amused moans of the porn starlet, while he pouts like Pierrot at the camera. And one type of pleasure one can imagine, a synthesis of porn and comedy, is the cruelty of the pornographic exhibition of women's bodies, bodies that one has, in effect, tricked into being humiliated. Another type of pleasure one can imagine, though, presumes that the three bodies performing this odd piece of vaudeville are coordinating their own arrhythmia quite democratically, and that the little moans correspond asymmetrically to Nikki's pout.

Trans women are often accused of broadcasting pornographic images of womanhood—in some sense, of *being* pornography.[37] The effect is more pernicious than a mere scapegoating, albeit that the minoritizing gaze that transforms trans women into wax (porn) women accelerates the general degradation of trans civil rights across the polity. But by leaving open the possibility of a return gesture, of treating the pornographic sign as an illustration of transness, contemporary antitrans ideology universalizes the pornographic gaze across the body of the social. In conclusion, then, let us consider the regime of "clockiness" that the porno-universalism of the present has produced. When we talk of "clockiness," we switch the conventional modes of active and passive assumed by most models of aesthetic judgment. If I refer to an aspect of my embodiment as clocky, I attribute to myself a capacity—what James Gibson might call an "affordance"—for a particular kind of interpretation, even as I distance myself from the interpretation itself. My Adam's apple, let's say, might mark me as someone whose embodiment is conditioned within the category of "male," but that claim alone does not amount to an ascription of clockiness, which is present if and only if the marking itself would be, in my view, incorrect—that is, if I would not categorize myself as male. So, clockiness is not exactly a symptom, but an openness to the symptomatology of the other; not a property of the perceiving subject, but an anticipation of observance.

FIG. 6. Still from *Edward Penishands*, directed by Paul Norman. Paul Norman Productions, 1991.

We see too, then, that clockiness exposes the transsexual body as, in the Marxian sense, a relational condition. There is no transsexuality that precedes either clocking, the anticipation of clocking, or the evasion of clocking; much as there is no use-value prior to exchange, whether of the laboring body or of any other commodity. On these grounds, trans Marxists have redeployed the otherwise contentious vocabulary of gender to explain aspects of trans embodiment as relation. In her important essay, "Gender as Accumulation Strategy," Kay Gabriel argues that gender is a set of claims made upon bodily pleasure; relatedly, the trans masculine Marxists Jordy Rosenberg and Paul Preciado have developed differently accelerationist accounts of gender as a species or capital peculiar to the capitalist mode of production. (Clockiness, of course, predates the modern transsexual, as anyone who has read Chaucer knows well.) It is true that the negative condition of clockiness, as a currency form of transsexual embodiment, generates a slew of oddball effects: while we may, of course, be frightened to be clocked (and for many trans sex workers, primarily Black trans women, who remain the central targets of antitrans violence, clocking can be a life-or-death matter), we may also view the very fact of being mistaken as a source of pleasure, of secret knowledge. Writers on t4t sexuality, like Cam Awkward-Rich and Hil Malantino, often emphasize the visibility of transness as an erotic token. Yet it isn't clear whether these enchantments fundamentally differ from immiseration by capital, or from the erotic relations between bodies conditioned by the coercive extraction of surplus labor power by capital. Perhaps we eroticize wealth, but it isn't clear that that condition prohibits an apparently countervailing delight in the bodies of workers—and this distinction is all the more important if we see, as Gabriel does (developing arguments by sex workers like femi babylon and feminist theorists of sex work), *hotness* itself as an effect of the extraction of feminized (feminizing) and racialized (racializing) labor. Rather than, for example, as a condition of consumption. Thus a key question of trans women's experiences—whether beauty is produced by laborers or purchased by consumers—reproduces in a curious way a central question of nineteenth-century aesthetics. In her indispensable history of the period, Regenia Gagnier argues that the "marginalist revolution" of the middle-Victorian period—a theory of value, developed by Stanley Jevons, focused on the relative values, or "marginal utility," of various priced commodities—overwhelmed prevailing aesthetic theories of productive labor (such as those of John Ruskin) with theories of consumption and taste (personified in Oscar Wilde).

What even is clockiness? Extracting a definition only from a context—the first and most fundamental principle of Marxist method—unfamiliar readers will have perhaps already realized that the term refers to aspects of trans embodiment, especially trans women's embodiment, that supposedly give us away, that undermine our attempts to pass. You have presumably also realized that the term indicates a certain ambivalence—fear, yes, but also, perhaps, a fond shimmer—as Charlie Markbreiter has written about in his recent essay on trans cringe.[38] What I suspect that you cannot have guessed, but which any trans person could confirm at a stroke, is that clockiness is not unidirectional—that, despite appearance, a clocky appearance is not one which exposes a trans woman as, secretly, a man; it is just as likely to expose a trans woman as, secretly, a woman. Because it is a symptom that only exists for the observer, one cannot determine in advance exactly what meanings will be assigned to it within a given setting. At Heathrow Airport on Tuesday, dressed up in my best "boy mode" so as to match the name on my legal travel documents, I was frog-marched out of the men's toilets by two agitated attendants, a man and a woman, both saying quite forcefully, "madam—madam—you are in the wrong place." Clockiness does not expose a referent, so much as muddle reference altogether. A couple of weeks earlier, similarly butch for an appointment at the American embassy, one cop said to his supervisor, "she's got an appointment," before his colleague, gently chiding, corrected him: "ahem, *they've* got an appointment."

Clockiness resurfaces once again the unfortunate problem of ontology—or, least, requires some calibration of how trans embodiment depends upon a strategic refusal of any and all demands for ontologization. With all its ambivalences, it thwarts any ontological position, demarcating as it does a social regime under which the body is transformed into language—or rather, by which the body's resistance to being so transformed occasions some form of crisis. To acknowledge one's own clockiness—an acknowledgment whose extent is in principle, although not by definition, universal—is to articulate the transsexual condition that, within psychoanalytic thought, precedes and conditions the developmental drama of sexuation. We can illustrate the negative, or rather instrumental, quality of clockiness through the perhaps surprising medium of cake simulacra—a comparison made to me by a British scholar of international relations, also an antitrans campaigner, named Colin Wight, albeit that he characteristically spectacularly missed the point. Showing me photographs of some cakes in the shape of burgers, Wight took issue with the claim that the basically unclockable trans porn actor Buck Angel is a man, suggesting that the claim amounted to saying that that these cakes were in fact burgers. Yet, since the cakes were utterly clockable—were meant to signify "burger," but not truly to *resemble* burgers—Wight inadvertently confuted his own position. As he may not have known, cake simulacra have been a popular and consequential meme type over the last few years, even spinning off a Netflix quiz show, *Is It Cake?*, in which contestants are invited to build cakes in the shape of various objects that they can then pass off. When one watches an "is it cake?" video, one experiences, for the first few seconds, incredulity, which only mounts as the knife (the agent of bisection, and thus of exposure) approaches. But as the knife pushes into the soft fondant exterior, the object being exposed as cake is revealed, simultaneously, to be substantial in an entirely distinct way. The fondant into which the knife presses warps slightly, producing a visual distortion akin to a lens flare or a switch in perspective, and although "cake" is the name for the object that is exhibited at the end of the video, that object can be cake only in an unusual sense: it isn't there to be eaten, only to be cut; its sensory and its substantial aspects are both allegorical, which is to say indexical. Somehow the "is it cake" video succeeds in depicting cakes that are less cake-like than even the objects whose shapes they've taken. The "is it cake" video thereby offers a rejoinder to Magritte's famous "ceci n'est pas une pipe," not because, in the end, *c'est un gâteau*, but because the videos expose the potential cake-like-ness of all objects; even a pipe, even a painting of a pipe. Trans flesh is flesh, regardless of which direction it has transitioned; regardless of whether, in fact, it has transitioned at all. The "is it cake" video exploits the porous border between two forms of visual observance: the skeptical observance ("surely this cannot be cake") and the pornographic observance ("the knife teaches us the essential nature of matter").

In his short and unusual book on Magritte's painting, Michel Foucault describes the work as a "calligram": that is, as a kind of text shaped like its referent. His basic claim about the painting is that it comprises a sort of negative tautology; it is both true and false, and works to convert meaning into shape and vice versa. He goes on:

> Pursuing its quarry by two paths, the calligram sets the most perfect trap. By its double function, it guarantees capture, as neither discourse alone nor a pure drawing could do. It banishes the invincible absence that defeats words, imposing upon them, by the ruses of a writing at play in space, the visible form of their referent. Cleverly arranged on a sheet of paper, signs invoke the very thing of which they speak—from outside, by the margin they outline, by the emergence of their mass on the blank space of the page. And in return, visible form is excavated, furrowed by words that work at it from within, and which, dismissing the immobile, ambiguous, nameless presence, spin forth the web of significations that christen it, determine it, fix it in the universe of discourse. A double trap, unavoidable snare: How henceforth would escape the flight of birds, the transitory form of flowers, the falling rain?[39]

We might think of clockiness as a related kind of trap (and "trap" itself, of course, is a term which denotes the precarity of the clockable woman). The transsexual is a calligrammatic woman, both reference and referent; index and indexed.[40] And the consequence of the transsexualization of flesh is no less epiphanic than those of the Foucaultian calligram: the irresistible ascription of meanings to forms one discovers in the world.

IV

Fear of Commitment

ADORNO CASTRATING BRECHT

> Male people cannot just become female people because they want to. Those words have meaning beyond feelings in our heads. Hormone therapy and gender reassignment surgery may enable people to live in the same way as the opposite sex (and they definitely provide evidence of commitment) but they don't actually change our sex. My chromosomes are as they ever were.
>
> —DEBBIE HAYTON, "NOT ALL TRANSSEXUALS THINK TRANS WOMEN ARE WOMEN," *THE SPECTATOR*, OCTOBER 17, 2018

why do we let him do this to us?

What does it mean to commit? And why are men stereotypically afraid to do it? At some point in the last, say, sixty years, commitmentphobia displaced sexual neurosis as the acceptable euphemism through which men could talk about (or at least be talked about as though they talked about) the obsessive fear of castration that, from Ovid to Freud, took as its sign the phallophagic vagina.[1] Thus, in one of the key contemporary representations of male commitmentphobia, the relationship between Chandler and Janice on *Friends*, our sympathetic horror derives not from Chandler's having been encompassed by Janice's body but by her postcoital laugh. To surrender, by surrendering to the feminizing procedure of commitment, one's contempt for women; to put oneself in the position where one had no choice but to put up with such a laugh—worse, perhaps, to feel compelled to *excuse* such a laugh among one's friends: such would be the anxious hypothesis of a heterosexual body magnetized toward feminization but just as strongly defended from it.

Transsexual women are likely to approach the question of commitment a little differently, if only because for transsexual women the prospect of *feminization*—however fearful or even contemptible it may remain in certain respects—is articulated on the terrain of biology, and subject to repeated avowals. But trans women, if we are women, are women who have chosen to become such, and so to those whose understanding of the subject "women" distinctively entails a predicate like "not choosing, unwilling," we present something of a conundrum. This conundrum endures whether or not anyone choose to ontologize "transness" as an innate condition of being, because even if we could agree that transness *were* innate as a form of desire or identification, its expression would still require an exertion of will—an exertion, moreover, often conducted at the stake of one's own life. Conceiving of a moment in which such a truth presents itself to a subject who may at some point transition, the psychic moment that defines a trans woman as such is not one of mere identity but of *commitment* to the truth of that identity, a commitment that could be contrasted from (say) living in the light of it, to confessing it or to asserting it, or simply to holding it to be true in a sense that requires no action on the part of the holder.

For such a subject, the term "commitment" names both an act of self-creation and an act of self-dissolution. Self-dissolution, because for trans women who were not raised as women, the subjection by a sudden awareness must interrupt the continuity of consciousness, must break into the story. The old name is thereafter "dead," as though choked off. This breach, after all, can occur with or without hormonal treatment, which likewise is supplied to trans women on the paradoxical grounds that it will both affirm our prevailing sense of ourselves and radically reorient the way we think.

This paradox disgorges new fables of monstrosity and reanimates old ones. Susan Stryker's analogy of the trans woman with Frankenstein's creature does not, exactly, stipulate who is Frankenstein, but in addition to the nontrans women she addresses, one must surely cast the author herself.[2] If the self-abolition effected by trans consciousness seems to align trans with the evocations of negativity that have proven so important to queer theory, it is by no means obvious that such an alignment can be brought to completion. An optimistic framing of a trans identity would frame it as the integration of a whole. But there is surely a more critical-theoretical account to hand. If truth breaks into consciousness with the kind of force that shatters previously maintained ego-architecture, could commitment to a proposition like "trans women are women" be anything other than a reaction formation through which a wounded ego could attempt to reinsert itself into a domain from which, by the emergence of the new truth, it has been (however temporarily) expelled? For Theodor Adorno, who will be the focus of attention for most of the remainder of this chapter, "commitment" was a complex way of asserting the autonomy of an artistic creation: a committed artwork possesses "an apoliticism that is in fact deeply political," and, because it is "necessarily detached as art from reality," subsumes both an available category and its antithesis.[3] An extrapolation that might make sense for trans women would be something like: a negation of the past self without the embrace of a new one; it would in that sense be aligned with an account of transness as "open-ended" and productive of "categorical crossings, leakages, and slips of all sorts."[4]

It would resemble, in perhaps surprising ways, the commitment that Debbie Hayton attributes to "hormone therapy and gender reassignment surgery" in the epigraph above—a commitment without an object, exactly, because the apparent object of commitment (I get surgery to prove I am a woman or to make myself one) is precisely that which the expression of commitment has been formulated to abolish. For, as the author of these words (herself a transsexual woman) thinks, the object of this particular commitment is nothing more than a paradox. A paradox, because the thing that the trans woman asserts that she *is*, a "woman," is precisely the thing that she cannot be as long as she is a trans woman; at least this would be the case if, as Hayton claims to think, the predicate "a woman" were indexed by the symbolic division demarcated by unfelt but determinative chromosomes.

One can, however, imagine forms of commitment that exist in the vicinity of negation, with rather more affinity to the claim "trans women are women" than this one has—once one takes account of the unscalable negation that what Hayton euphemizes as "gender reassignment surgery" makes unavoidable: the negation of the phallus, its subsequent inversion and invagination. This negativity endures precisely *as* the form of the realist proposition. As Eva Hayward writes, "My cut is *of* my body, not the absence of parts of my body. The regenerative effort of my cut is discursive; my transfiguring cut is a material-discursive practice through which I am *of* my body and *of* my transself. My cut penis entails being and doing, materiality and affect, substance and form."[5] I cannot write on my own body in these terms, but the same cut encompasses me no less than it does Hayward, for I also am a transsexual woman caught within a dialectical structure of predication. I have said, I shall become a woman, and thereby cease to be "I"; but as soon as I have said it, the "I" that will have done so will not possess the authority of the one that began to utter this sentence. This very setup is, according to Hegel, in fact the representational form (*Vorstellung*) of dialectical reasoning as such: "Starting from the subject, as if this were a permanent base on which to proceed, [this way of thinking] discovers, by the predicate being in reality the substance, that the subject has passed into the predicate, and has thereby ceased to be subject."[6] In predication, some aspect of the subject's subjecthood is left behind; or, in more colloquial language, definition is an act of cutting. If only, of course, the thing left behind could be fully done with—but those pesky chromosomes make themselves known in the Hegelian dialectic too, since the new subject (the one formed by predication) can no more rid itself of the old one (the one pre-predication) than a leopard can change its spots:

> The subject in the second case—viz., the knowing subject—finds that the former, which is itself supposed to be done with and which it wants to transcend, in order to return into itself,—is still there in the predicate: and instead of being able to be the determining agency in the process of resolving the predicate—reflectively deciding whether this or that predicate should be attached to the former subject—it has really to deal with the self of the content, is not allowed to be something for itself, but has to exist along with this content. (Hegel, preface to *Phenomenology*, §60)

The surplus subject present in its existence at the beginning of the proposition (eggplant emoji) will be lost in the act of predication (scissors emoji) but now finds its own subjecthood determined by the plenitude of loss that characterizes the new condition. Trans women are women; are "not allowed to be something." For trans women, as for Hegel, the act of commitment (eggplant emoji, scissors emoji) entails the dialectical absorption of a logic of predication whose truth-value is literally impossible to determine, because there is no subject ("trans woman") that does not include the predicate ("woman"), nor any predicate that can fully divest itself from the subject. So, then, an urgent question that, for us, arises within the discourse space of feminist ethics: Is it possible to separate ("separate"; cut off) the tendency toward commitment from the necessity of proving a falsehood? The question applies to men, not just trans women. Does anyone really want to be a man? Perhaps not, says Valerie Solanas: "Since he's trying to prove an error, he must 'prove' it again and again."[7] Is commitment to a thing finally a decision to stick with it *right or wrong*, and therefore to acknowledge that one's commitment is made, not on the basis of rightness, but on the basis of commitment for its own sake?

how to castrate your friends

In the "Commitment" essay, Adorno ladles some of his liveliest acid onto those enfeebled creatures, among whom are doubtless numbered some of our own, who publicly espouse a radical politics but do so in bad faith. Scanning the souls of these creatures with his characteristically unblinking eye, Adorno cannot neglect to observe a whole suite of tells, each disclosing that beneath the carapace of this or that would-be revolutionary hero cowers a milquetoast romantic lead. So, for example, Brecht's "exaggerated adolescent virility . . . betrayed the borrowed courage of the intellectual";[8] he has fallen prey to "the theatricality of total plain-spokenness"; consequently, the "simplicity of his tone is thus a fiction."[9] The feeling of being thus scanned by Adorno is, doubtless, part of the pleasure that only a German disciplinarian can still supply to that type of earnest young man who believes that beginning a PhD in literary studies will sublimate the violent cravings, sadistic and masochistic, that are aroused when he meditates on revolutionary themes. Indeed, it would not take Hélène Cixous to detect in this very rhetorical move a kind of self-scansion, a no less enfeebled desire to be released from the violence of the author's notoriously, even comically, self-serious prose and allowed, if not to chill out, at least to join in; "works of art, even literary ones, point to a practice from which they abstain."[10] Thus it is not just startling to learn, at the essay's end, that the villain all along has been "the petty-bourgeois hatred of sex" that unifies the "Western moralists" with the "ideologists of Socialist Realism"[11]: it is also disturbing, since the opposite of hating sex is not, as it turns out, enjoying it (whatever that would mean), but hating those who hate it, reversing the bourgeois aversion to sex and situating theory itself as an interminable, asymptotic approach toward pleasure, good faith, and practice.

Is "trans women are women" a commitment after all, then? That possibility would be suggested, partly, by the gendering of the would-be radical intellectual in "Commitment" toward which I have already gestured—hard on the outside, with a gooey center. To be clear, I'm not saying Adorno's conscious understanding of these terms is one in which sex is dispositive or definitive. Adorno doesn't want to avow masculinity—maybe nobody does—it's just that the nonavowal of masculinity is a constitutive gesture in his performance of masculinity. It is therefore also part of the proposition Adorno advances of an artwork's discovering its commitment. Where do commitments come from? Do they "develop," come into being, or change—or are they "natural"? The coming-into-commitment has at least this in common with the logic of coming-out-as-transsexual: it is both a recognition of something that is already true and a promise of a future truth that will, everybody understands, never be fully realized. In respect to that first problematic, Sartre's mistake is to believe that it is possible to represent "a just life" under the present conditions of injustice—the "feigning of a true politics here and now,"[12] which generates mere radical kitsch.

It will seem picky to take issue with an aspect of Adorno's writing that he does not openly avow: the analogy of artistic commitment with the feminizing humiliation of the wannabe radical. Especially since, if this thread in his writing were pointed out to him, he could probably explain it as an inverted symptom of bourgeois prudishness, or else perhaps one of the cognitive biases swallowed along with his Freud. Nonetheless, this critique will feel familiar to readers of nineteenth-century literature, since the feminization of interiority was one of the most consequential cultural projects of the nineteenth century, as such feminist scholars as Nancy Armstrong and Rita Felski have explained so powerfully. One of Adorno's greatest virtues for contemporary scholars is the tonic he prescribes to treat our bad-faith politicking. But the shock of the sexed body as it arises, spasmodically, toward the end of "Commitment" cannot (or at least does not) treat the pathological conception of "bad-faith politics" as the masculine concealment of primary femininity that underwrites modern metaphysics as such. This is why, I take it, Sianne Ngai turns to Adorno to theorize the cuteness of the avant-garde as the disavowed but finally desired fantasy of its own inefficacy: the fictitious but comforting belief that poetry makes nothing happen. "Poetic explorations of cuteness," Ngai writes, citing Gertrude Stein and Francis Ponge alongside Adorno, "can be read as a way of acknowledging but also critically addressing oft-made observations about the literary avant-garde's social *powerlessness*, its practical ineffectualness or lack of agency within the 'overadministered world' it nonetheless persists in imagining as other than what it is."[13] In the framework of "Commitment," where men stand alone, the question of how to be a good political subject can only be resolved by either negating the feminine object of self-identification (the dimension of the artwork and the radical alike that is both ornamental and anaclitic) or else deferring until some postpolitical future the question of sex altogether.

Sometimes it seems as though the work of "Commitment" is to model the former action, to strip feminine objects of their glamour and spoil their shine: "A work of art that is committed strips the magic from a work of art that is content to be a fetish."[14] Elsewhere, it seems like the best resolution to the problem of feminine interiority is something a good deal more negative—the "menacing thrust of the antithesis,"[15] perhaps. If there is an irony here, it is only that the division of the political into which "Commitment" finally collapses requires the separation of the political not only from politics, which it has coded not merely as risible but also as feminine from the start (as mere "ameliorative measures"), but also from the domain of the body, which is arranged among other objects of "brawls of the cattle dealers over their shares of the booty."[16] Political commitment requires not merely the blotting out of that which the world (wrongly) calls politics, but also the negation of embodiment as such: proper (negative) commitment gets figured as an immanent, quasi-material tensility inherent within the writing of, particularly, Kafka and Beckett. Of course, these men cannot be praised without someone else being correspondingly feminized: they "have an effect by comparison with which officially committed works look like pantomime" (86). Commitment is a zero-sum game. In another of Adorno's notes on Kafka, it is not his competitor but his reader who is railed by Kafka's irresistible force: "He over whom Kafka's wheels have passed has lost forever both any peace with the world and any chance of consoling himself with the judgment that the way of the world is bad."[17]

Unanchored in the flesh, and with no hooks in the institutional fabric that would designate the political as an ideological or even—to others less aversive of the critique of that which the world calls politics—a repressive state apparatus, Adorno can't avoid his own pratfall into confessional: "Formal structures which challenge the lying positivism of meaning can easily slide into a different sort of vacuity, positivistic arrangements, empty juggling with elements. They fall within the very sphere from [which] they seek to escape."[18] This is surely the humanist radical's pessimistic credo, and it is worth repeating: "They fall within the very sphere from [which] they seek to escape." The "[which]" is in brackets because, incredibly, the *New Left Review* publication of Adorno's "Commitment" available as a PDF through the *NLR* website omits the pronoun through, one assumes, typographical error. The error draws the Anglophone reader's attention to the setting out of a logical formula (x "falls within the very sphere from which [x] seeks to escape") that, though it does not precisely encode the propositional form of bad faith, expresses that condition in a historical setting: the species of unwilled intellectual enfeeblement through which critique fails to obtain escape velocity and reinstantiates its own premises. Does this ever happen in "spheres" that are not already entirely accommodated by cushions of sublime abstraction? In fairness, Adorno doesn't say so.

"Commitment" finally describes a process of subjectivization (eggplant emoji, scissors emoji) rather than a politics in the conventional sense of the word. So it is difficult to know what an account of bad faith would look like, for either Adorno or Sartre, if it did not depend upon some negation of the feminized interior. Does either conceive of a model of subjectivity, intellectual or otherwise, that is not hard on the outside but soft in the middle, or are both doomed to endlessly introject the terrifying masculine authority that ever tries, and ever fails, to choke out the interior femininity, which, in reality, exists for that masculine identity only so that it *can* be choked out? I think it is worth wondering from where would Adorno (or where would we) have inherited this bafflingly misogynist conception of the political subject, the subject at the scene of politics: this political man is the unhappy participant in an endless gauntlet in which the failures of his (it is always his) own acts of linguistic expression are routinely and humiliatingly exposed. It becomes a kind of drama of telling and not telling, what I see but you can't: "The less works have to proclaim what they cannot completely believe themselves, the more telling they become in their own right" (83).

Opposite Sartre and Adorno, Solanas and Andrea Long Chu both think that *all* men are afflicted with a repressed transsexual desire. A strong case for that position could be derived from observing the case of Chandler Bing, in the very second scene of the first episode of *Friends*, "The One Where Monica Gets a Roommate," which broadcast on September 22, 1994. A Truffaut fade overlaps one shot of our new buddies in a coffee shop with another almost identical shot, the buddies in a minutely different configuration on the upholstery and their costumes slightly changed. Chandler is reciting a dream:

> So I'm back in high school. I'm standing in the middle of the cafeteria, and I realize, I am totally . . . naked. (Monica: "I've had that dream.") Then, I look down and I realize there is a phone . . . there. (Joey: "Instead of?") That's right. (Joey: "Never had that dream.") All of a sudden, the phone starts to ring. And it turns out it's my mother. Which is very, very weird because . . . she never calls me.

Another gentle cross-fade onto a minutely different shot. What, exactly, is Chandler doing, in order to realize that it is his mother? Does he . . . pick it up? Or . . . press a button? Is she on speakerphone? What must this wretched, defeated man do to his genitals to enable him to communicate with his mother, by whom he feels so permanently abandoned and deferred? It might be worth recalling, too, that the term "mother" could at this point be one of two women—for Chandler, though he doesn't acknowledge the fact, has two mothers. The first one we meet, the one he calls "Mom," is Mrs. Bing, played by the almost transsexually glamorous Morgan Fairchild; but the second, the one he calls "Dad," is otherwise known as "Helena Handbasket," formerly Charles Bing, and played by Kathleen Turner.

commitment to the beat

I have been arguing that Adorno's framing of the faithless intellectual describes a masculine shell concealing a feminine soul; I have argued that his work is still read and circulated at least in part because of the pleasure readers derive from his virtuosically cruel performances of antifemme discipline. And I have argued that among the consequences of that discursive practice has been the opening of a question concerning the place of trans women within critical theory. I am, in one sense, substantiating an argument made by Chu in her dialogue with Emmett Harsin Drager entitled "After Trans Studies," in which she argues that scholarship dealing with trans life has been, in general terms, in hock to the account of gender offered by queer theory, at the expense of the claims and self-descriptions particularly advanced by trans people, and profoundly uncomfortable with the figure of the transsexual woman, which should have been at least a major, if not the central, figure of trans life but is instead too often cast by scholars as an embarrassment, a throwback, an anachronism.[19] For the record, I don't agree with Chu's diagnosis of the state of the (inter-)discipline of trans studies. It is true that plenty of essays in the field have worked to dilute or excuse the experience of trans women and to promote heuristic or metaphysical accounts of transness within which the singularity of many trans women's experience (eggplant emoji, scissors emoji) seems almost pedantic. But it is equally true that the figure of the transsexual woman returns again and again in the founding and refounding statements that comprise trans studies as a series of intermittent events: in Stryker's "My Words to Victor Frankenstein," in Sandy Stone's "The Post-transsexual Manifesto,"[20] and in the work of Eva Hayward, whose writing circumvents the drive to lay down the law to which Chu, Stryker, and Stone all give powerful voice, but whose experience of surgical and hormonal treatment forms the ontological grounds on which inquiry is possible. But for all that, I think that trans studies has maintained more of a distance from this particular kind of theoretical transmisogyny than Chu allows, I would argue that critical theory as such has maintained a strange proximity to the rhetorical configuration of the trans woman's bad faith.

By way of a brief conclusion, I want to consider an alternative genealogy of the relationship between criticism and sexual embodiment, toward the possibility of a realist commitment to female transsexuality—a commitment that would uphold the possibility that trans women are distinctive people and that "trans womanhood" is not merely an overstated formulation of the condition of maleness as such—through a very brief reading of an even briefer lyric (if one can even call it that) by the Victorian poet Alfred Tennyson. And to the Tennyson who, toward the end of a very long career, stuttered to articulate a difference that has puzzled every reader since its 1889 composition. The lyric is called, rather pleonastically, "To One Who Affected an Effeminate Manner":

While man and woman still are incomplete,
I prize that soul where man and woman meet,
Which types all Nature's male and female plan,
But friend, man-woman is not woman-man.

Christopher Ricks tells us that the manuscript version of the second line reads, "In earth's best man, the men and women meet," which raises the question of who Tennyson thought, in 1889, was the earth's best man. But by the end of the verse, a cryptic but rather stern injunction appears to have been issued: man-woman is not woman-man, "friend." The title, "to one who affected an effeminate manner," seems itself oddly pleonastic, since among the properties Victorians were wont to associate with effeminacy was, precisely, "affectedness"; affecting an effeminate manner, while technically possible, thus feels like a kind of redundancy. What could the lyric's terminal distinction, between "man-woman" and "woman-man," actually distinguish? Benedick Turner offers the following assessment: "The best people combine the virtues associated with both genders, but those who fail to live up to the standards of their sex cannot hope to compensate by evidencing the virtues of the opposite one."[21] Happy fault.

It is a startlingly strange poem and not one, I think, that it is easy to habilitate in a world where we tend to assume gendered interiorities and sexed exteriors, where trans women are, for example, required to pretend to be "women trapped in the bodies of men." It speaks, for example, to the possibility of a utopian trans future, since, at the moment of the poem's delivery, sexed beings, apparently, "still are incomplete." Tennyson does not gesture toward the question of their completion; or help us answer whether or not that completion may involve their becoming merged in a single, hermaphrodized, or otherwise nonbinary or two-spirit being; or whether their completions would follow separate tracks. Were such completion arrived at, would the poet stop prizing the true androgyne, or would the androgyne be contained within or prefigurative of their completion, or rather rendered redundant by that completion, subsumed in the act of sexual becoming? Neither of these questions is resolved by one of the most tricky verbs in Tennyson's idiolect, "types," which names the action of the true androgyne soul on behalf of "Nature." In *In Memoriam*, written nearly three decades before "To One Who Affected," "type" had been the occasion for one of Tennyson's most destabilizing wobbles, which leads the poet to correct a characterization of "Nature" between one canto and the next. In canto 55, Tennyson had found some comfort in the notion that although Nature seemed prepared to do away with any individual organism ("so careless of the single life"), she nonetheless protects and preserves classes of organism ("so careful of the type," where "type" means something like "species"). But then in canto 56, Nature herself responds scornfully:

> "So careful of the type?" but no.
> From scarped cliff and quarried stone
> She cries "a thousand types are gone:
> I care for nothing, all must go."

In other words, in one of Tennyson's most conspicuous acts of self-correction, "type," as noun, had been rejected by Nature herself. Yet in the later poem, "type" returns as, now, a verb, whose direct object is "plan" (suggesting now, as probably not so distinctly in the early plan, the act of typing out on a typewriter) and whose subject is an androgynous person. It is easier, I think, to cast the androgyne as a figure of negativity (which is more or less how I think gender dissidence works out in Adorno) than it is to take the androgyne as the subject of a future for men and women. Such, at any rate, is the strategy specifically avoided by the period's more explicitly queer texts that deal with male femininity: Wilde's "The Portrait of Mr. W. H.," for example, in which the effeminate boy of the story's title is lost to history but felt as an irresistible archival presence; or Pater's "Diaphanèite," in which the androgyne heralds a future in which sex, properly understood, is abolished rather than completed. Wilde and Pater share a sense that the object of queer negation is and should be masculinity, and that the effeminate boy, who circumvents masculinity and authority, thus also negotiates a path for the undoing of gender as such.[22] In that way, they play Adorno in a major key and write out the fugue of commitment with the same countermelodic negativity.

PART TWO

How to Survive Negation

FIG. 7. Still from *The Silence of the Lambs,* directed by Jonathan Demme. Orion Pictures, 1991.

As I invent Being starting from Being, and return to Being in order to sketch out Being on the surface of Being, I am exactly in the situation of the creator. But, conversely, by gathering itself together under my operational vision, by rising up congealed and indestructible under the temporal link that I bring about [*intuition is not instantaneous: all intuition temporalizes itself*], Being becomes the truth of my anticipation, or, rather, Being pours my anticipation into Being. . . . *Enjoyment* is precisely this irritating and voluptuous proximity without distance of the For-itself to what is not itself.

—JEAN-PAUL SARTRE, *TRUTH AND EXISTENCE,* 1989

V

On Being Criticized

Several of the Essays which are here collected and reprinted had the good or the bad fortune to be much criticised at the time of their first appearance. I am not now going to inflict upon the reader a reply to those criticisms; for one or two explanations which are desirable, I shall elsewhere, perhaps, be able some day to find an opportunity; but, indeed, it is not in my nature,—some of my critics would rather say, not in my power,—to dispute on behalf of any opinion, even my own, very obstinately.

—MATTHEW ARNOLD

But all his homeless reverence, revolted, cried:
"I am my father's forum and he shall be heard,
Nothing shall contradict his holy final word,
Nothing." And thrust his gift in prison till it died,
And left him nothing but a jailor's voice and face,
And all rang hollow but the clear denunciation
Of a gregarious optimistic generation
That saw itself already in a father's place

—W. H. AUDEN

in criticism

A history of literary criticism derived from the "Acknowledgments" pages of the genre's major texts might tell us a number of things we already know. Chiefly, it might confirm that while the particularities of marital devotion with which such encomiums traditionally conclude have changed since F. R. Leavis reported writing out of a "sense of my immeasurable indebtedness" to his wife and colleague, Queenie, and our more familiar paeans to *my most assiduous reader*, the couple form itself has proven more durable than readers who skip over the paratext may have felt inclined to predict.[1] Yet the language of *debt*—which Leavis, conventionally enough, treats as a prior condition of writing literary criticism—conceals as much as it reveals. Since the body of *The Great Tradition* concludes with a celebration of the "really great" Joseph Conrad, for instance, a reader might be interested to learn that the phrase "sense of immeasurable indebtedness" is taken (presumably unwittingly—but, seriously, who knows?) from Conrad's 1919 essay "The Crime of Partition," an encomiastic acknowledgment of what the *Collier's* editor calls "the 'irrepressible vitality' of the Polish nation."[2] In that case, however, Conrad insists that "a sense of immeasurable indebtedness" will *not* serve as a basis for self-determination, since any such gratitude "is always at the mercy of weariness and is fatally condemned by the instability of human sentiment to end in negation."[3] Leavis, no doubt, can hardly be faulted for having failed consciously to register any wariness around the language of debt in Conrad's argument. Leavis's flagging, paratactical syntax seems to know, as his lexis does not, that criticism has not been born, sinless, from a sentimental attachment: "my sense of my immeasurable indebtedness, in every page of this book, to my wife cannot be adequately expressed, and I cannot express it at all without an accompanying consciousness of short-comings—no one but myself has any part in them—that makes me insist at the same time on my claim to all the responsibility."[4]

Any attempt to embed the work of criticism in the social and psychic network glimpsed, disavowed, exhibited, or peacocked in such textual acknowledgments would inevitably have to confront a countervailing account that might call itself "Arnoldian"—an account according to which any critical project worth the name must begin by divesting itself of such "interest" in the pursuit of "the object as in itself it really is."[5] The source for such an argument would likely be Matthew Arnold's essay "The Function of Criticism at the Present Time," which is generally taken to argue (to two readerships: poorly read but sentimental romantic poets and philistine British liberals) that the critical enterprise must absent itself from practical concerns. "Let criticism leave church-rates and the franchise alone," as Arnold puts it.[6] The purpose of the present chapter, however, is to render such a rebuttal more difficult by demonstrating that Matthew Arnold himself, relentlessly and at substantial psychic expense, understood criticism as a socially embedded act of responding to the more primary condition of being—and, no less importantly, feeling—criticized. The two steps of reasoning here will sometimes blur in my own argument, but they can be logically discriminated: (1) Arnold's language of objectivity only thinly veiled a set of social and subjective conditions that variously enabled and disabled possible critical interventions; (2) the thematic substance of those conditions is felt as a governing sense of persecution and, in the extreme, offense—that Arnold criticized because he felt himself already in criticism. Pursuant to the latter of these claims, it will already be noted that I take Arnold's use of the word "criticism" to be far less specialized and technical than is generally held—as we will see, his personal correspondence composed around the time of the *Essays in Criticism* uses the word in its most conventional sense, of being mean about somebody, of grousing.

My rebuttal is not purely preemptive: it is necessitated by a set of mischaracterizations of criticism as naively objectivist or unfashionably confident in the correctness of its opinions. Distaste for critical writing has been evinced most forcefully by Sharon Marcus and Stephen Best's coauthored essay on "surface reading" and by Rita Felski in her recent monograph *The Limits of Critique*.[7] Arnold is not mentioned by name in those works; his style is too obviously affirmative ("the best that is thought and known") to lend itself to the dedramatizing arguments of Best and Marcus or to Felski's anticontext historiography. And in certain senses, the account of Arnold's *Essays in Criticism* I am going to offer resembles Felski's own method: her premise that "arguments are a matter not only of content but also of style and tone" enables her to treat the "hermeneutics of suspicion" as a particularly pervasive kind of rhetorical mood without "peering into or diagnosing anyone's state of mind."[8] This latter phrase discloses Felski's impatience with psychoanalytic (or other "depth") conceptions of a writing subject and aligns the "affect" of a text—the way it feels—with what Best and Marcus understand as a textual "surface." So, Felski's prescribed method allows readers to speculate about the way a writer or a text feels, but without assuming that such feelings can produce knowledge about the *interiority* of text, author, or context. The language of "affect" conveniently relocates psychological speculation from the *psyche* to the *soma*.

Although this kind of writing has been called "nondualistic," the conception of the world upon which it depends is profoundly dualistic. There is mind, and here is matter; we cannot deduce anything about the former from the latter. What Arnold has in mind when using the word "criticism" is, I think, a much bolder nondualism, whose "function" (which indeed serves as a decent synonym for "symptom") is to toggle *between* mind and matter, to externalize the affective condition of feeling criticized, and thereby to recirculate that affect and stimulate other affective productions elsewhere. Criticism, in other words, has always been both more excruciatingly pained and more exultantly joyful than Arnold's readers have been prepared to believe: neither a rhetorical operation for denuding ideological structures, nor a vehicle for disseminating moral and cultural lessons, but a mechanism for managing and weaponizing a particular kind of shame. In the case of Matthew Arnold, a foppish son of an eminent Victorian and his fond widow, the melodrama of criticism frequently entailed a trio of stock characters: hopelessly embattled effeminate boy (author); malicious masculine authority figure (interlocutor); and caring but inadequate maternal auditor (reader). My purpose in describing the critical scene in such terms is not to make Arnold more palatable to readers for whom affect/description will always best critique/conceptualization, but rather to suggest that the latter-day polarization of those positions (ahistorically) presupposes their ontological differentiability.

I do not wish too quickly to assimilate "critique" (the object of Rita Felski's study) with "criticism" (the practice advocated by Arnold): despite their convergence in the adjective "critical," opponents of the former rarely object explicitly to the latter—a position synthesized and elaborated in Heather Love's essay "Close but not Deep." What Love calls the "opacity and ineffability of the text and the ethical demand to attend to it" has sustained a "close reading" practice that, although its methods were formulated by modernist New Critics, has been continually nourished by a Victorian humanist tradition whose touchstone, explicitly for the modernists and implicitly for their inheritors, is Arnold.[9] Yet in the postcritical re-enchantment of a criticism deprived of critique, the distinctive value of Arnold's criticism has been first mischaracterized, then abandoned: mischaracterized by the modernists as an alibi for an objectivist critical stance that would "see the object as in itself it really is";[10] abandoned by the postcritics as a strong epistemology entailing an unseemly penetration into the ethically and erotically (im)permeable object. What might we gain by reversing these terms, and treating the (Arnoldian) critic as the (im)permeable object, already violated and writing out of a sense of that violation? This, I think, is the weak position in which Arnold found himself; I also hope that, through the elaboration of what I take to be that position, I can make a case for its utility as a contemporary heuristic, capable of renegotiating the subject/object relations that govern our contemporary critical practice.

you bastard

Arnold's reputation as a critic is founded largely on the short pieces collected in *Essays in Criticism*, many of them initially delivered as lectures or published occasionally elsewhere. The most exemplary of these remains "The Function of Criticism at the Present Time," whose title joins Sigmund Freud's "Civilization and Its Discontents" and Walter Benjamin's "The Work of Art in the Age of Its Mechanical Reproducibility" among the most adaptable and flexible formulas for generating new work. That very flexibility, which I take to indicate the openness, clarity, and ambition of Arnold's piece, is nonetheless supervened at the very start of the essay, which immediately confronts readers as more querulous, brittle, contradictory, and playful than the essay's many commentators generally acknowledge.[11] "Many objections have been made to a proposition which, in some remarks of mine on translating Homer, I ventured to put forth," Arnold opens *Essays in Criticism*, wearing his litotes heavily and awkwardly, molding what in "On Translating Homer" was a proper noun into a regular modifying clause with a cumbersome irony.[12] His critics are not named, though they are further characterized (again with a pungent vagueness): "more than one rejoinder declared that the importance I here assigned to criticism was excessive."[13] In any case, the objections had been dealt with quite thoroughly by the time a reader of Arnold's *Essays in Criticism* made it a few paragraphs into the preface. The second paragraph of that preface, indeed, nominates "Mr. Wright" to stand in as the stooge for all that is wrong, having himself taken too much offense at one of Arnold's jibes in *On Translating Homer* (1861). Arnold had written that Wright's translation, which "repeat[ed] in the main the merits and defects of Cowper's version" had therefore "no proper reason for existing";[14] Wright swiped back that Arnold had "declared with much solemnity that there is not any proper reason for his existing";[15] Arnold therefore takes pains to note "not that Mr. Wright, but that Mr. Wright's version of the *Iliad*," etcetera.[16] The preface to a collection of obvious intellectual ambition opens, remarkably, by reassuring the reader that one translator of Homer does not, in fact, wish another dead.

The reason quickly becomes clear, with a decisive shift in tone away from the lightly ironical engagement with Mr. Wright—an irony, nonetheless, that does not succeed in sanding down the passage's sharp edges—to a lyrically apocalyptic defense of the author's frivolity: "My vivacity is but the last sparkle of flame before we are all in the dark, the last glimpse of colour before we all go into drab,—the drab of the earnest, prosaic, practical, austerely literal future."[17] Such a rejoinder against literality will chafe against the injunction "to see the object as in itself it really is," but placed in the preface it possesses at least a rhetorical, and surely an affective, priority over that commonplace. Especially since, as we are reminded by R. H. Super's meticulously edited *Complete Prose Works*, that sentence beginning "My vivacity is but the last" is the only remaining vestige of three anti-Wright paragraphs excised from the first edition, in which Arnold's deep anger and frustration had been vented at much greater length: "He has held me up before the public as 'condemned by my own umpire'"; "he has himself made game of me"; "Partly, no doubt, from being crest-fallen . . . I will not raise a finger in self-defence."[18] These, too, culminate in the histrionic protestation that, after all, the critic is guilty merely of "the unpardonable crime of being amusing,"[19] Privately, in letters, Arnold would describe his vivacity in erotically lucent terms: "my sinuous, easy, unpolemical mode of proceeding."[20] An obliquely sexy description of a style that bears the woundedness of its heart on its sleeve, this is both an apt and an incomplete description of the campiness of Arnold's writing, its inability to perform the gentlemanly equanimity required by his father's forum when confronted with criticism: its refusal not to get upset.[21]

Before launching into its counterargument to the totality of critics for whom Wright has served as synecdoche, "The Function of Criticism" goes on to praise "Mr. Shairp's excellent notice of Wordsworth," adding in a footnote the observation that "a notice by a competent critic" should be appended to new editions of the works of eminent authors.[22] Specifically, Arnold suggests, the notice should be written by "a critic, a man of letters, not, as too often happens, some relation or friend with no qualification for his task except affection for his author."[23] The critic here is distinguished from the creative artist (as he had been in the Homer essay), but also from the affectionate or personal relation. The commonsensical character of this division notwithstanding, Arnold passes into citation and argument without having offered any positive description of "criticism" or "critic" whatsoever; we have these two distantiations and then a gush of commendation. The sheer repetition of the word "criticism" produces an anesthetic effect, as if the concept could be defined by insistence alone: "Wordsworth was himself a great critic, and it is to be sincerely regretted that he has not left us more criticism; Goethe was one of the greatest of critics, and we may sincerely congratulate ourselves that he has left us so much criticism."[24]

The middle part of the "Function" essay offers two further discriminations of criticism—without, again, offering much by way of positive definition. First, Arnold distinguishes between creative and critical faculties, arguing that while the former constitutes "the highest function of man,"[25] creativity exudes from "materials and a basis"[26]—those being a broader intellectual culture that has been furnished by the latter. Criticism, which appears as mere commentary on and transmission of preexisting matter ("the best that is thought and known") in fact *precedes* creativity and serves as its ground: it is the uncompensated reproductive labor that enables the creative power.[27] Arnold is careful to distinguish criticism as a logical ground—with its two attendant metaphorical repertoires of *nature* and *nation*—from the mere fact of established institutions of learning. The romantic poets lacked power, but not because they lacked books and reading: because they did not live "in a current of ideas in the highest degree animating and nourishing to the creative power."[28] The vitalist imagery associated with the establishment of a state of criticism is neither, then, arboreal nor rhizomatic, but rather liquefacient, ambient, and rhythmic: a "current," the "nationally diffused life," "a national glow of life."[29] The political complexity of Arnold's determinations seems to land most forcefully in his phrase "the general march of genius and of society," where "march" hews most closely to the meaning listed in the *OED* Online as "n. 5"—"an intention; the tendency or drift of thought"—which is up the etymological stream from the more familiar meaning of military maneuver or rhythmical collective walking.[30] Arnold means to indicate a weakly determinist causality, but one on the cusp of becoming militarized.[31]

The essay's third and longest movement is from "immediate political and practical application"—that is, from policy.[32] It is in this movement that we become aware of the presence of Arnold's gentlemanly critics, who are introduced and rebutted in sequence ("A member of the House of Commons said to me the other day";[33] "the Englishman in general is like my friend the Member of Parliament";[34] "He is like the Lord Auckland of Burke's day";[35] a string of newspapers; and then Sir Charles Adderley, whose appearance marks the essay's turn into its own version of practice.[36] Much has been written on the aversion to politics in Arnold's criticism, but less on the rhetorical mode in which he responds to his own dismissal in advance, which involves cagey citation and ambivalent repetition:

> Joubert has said beautifully: "C'est la force et le droit qui règlent toutes choses dans le monde; la force en attendant le droit." (Force and right are the governors of this world; force till right is ready.) *Force till right is ready*; and till right is ready, force, the existing order of things, is justified, is the legitimate ruler. But right is something moral, and implies inward recognition, free assent of the will; we are not ready for right,—*right*, so far as we are concerned, *is not ready*,—until we have attained this sense of seeing it and willing it. The way in which for us it may change and transform force, the existing order of things, and become, in its turn, the legitimate ruler of the world, should depend on the way in which, when our time comes, we see it and will it.[37]

This blizzard of deconstructive nuance, nestled within which is one of the more frequently excerpted dicta from Arnold's prose, has been taken to argue that the world of politics ("force") should not be influenced by the world of morality and culture ("right") until a deferred future.[38] Bending the syntax to extrapolate that motto is impossible, however, without ignoring the complex position of the "we," which is introduced only belatedly and only through a further twist of Joubert's French—which Arnold has already bent a little out of shape.[39] "Till right is ready" does not equate to "we are not ready for right," and by the end of the passage, the "we" has been transformed from mere by-stander to active determinant of right: "the way in which *for us* [right] may change and transform force, . . . should depend on the way in which, *when our time comes,* we see it and will it."[40] Arnold has transformed an objective statement into a subjective one, through the interposition of a pronoun that, earlier on in the same paragraph, he had used to designate "the English" as distinct from "the French." It is not at all clear, in other words, on which side of any number of binaries—public/private, English/French, force/right, we/they, see/will—Arnoldian criticism will finally come to rest.

Private letters, too, amplify Arnold's sense of "criticism" as something liable to be misread, a process whose apparent objectivity broadcasts what it was, indeed, never intended to conceal: the vulnerability of the critic. Invited by J. Dykes Campbell to supply a review of Tennyson's "Enoch Arden" (1864), Arnold pulls his pen up from "The Function of Criticism at the Present Time" to talk of criticism rather more secretively: "is it possible for one who has himself published verses to print a criticism on Tennyson in which perfect freedom shall be used?"[41] Arnold makes clear to Campbell that he does not "think Tennyson a great and powerful spirit in any line" but worries that saying so publicly "would inevitably be attributed to odious motives."[42] Tennyson and, later, Browning were cast by Arnold himself as the greater men from whose shadow he might retrieve some dignity and even glory: he wrote to his mother in 1869, "it might be fairly urged that I have less poetic sentiment than Tennyson and less intellectual vigour and abundance than Browning; yet because I have perhaps more of a fusion of the two than either of them, . . . I am likely enough to have my turn as they have had theirs."[43] That poignant self-laceration has been affirmed by at least one of his critics.[44] In the case of poetry, Arnold could allow posterity to make its final judgment on his merit—in the sphere of criticism, however, the social contingencies of opprobrium and suspicion held sway. He never wrote publicly against Tennyson. We may note, however, that in his letters to his mother, Arnold did write himself into *her* place; distinctively, amidst an admittedly limited correspondence, he signs his letters to his closest confidante with his initials, or her own pet name, "your ever most affectionate, M. A."

The psychic space through which the parade of gentlemanly *eminences grises* (Wright, Tennyson, etc.) passes, in Arnoldian criticism, might be designated that of "the Victorian daddy." And in a sense, it is ironic that any authorized style should bear the eponym "Arnoldian" since, as both his contemporaries and later commentators have noted, the poet-critic bore heavily the weight of a patronym associated with his father, Thomas, the grand Victorian educationalist. Thomas was the very archetype of Victorian "eminence": Lytton Strachey barely glances at the career of Arnold *fils* in the chapter of *Eminent Victorians* dealing with Dr. Arnold, and the essay's glib appreciations of Thomas seem to mock Matthew by ignoring him: "He held decided opinions upon a large number of topics; and he enunciated them—based as they were almost invariably upon general principles—in pamphlets, in prefaces, and in magazine articles, with an impressive self-confidence. He was, as he constantly declared, a Liberal."[45] To others—including, as we will see, Charlotte Brontë—the foppishness and frilliness of the son shamed the father. If it is an irony, however, it is of the kind that affirms the ostensive rather than negates it: if "Matthew Arnold" was understood as in some sense a bad copy of "Thomas Arnold"—an embodied threat to the version of narcissistic reproduction entailed by patronymy itself—that structure could also be made to characterize Arnold's version of criticism as such: a generalized secondariness. More pressingly, the overbearing presence in Arnold's essays of authoritative men—of whom Mr. Wright is the first of many examples—might, on first glance, be grafted onto a conveniently reworked but nonetheless recognizable oedipal scheme. Unable to displace the tough guy from his perch of ontological security, Arnold generates a secondary terrain—criticism—in which the manly virtues of Rugby School and orthodox liberalism might be more subtly thwarted. Criticism not on the other side of weakness (or surface, or description), but *as* the position of weakness itself.

murmur, mama, murder

Arnold does not permit his readers to make a fetish of such weakness, however; rather, he equips them with a set of rhetorical techniques with which to make both pleasure and political virtue of the abjected position. The final section of "The Function of Criticism at the Present Time" draws together many of the rhetorical and formal techniques we have been discussing in the operationalization of criticism *against* the masculine figures of orthodoxy and tyranny whose presence has hitherto been sensed only at the margins. There are many more such personifications of masculine intimidation than Mr. Wright. In his essay on "Arnold and Pater," published in *The Bookman* in September 1930, T. S. Eliot notes a couple, admitting that "where Sir Charles Adderley and Mr. Roebuck appear, there is more life than in the more literary criticism."[46] Those two are the primary antagonists of "The Function of Criticism," whose animalish names are arrayed among other, equally repugnant (and, as Marc Redfield points out, suggestively anal) English names ("Higginbottom, Stiggins, Bugg!") as counterevidence to their chauvinistic, and no less animal, assertion that the "old Anglo-Saxon breed [is] the best in the whole world!"[47] It is against that bestializing assertion that Arnold begins not merely to mobilize but also to theorize the function of criticism, which has hitherto been felt primarily either as evasion or as a subtle tonal shift operating at the level of repetition; this, Arnold comes to understand, is the condition of the *murmur*. Towards the end of the essay, Arnold begins to imagine the voices of these antagonists converging in a "dithyramb," a choric and collective enunciation to which the voice of criticism must find an alternative.[48] "Criticism"—here the subject of the action, though Arnold will reappear to take its place in due course—should "leave church-rates and the franchise alone, and in the most candid spirit, without a single lurking thought of practical innovation, confront with our dithyramb this paragraph on which I stumbled in a newspaper immediately after reading Mr. Roebuck:—."[49] At this point, cataclysmically, Arnold introduces a short item from a newspaper:

> "A shocking child murder has just been committed at Nottingham. A girl named Wragg left the workhouse there on Saturday morning with her young illegitimate child. The child was soon afterwards found dead on Mapperly Hills, having been strangled. Wragg is in custody."[50]

It is then these last words, "Wragg is in custody"—"the sex lost," he adds—that Arnold proposes "murmuring under his breath" in response to the coryphaeic Mr. Roebuck.[51] Note, too, the weirdness of Arnold's "with," positioned before "our dithyramb" so as to leave bizarrely open the question of where exactly Arnold stands during the confrontation between dithyramb and paragraph: reading alongside the Roebucks, in a spirit of winsome discord, or presenting the paragraph, as though it were a sick note justifying his perversity, to frustrate them.

The anagogical pressure placed on this anecdote cannot but recall *Adam Bede*, George Eliot's novel-manifesto for "seeing the object as in itself it really is" that, likewise, derives from a narrative of maternal infanticide its fullest articulation of the moral complexity of realism.[52] Yet, where that novel invests in the capacity of the real to save readers from brutish condescension, Arnold's position is in one sense much more radical than Eliot's. More radical, because the virtue of the Wragg anecdote is, in a sense, its inability to function as an anecdote: it will not be allowed to *prove* anything, lest it be dragged thereby into the circuit of pragmatic reformism from which criticism, at all costs, must be exempted. The meaning of the words "Wragg is in custody" is, in this sense, phonic rather than semantic, performative rather than constative; they vibrate with half-articulated suggestiveness. As the choric setup might have led us to expect, its importance is in the sounds of the words themselves and in the affective disposition ("murmuring") with which they are articulated. In the address to Mr. Wright excised from the preface, Wragg reappears (despite, one presumes, her having yet to be introduced to the proposed reader) and again Arnold emphasizes the vocal quality of the story, framing whatever "Wragg" has become by this point, the object of a murmur, almost as a kind of vomit: "I will not even ask him,—what it almost irresistibly rises to my lips to ask him when I see he writes from Mapperly,—if he can tell me what has become of that poor girl, Wragg?"[53]

The murmuring, however, encapsulates if not criticism's practice, then at least Arnold's conception of its utility. It is an oddly masochistic operation, which takes alien language and merely repeats it; indeed it is the *mereness* of the repetition that distinguishes its affect as such. It is a technique without efficacy, a rhetorical device designed to minimize, through its minor-keyed reproach, the subjective presence of the rhetorician. It was a strategy Arnold used elsewhere: to theatrical effect, for example, in the introduction to *On the Study of Celtic Literature*, written when he collated his articles for the *Cornhill* into a monograph for Smith and Elder in 1867. The introduction begins by setting up the familiar chorus of philistines, whose mouthpiece this time is the *Times*, which has attacked Arnold's philo-Celtism "in its usual forcible style" and addressed him specifically as "a sentimentalist who talks nonsense about the children of Taliesin and Ossian, and whose dainty taste requires something more flimsy than the strong sense and sturdy morality of his fellow Englishmen."[54] In the remaining few pages of the introduction, Arnold repeats "strong sense and sturdy morality" six times, the proper masculinity gracelessly entailed by the *Times*'s effeminization of the Celts getting stuck in his mouth in much the same way as the word-woman Wragg: "Did any one ever hear of strong sense and sturdy morality being thrust down other people's throats in this fashion?"[55]

Criticism, then, may be "powerless to aid or to harm," as T. S. Eliot suggests, but for Arnold it is eminently capable of vocalizing the conditions of its own powerlessness, a wound that it opens over and over again.[56] And, although the murmur in "The Function of Criticism" and the repetition in the introduction to *On the Study of Celtic Literature* are more self-consciously performative than most of Arnold's prose, the subvocal murmur lurks within most, if not all, of his acts of "situating." This "murmur," with its phonic associations (via Wragg) of both "mama" and "murder," serves as a name for Arnold's own critical affect, the shadow state that occupies the position in relation to "theory" that has been vacated by "practice." It is a word that Arnold gravitates towards in the many citations in the *Essays*: from "Marcus Aurelius," "art thou compelled, through being defectively furnished by nature, to murmur"; from "Maurice de Guérin," "a melodious murmur, which dies away in the soul," "the murmur of that world of thought and feeling," and "the murmur of night."[57]

The ambivalent rhetorical power of Arnold's murmur may go some way to explaining an oddity within his reception, especially among the modernists to whom he appeared an early advocate for critical objectivity. Despite the frequency with which he has been treated as the originator of that tradition, his critics have generally experienced their own kind of tremulousness when describing his work, as if feeling keenly the inadequacy of his criticism. Lionel Trilling calls him "the great continuator and transmitter of the tradition of humanism,"[58] and goes on to further define this category—it entails urbanity, sociality, and intelligence—in terms strikingly similar to those that appear within T. S. Eliot's essay. Eliot exhibits Arnold as the "forerunner," "ancestor," and, again, "father" of humanism.[59] For Eliot, as for Freud, the paternal relation was nonetheless founded on a kind of miscomprehension and competition, and so Arnold's fatherliness is a sign of his inefficacy and impermanence: "He was a champion of 'ideas' most of whose ideas we no longer take seriously."[60] Trilling grants that Arnold has "stayed . . . fresh," but muses that "it is not entirely easy to understand why this should be so," and opens the introduction to his 1949 *Portable Matthew Arnold* with an awkward list of Arnold's defects as a man and as a writer.[61] Harold Bloom, another of the twentieth century's most vocally oedipal theorists of criticism, was simply scornful of Arnold, the inadequacy of whose oedipalization derived from a refusal to avow his filial relation to the Romantic poet that (in Bloom's view) endowed Arnold with his model. As a result, there is no creative misprision, only a "highly derivative" poetic practice that remained "embarrassingly close to Keats."[62]

These evaluative oddities make manifest, among other things, a profound uncertainty in Arnold's critical essays about how readers are supposed to relate and rank the terms in circulation, some of which feel at times interchangeable: "culture," "Hellenism," "criticism," "objectivity," "disinterestedness," "the best that is thought and known," "humanism," "sweetness and light," etc. This thread of positively valued but hazy categories does not, as Amanda Anderson argues persuasively, amount to a system. It amounts, rather, to a "range of forms of detachment" in merely "loose relation to one another."[63] (Funnily enough, it was only when the critical essays were collected into a single volume that their introductory piece, hitherto "The Functions of Criticism at the Present Time," was reconceptualized in the singular.) These blurs, I would add, are not the accidents of a haphazard mind, but foundational features of Arnold's conceptualization of criticism as entailing an affective asymmetry to which the murmur is the most dynamic possible response: criticism is eminently more fun for one to do than to have done to one.

I am in love with Arnold's inadequacy and with the rage and wit he musters against it. It is this glass-jawed grandee, the dullest of dullards, who among nineteenth-century prose writers most inflames my narcissism, whose bloodless commitment to learning "the best that has been thought and known" and to murmuring it into the granite faces of power, most intensifies in me the dubious feelings of insuperability and isolation. No less so since, to date, I have yet to persuade a single person that this version of him exists. Most readers and biographers have found grounds to affirm the judgment passed by his friend Benjamin Jowett, who believed himself to be eulogizing Arnold when he wrote, "He was the most sensible man of genius whom I have ever known, and the most free from personality."[64] Of course, as everybody (here, Trilling) points out, "it was not our present sense of the word 'personality' that Jowett intended—he meant that there was no impulse in Arnold to make any special claim for himself."[65] But just as I have been attempting to drag Arnold's "criticism" back to the colloquial mode of chiding and griping that, as we have seen, preoccupied him deeply, I will take Jowett at his word that a lack of personality is precisely what it sounds like—an antisocial vagueness, distinguishable but finally inseparable from the function of criticism.

The idea that criticism is written out of a condition of being criticized will feel achingly familiar. Situating one's intervention in the terms established by those one wishes to engage has become, for those of us Trilling and Eliot would place in Arnold's line, such an indispensable element of the scholarly essay that we have missed the complex rhetorical work the *Essays in Criticism* do with it, the wound it opens up for their author. The work's composition raised, for Arnold, the problem of how to nominate and nominalize its objects; how to intervene into a critical field that, he also felt, did not yet exist and it was the collection's task to convene. The collection was assembled in 1865 inductively: mostly from preexisting work, with Arnold adding an introduction (the "Functions" essay, which he also delivered as a lecture at Oxford and published in *The National Review* in November 1864) and the above-quoted preface. Letters to its publisher, Alexander Macmillan, reveal Arnold's doubts and hesitations about the piece, which is conceived with the same kind of querulousness he brings to the dispute with Wright: he would prefer a cheap edition because "I am the most unpopular of authors, but I think this volume will pay its expenses." More striking yet is the difficulty Arnold has titling the collection. His first suggestion, "Orpheus," is abandoned for similarly defensive reasons ("I shall certainly be torn to pieces for presumption by the Thracian women of the periodical press"), but finally it is the prepositional problem of criticism that detains him: "I had thought of 'Essays of Criticism' in the old sense of the word *Essay—attempt—specimen*; but perhaps this would hardly do. What do you think of 'Essays *in* Criticism'?"[66] The "of" title would have sounded strange, as Arnold realized, but would have preserved one of the essays' foundational curiosities: that they are attempts both to reach "the best that is thought and known" and to operationalize that knowledge against an array of third parties, from the philistines to the various Mr. Wrights who personify that class. On the other hand, to be *in* criticism is to be, in some sense, already in the wrong.

unupbraided for once

Thematically speaking, there is nothing remotely radical about Arnold's troping of the bad mother as a figure of ruin and disaster: it remains one of the most recurrent figures in European semiotics, as well as one of psychoanalytic theory's most persistent ghouls. Nothing radical either, to paraphrase Redfield again, in the anecdote's tremulousness about menstruation ("Wragg") and its anxiety over castration ("the superfluous Christian name lopped off"[67]). Yet it is worth noticing that Arnold's mobilization of maternal relation via Wragg against Roebuck and Adderley might also exemplify a shift in his relation to the figure of the bad *father* during the period of his major productivity.[68]

Arnold contemplates the idea of *mercy killing* the father (putting him out of his misery) in a poem published in *Fraser's* in 1855 to mark the death at thirty-eight of Charlotte Brontë, predeceased by all three of her gifted siblings but survived by her father. After a brief reminiscence of a meeting with Brontë and Harriet Martineau, whom Arnold also believed to be close to death (she lived another twenty years), the poem comes to contemplate the sad condition of a "childless father":

> See! in the desolate house
> The childless father! Alas—
> Age, whom the most of us chide,
> Chide, and put back, and delay—
> Come, unupbraided for once!
> Lay thy benumbing hand,
> Gratefully cold, on this brow!
> Shut out the grief, the despair!
> Weaken the sense of his loss!
> Deaden the infinite pain![69]

The poet was evidently self-conscious enough about appearing to express a sincere desire for the mental decline of Rev. Patrick Brontë that the passage was excised from the version of "Haworth Churchyard" that appeared in *Poems: Lyric, Dramatic, and Elegiac* in 1877.[70] And indeed the passage seems scarcely in possession of its own marbles. The polysyndetic "delay" enacted by the irruption at "Alas!" not only stutters and repeats, but also swallows its own subject: "Age" is glossed between the dashes, but then apostrophized after their closure. Awkwardly, too: "unupbraided" had appeared in Edward Young's *Night-Thoughts* in 1745 ("Nor stands thy wrath deprived of its reproof / Or unupbraided by this radiant choir"); it would appear again in Swinburne's *Atalanta in Calydon* in 1865 (in Althaea's ironic description of a future in which she and her son might live "each unupbraided, each without rebuke / Convicted, and without a word reviled / Each of another").[71] The word was otherwise Arnold's, and this is his only usage. There are other questions: why is the hand of age "grateful"—because it is unupbraided for once? And what is to be said of the rhyme—visual, rather than phonic—of those verbs "weaken" and "deaden"?

Of Charlotte Brontë herself, Arnold had written less charitably in his private correspondence: writing to his future wife, Frances Wightman, in December 1850 to record the meeting he treats at the beginning of "Haworth Churchyard," Arnold complained that Martineau "blasphemes frightfully" and that

Brontë was "past thirty and plain, with expressive gray eyes, though."[72] *Villette*, he wrote as late as 1853, was "hideous undelightful convulsed constricted [*sic*]."[73] It is indeed easy to find evidence of what Antony Harrison calls Arnold's "notorious misogyny"—what he himself called his "feeling with regard to (I hate the word) women."[74] (In the context of Arnold's passionate letters to Arthur Hugh Clough, who is addressed throughout as "my duck" and "my love," incidentally, that odd admission feels at least as seductive as symptomatic.[75] Brontë's recollection of the encounter was no kinder:

> Those who have only seen Mrs. Arnold once will necessarily, I think, judge of her unfavourably; her manner on introduction disappointed me sensibly, as lacking that genuineness and simplicity one seemed to have a right to expect in the chosen life companion of Dr. Arnold. On my remarking as much to Mrs. Gaskell and Sir J. K. Shuttleworth I was told for my consolation it was a "conventional manner," but that it vanished on closer acquaintance; fortunately this last assurance proved true. It is observable that Matthew Arnold, the eldest son, and the author of the volume of poems to which you allude, inherits his mother's defect. Striking and prepossessing in appearance, his manner displeases from its seeming foppery. I own it caused me at first to regard him with regretful surprise; the shade of Dr. Arnold seemed to me to frown on his young representative. I was told, however, that "Mr. Arnold improved upon acquaintance." So it was: ere long a real modesty appeared under his assumed conceit, and some genuine intellectual aspirations, as well as high educational acquirements, displaced superficial affectations. I was given to understand that his theological opinions were very vague and unsettled, and indeed he betrayed as much in the course of conversation. Most unfortunate for him, doubtless, has been the untimely loss of his father.[76]

What is the connection, if any, between the recurring sense of Matthew Arnold as foppishly overshadowed by his eminent father and his having been established as the "father" of the poetastic style of writing on culture? In concluding this chapter, I will attempt to answer that question by aligning Arnoldian criticism with what I take to be a related phenomenon: the concept of narcissistic desire as it is understood in psychoanalytic theory. Narcissism will seem an odd context in which to describe an intellectual project so oriented towards (textual, cultural, human) objects as Arnold's. Yet the two concepts describe an allergenic response to the fact of one's own objectivity—to the empirical fact that one is, indeed, treated as an object by others.

Recently, Arnold has recurred in a different guise than as the patriarch of the New Criticism. In a recent essay entitled "The Function of Criticism at the Present Time," Virginia Jackson contrasts Arnold's criticism with that she derives from Lauren Berlant, whom she calls "our Arnold in drag."[77] (We have already seen Arnold himself in full Norma Bates mode.) Jackson retrieves from Berlant a phantasmatic compensation for Arnold's melancholic condition: where the Victorian glumly remained on top of Pisgah, the "current diva performer of the function of criticism" dreams her way into the promised land, because "after all, what forms of desire are not fictive?" True, but it is not clear that Arnold's criticism is, precisely, a desire—or, at least, not in the psychoanalytic sense evoked by Jackson. (Criticism is, to be sure, introduced in *On Translating Homer* as "just that very thing which now Europe most desires," but there criticism is the *object* of desire, rather than a motivating force.) In the *Essays,* the critical power works to "make an intellectual situation of which the creative power can profitably avail itself";[78] it is not, in itself, such an availing, or even an agency. Creative power is the source of "man's true happiness"; critical power seems, by contrast, a far more affectively ambivalent phenomenon.

There is one kind of psychoanalytically expressed desire that *does* suggest Arnoldian critical affect, though: narcissistic desire. Libido, as Freud develops the idea in "On Narcissism: An Introduction," is subdivided into ego-libido and object-libido, with the latter encompassing most psychic states commonly called "desires," and the former encompassing similar tendencies directed towards the self, experienced either by the secondary (i.e., adult) narcissist or any subject in a narcissistic state.[79] (These "ego-desires" are nonetheless categorically distinct, Freud thinks, from the "ego-instincts" of self-preservation, which are emphatically nonlibidinal.) The presence of ego-libido inhibits the subject's incorporation into normal object relations, because the narcissist is uniquely capable of treating *himself* as an object, should an object seem like a useful thing to interact with. "The creative power has, for its happy exercise, appointed elements, and those elements are not in its own control": Arnold's search for a spirit of criticism resembles Freud's lifelong attempt to explain those cognitive states which do not tend towards the generation of new meanings, or of newness in general.[80] Freudian narcissism, like the Arnoldian criticism, both is and is not relational: the symptoms of each are visible in the subject's treatment of objects, but the condition of each is felt as the subject's growing sense of his own objecthood. One of the many ironies of Arnold's famous formulation that "criticism obeys an instinct prompting it to try to know the best that is thought and known in the world" is that criticism must, perforce, recuse itself from the privileged field of "the best that is thought and known." Yet we have seen that Arnold recognizes, in Burke, Joubert, and the other autoerotically charged objects Cain calls his "touchstones," analogues to his own isolation and abjection; men into whom he may merge both himself and his antagonists.[81] I offer this observation not in a spirit of diagnosis, but to return Arnold to the world of acknowledgment and reproof that left its lacerations on both his own prose and the critical style that continues to bear his name.

When the *Pall Mall Gazette* falsely attributed to him the view that Arnold was "a Philistine of the Philistines," the philologist F. J. Furnivall wrote a letter of correction, reporting instead that he took his fellow Homerian to be "one of the larkiest writers I ever came across," and added "if I have mistaken so august and reverend a sage, he may, or may not, condescend to hold me up to ridicule in that delightful way of his, which the victim gets as much pleasure from as the writer himself."[82] Some version of this Arnoldian frippery found its way into the modernist reception, in Stephen Dedalus's fond Oxonian imaginings at the opening of *Ulysses*: "Shouts from the open window startling evening in the quadrangle. A deaf gardener, aproned, masked with Matthew Arnold's face, pushes his mower on the somber lawn watching narrowly the dancing motes of grasshalms."[83] With full Marvellian bathos ("the mower, mown"), Joyce plasters Arnold's face onto a figure of architectural impermeability: the permanently bemused gardener, cognizant of but unmoved by the Schillerian play of nature in his wake. Auden's imagination of an Arnoldian face-transplant ("left him with nothing but a jailor's voice and face") was, however, the more common judgment: M. A. became, for Auden and his contemporaries, his "father's forum," morphing into his own Victorian daddy on account of the very narcissistic strategies he had deployed *against* him. Larkiness, perhaps, has a shorter half-life than seriousness; it's also, perhaps, more difficult to retrieve once lost. But the problem with Arnold's larkiness is something more than its tendency to degrade over time, even its tendency to self-erase in its own pompous projections; it's that even the maximalist expressions of critical affect one encounters, in plain sight, miss their apparent object entirely and redound on the wounded narcissistic ego itself. What could we learn from a history of literary criticism composed of acknowledgments, not of marital devotion or familial care, but of the spite, neglect, and resentment that propelled Arnold, madly, into his larks?

VI

The Egg and the Essay

"Obviously, its metaphor of life as theatre is peculiarly suited as a justification and projection of a certain aspect of the situation of homosexuals."[1]

—[*YOU KNOW WHERE IT'S FROM*]

"Essays! Pooh! Forget essays! That was the past. From now on, I'm writing fiction. I have a whole new life. It's going to be terrific!"[2]

—[*SAME PERSON, A FEW DECADES LATER*]

OF COURSE THE CONSERVATIVE COMPLAINT that "one can't say anything any more" disguises a primary naivety concerning the nature of language and meaning—it presumes that, absent certain historical contingencies, *anything* could be said by *anyone*, and that the fact is fundamental to the possibility of freedom. Yet as we have seen, "I am a woman" remains a statement unsayable on the grounds of its intrinsic, rather than extrinsic, properties: Hegel (as we have also seen) would add that all self-statements remain unsayable on the same grounds. Yet if it is true that "I am a woman [now]" is unsayable; or "I will become a woman"; or even "I would like to have become a woman"; one might wish to investigate nonetheless why so many people who feel the need to say this—for whom the impossibility of the saying stands in for the necessity of the predicate—do, in fact, say it. Again and again, in the form of the personal essay. Why are there so many trans women essayists?

The answer may have to do with the condition of the egg having hatched. One only becomes an egg in retrospect, when one has hatched, and the chick has emerged. So I remember being told in the very early part of my transition, that I had been, until now, an egg, and—as powerfully rooted in a belief in latency as I found myself—I resented it deeply, this unlovely shadow of an unchosen object that, therefore, I had always (not yet) been. Thirty-four years of one's life, one's hopes, are more than mere latency—and less, too—and I recoiled from the notion that I was in a shell, "a shell of a man," as the cliché goes. D. A. Miller begins his monograph *Bringing Out Roland Barthes* (1992) with a fantasy of having been close to the man himself: "Twenty years ago in Paris, long before I, how you say, *knew myself*, a fellow student told me he had seen Roland Barthes late one evening at the Saint Germain Drugstore."[3] The pleated temporality of this line is the centerpiece of Barbara Johnson's 2002 essay "Bringing Out D. A. Miller," an important appraisal, in the aftermath of the first wave of queer theory, of the queerness evinced by and through Miller's signature mode of critical analysis. I never met Roland Barthes or Barbara Johnson, but if I had, it would have been in boy drag. Was I, even then, tucked into a shell—insincere or stupid, or both? *Mais non,* of course not. Still, to be called an egg is not to be insulted: by the time one is called one, it must be understood that one is *not* one, or not one any longer. An egg is displaced in time, "retconned" back into one's own being; a protocol for a new, and newly incommensurable, sense-making procedure. Just because one cannot say, "I am an egg," then, without falling afoul of the liar's paradox, does not mean that there aren't eggs—any more than the same problematic proves that there are no liars. (Eggs are not liars, again by definition.) Just because one cannot point to a text as an egg text, therefore, does not mean that there are none as such. It simply means that "egg" is a heuristic that necessitates deployment of the judgment of the interpreter, that any such deployments reflect the observer's judgment as much as they depict the egg.

But: eggs have theories. Chiefly, the egg's theory is that they (he, she, ze, etc.) cannot transition. Not, generally, *must* not—though doubtless beneath the sacerdotal cassocks of a few "gender critical" ministers one can catch a glimpse of chalazae.[4] Egg theory is not generally ethical, but technical. One simply cannot. Which among us, given the chance, would not? But of course it is not so simple; indeed, the categories at issue are endlessly complicated, existing on different ontological orders (sex and gender, for example), and battened by chaotic forces so powerful and incoherent (desire, say, or sexuality, or "socialization") that to attempt something like a sex change would not so much be malicious as it would be gauche.

The second step of egg theory is its abstraction, via a curious and ambivalent universalism, into a set of general observations about a system in which the desire is found aerosolized into a fine spray. Here is egg theory at its purest, a medium of thought-form and desire, a desire with no object and with, perhaps, not even a subject to speak of; here, at last, is the compensatory hallucination of a system of delight and foreclosure. We may have different names for this system—we may call it "affect," we may call it "queer," we may call it "aesthetic"; there are plenty of other names—all that is required is its ontology be both virtual and plastic. And it must assure us that transition is both impossible and irresistible, without exposing the dialectical negative of that image to too much light.

The punk trans poet and novelist Sybil Lamb lays out the logic of egg theory in a broken, split manifesto titled "You Best Never Ever Tr*nsition, Tr*nny." It begins:

> DETRANSITION !!! if you are one of the 1:12000 people born with GID, if your assigned gender is not your gendxer ID, if you are a fag who thinks dressing like a woman will get you more boyfriends, then you are crazy. your head is all fucked up and you are a social pariah. NEVER EVER TRANSITION. becoming a tr@nny these days means comiting yourself to years of being a gender mutant on the fringes of society. alientaion and discriination and violence are your only possible rewards. best case scenario you can get a job in porn. she-male yum dot com pays $500 for a 2 hour photo shoot. all tr*nnys get to do for the rest of their life is attend support groups and write volues of tr@nny essays. do you really want to spend the rest of your life as a trans intellectual ?? i mean sometimes get invited to do a workshop at a tr*nny conference but its been a while since that happened and people know i talk alot of nasty hatefull dhit and swear too much. and i never got a free train ticket or motel room outta doing a tr4nny conference.[5]

It hits like a blizzard. Lamb's irony is of that relentless, manic kind that cannot finally be forced to line up on one side or the other of its apparent meaning: it is both a bitter pastiche of egg ideology and its no less bitter reinstantiation. It begins with scarcity: only "1:12000" are "born with GID," and access to transition depends on, even in the virtual domain of desire, a kind of mathematical accreditation—unless I can say with confidence that I am one of this number (and who could?), then I count myself out. The irony begins to separate into yolk and albumen in the following sentences, however, with the alienation of the "tr*nny" being, also, a ticket to a more romantic being, "fucked up" and "a gender mutant." A little more sexy. Yet the irony does not settle into mere parallelism. Rather, a second pairing takes precedence over "pariah"/"mutant," which opposes the two jobs that a "tr*nny" is qualified to discharge: porn ("best case scenario") and being a "trans intellectual," which pays less well and seems, perhaps, to require one to moderate one's language. Another specifically trans dyke dimension of this reasoning, another clue that this is egg theory cast back in time from a hatched present, rather than simply propaganda: under the conditions of patriarchy, to be a woman is to desire not to be, so the transsexual desire oscillates around a gravitational center that can never be inhabited until the abolition of patriarchy in general. Lamb continues:

> BROTHERS AND SISTERS ! TR*NSEXUALITY IS FUCKING HORRIBLE ! never ever transition. I mean first off do you really identify as the other gender ?? do you even act more like or kinna physically resemble the other gender ?? such qualifications are highly subjective and arbitrary. If your a tr*nny or junior tr*nny cadet then you should know by now that gender, at least in the modern western understanding is actually about 8 factors including a lot of socialization and other peoples perceptions. Once again we are living in the eye of the hurricane of the 20th century western world. Now is a great time to be a dyke or fag. Or if your not that way you can be a Nelly boy or a Rosy the Riveter tough lady. Or if you really want to, what with all the punks and weirdos around there's people with face tattoos and 20 rings in their face working at the coffee shop. So it shouldn't be to big a deal for you to cut your tits off or get some installed or whatever. Similar like sexuality is biological and its near impossible to sufficiently brainwash someone out of being a queer. And penguins and dog are queer so that's cool. Butch women and nelly boys is also just part of how society is way over genderpated and needs to stop telling kids which toys are appropriate. So to be perfectly clear and make complete sense: gays and lessies and bull daggers and swishy fops: all natural normal members of society. Tr*nsexuality is some kind of government plot to sell penises and 'ginas!!!

Switching into another register, the egg speaks to us as a pedant ("actually about 8 factors"), even a mansplainer ("highly subjective and arbitrary")—that is, as a kind of professorial authority. An authority that positions trans people against other queers—"all natural normal members of society"—whose thriving depends on the exclusion of the "tr*nny," a figure scapegoated for the fact that "society is way over genderpated" and somehow responsible for the gendering of toys. The sheer incommensurability of the various registers deployed against the would-be transitioner, whose character Lamb revises through turns (romantic outsider, cheap fuck, tiresome intellectual, inattentive student) must culminate in a conspiratorial unity—and so it does, with the "government plot" that alone can explain the phenomenon of transsexual desire. Egg theory contends with a distinctive kind of paranoia, not without its love for the "gender mutant," but which must contend at some point with the friction between the life of the "tr*nny" and that of the queer others whose transness has been sublimated into a more nuanced, sophisticated orientation toward gender. Like Leslie Feinberg, whose *Stone Butch Blues* Lamb positions as a futurological egg theory, the post-detransition text that completes the cycle of foreclosure: "Or remember Les, the stone butch blues guy ?? He's my fucking hero cuz stone butch was all about how freaking scary and upsetting tr*nnsexual life is and after forcing himself through 20 years of loneliness and workplace discrimination he called bullshit and ripped his beard out with tweezers and proclaimed him self *neither yet both*." The reduction of the text to a violently detransitioned body: pushing back in Leslie Feinberg.

As Lamb's reference to Feinberg implies, queer theory is, in certain of its guises, indistinguishable from egg theory—not because the two habits of thought are the same, but because egg theory is drawn to queer theory's engagement with a sexuality athwart identity, an account of sexuality that derives from something more, less, or other than identity. And perhaps one can say something more direct, even, than that. Among the blueprints of queer theory—the foremothers—one finds some egg theory: several figures within queer theory either wrote, at the time, about a transsexual desire that they kept at arm's length (most famously Eve Kosofsky Sedgwick), or made late-career pitches to trans identity claims. Since describing the latter would entail dreaming a dream as dreamy as Miller's reverie of the Saint Germain Drugstore (though major queer theorists are interviewed enough that it isn't hard to google what I'm gossiping about), I will restrict myself to the case just mentioned, with the proviso that I am not attempting to do justice to Sedgwick's complex and nuanced account of queerness or sexuality, and simply to ask a question about the egg-theoretical style as it is explored in a body of work whose importance to anti-essentialist practices of queer criticism can be followed quite easily.

Egg theory gets in at the root; it seems always to be felt as the historical-dialectical antecedent of any position. It can be grown, for example, in this kind of soil, from *Epistemology of the Closet*: "Axiom 1: People are different from each other."[6] This is a statement that has been formulated not to provoke an argument or to clarify a difference, but to accomplish two quite contrary rhetorical goals. On the one hand, the statement seeks to ground and to found a discipline in difference, and therefore to establish incommensurability, division, discrimination, and distinction as its characterizing techniques. On the other hand, Sedgwick boils down this new discipline, which we have come to call "queer theory," into an unobjectionable, even quite staggeringly bland, position. By virtue of being unexceptionable, the position is thereby also universalist: the axiom, if it is true at all—and how, of course, could it not be—it follows that it must be true for every "each other" that one could conceptualize. People may be different from each other, but everyone is differenced in the same way. In the sentence that follows, "it is astonishing how few respectable conceptual tools we have for dealing with this self-evident fact" (22), Sedgwick seems to evoke the first axiomatic of the United States Declaration of Independence, if not in a citational form then at least in a tonal shift into mock epic—as well as, in this case, a politics of the "respectable." (Respectable according to whom?) The rhetorical bind is similar too: we may hold these truths to be self-evident, but to the degree that we are required to hold them, they are not self-evident but require evidencing and instantiation. Likewise, though perhaps it is a "self-evident fact" that "people are different from each other," that fact nonetheless requires the ancillary labor of "dealing with." Yet why anything so grandiose as "conceptual tools" are necessitated by a statement as bland as "people are different from each other" remains, at the very least, an open question.

queer oviparity

Perhaps an answer is supplied in "White Glasses," a short paper of Sedgwick's delivered at the City University of New York (CUNY) Center for Lesbian and Gay Studies in 1991, the year after the publication of *Epistemology of the Closet*, and collected in *Tendencies* (1993). It comprises a lyrical reflection on Sedgwick's friendship with the queer poet and intellectual Michael Lynch. It is a text whose egg theory seems designed to provoke trans readers to bifurcated rage and sympathy, much like Lamb's. "One of the first things I felt when I was facing the diagnosis of breast cancer was, 'Shit, now I guess I must really be a woman,'"[7] Sedgwick writes, marking a shift into cancer memoir with one of the genre's characteristic discursive modes—gallows humor. The gallows humor in question, moreover, is one that conditions the speaker not merely to mourn the fantasy of bodily integrity that cancer threatens—in fact, it is explicitly not bodily totality that is under siege, since Sedgwick explicitly rebuts the notion that breast cancer could be "the secret whose sharing defines women as such."[8] Rather, the joke is that cancer has forced Sedgwick into a position where she has to reject a political alignment (that of "women as such") that has, within her community, attempted to force a competition for resources between research on breast cancer and research on AIDS. "As though AIDS were *not* a disease of women, of lesbians!" as Sedgwick exclaims.[9] That disgraceful attempt to draw a line between two different kinds of disease determines, for Sedgwick, a difference not between men and women but between queer men and "that-thing-that-is-not-man, that is not the male labeled queer, that thing not vulnerable through poverty or racism, through injection, through an insertive or hot and rubbed-raw sexuality to the bad luck of viral transition."[10]

In the paragraph of most direct interest to the trans reading of Sedgwick, we acquire a discipline of identity:

> Now, I know I don't "look much like" Michael Lynch, even in my white glasses. Nobody knows more fully, more fatalistically than a fat woman how unbridgeable the gap is between the self we see and the self as whom we are seen; no one, perhaps, has more practice at straining and straining to span the binocular view between; and no one can appreciate more fervently the act of magical faith by which it may be possible, at last, to assert and believe, against every social possibility, that the self we see can be made visible as if through our own eyes to the people who see us. The stubborn magical defiance I have learned (I *sometimes* feel I have succeeded in learning) in forging a habitable identity as a fat woman is also what has enabled the series of uncanny effects around these white glasses; uncanny effects that have been so formative of my—shall I call it my identification? Dare I, after this half-decade, call it with a fat *woman*'s defiance, my identity?—as a gay man?[11]

Like Lamb's, Sedgwick's disclosure here comes from a setting-into-the-past of an identity that can be claimed, overtly, because it has been earned over time—"after this half-decade." Yet if there is irony in the remainder of "White Glasses," there is here a rather different affect, and one that—unlike irony—can name itself safely: "stubborn magical defiance." Though the sentence in which something is defied without being named is complex for more reasons that that, and for reasons more submerged than the characteristic rhetorical pyrotechnics (em dashes) with which Sedgwick interrupts the articulation of an identity claim. Where, after all, does the sudden surge of defensiveness come from? Has someone been telling Sedgwick that she shouldn't identify as a gay man? If so—and here is where the ironic bifurcation of interest in "White

Glasses" reveals itself as egg theory—then the dominating voice against whom Sedgwick articulates her defiance is not the voice of (let us risk being embarrassed and call it) the patriarchy; rather, the voice that must be forced back is the voice of the tr*nny herself, for whom only an elect cadre can be allowed to make such identifications. Sedgwick's rage is not directed at anyone who might, indeed, impede the expression of gay male identity, but at those who are perceived as already having made the crossing.

If we contrast, for example, these reflections on identifying as a gay man with AIDS and those of Lou Sullivan, Sedgwick's contemporary and a gay trans man who had died from complications due to AIDS two months and seven days before Sedgwick delivered "White Glasses" at CUNY (Sullivan passed on March 2, 1991), we can notice some similarities and some differences. Consider this letter from Sullivan to Judy Van Maasdam of the Gender Dysphoria Program in Palo Alto, dated May 21, 1987:

> Dear Judy,
>
> I'm writing to let you know what's happening with me:
>
> Have finally completed my genitoplasty via Michael Brownstein. It was a long haul, as I had trouble keeping the left testicular implant, and it had to be reinserted two additional times before it "took." But I'm all there now.
>
> Don't know if you've heard it from Paul Walker, but this past New Year's Eve I was diagnosed with pneumocystis pneumonia AIDS. Brownstein was good enough to finish my surgery despite the risk. So, Judy, even though your Program did not believe I could live as a gay man, it looks like I'm going to die like one.
>
> Yours in liberation,
> Louis G. Sullivan

By this point, the egg has fully hatched—hatched athwart the grave. The enormous moral seriousness of the letter does not deter Sullivan, any more than it deters Sedgwick, from deploying a little genre-craft: in this case, a sharp escalation in seriousness from the difficult, but still broadly comical, tale of repeated ball insertion into a disclosure of AIDS status that can be asserted, explicitly, with pride, a pride that overwhelms the vacillation of egg futurity ("I could [not] live as a gay man") with the finitude of trans certainty ("I'm going to die like one").

Do Sedgwick and Sullivan have anything to say to each other? Perhaps the question is rather, what is the futurity of egg theory? How do we understand the choices that transsexual orientation (a word I am using here as distinct from, but not in contradiction to identity and desire) can enable or tolerate? I will say, for my part, that an identification that remains psychic or notional, as Sedgwick's does, is not merely the theory-of-an-egg voice that prevented me from seeking transsexual health care for a couple of decades, and still admonishes me for having done so; it is also, and more consequentially, the voice that harasses trans people for the force of our identifications in the name and voice of queer theory. For example, Christopher Reed constructed his 2018 antitrans manifesto out of axioms, "a format that pays homage to Eve Sedgwick," and—explicitly of the post-1980s moment, which he associates with a kind of anti-"essentialist" queer liquidity—a pleasing slipperiness that allows one to aestheticize and thus incorporate difference without it departing from the ambit of "play."[12]

Others—Aren Aizura (2018), Blu Buchanan (2018), and Ellen Samuels (2018) especially—have assessed the irony of a text that speaks for "English professors" in laying down the law of queerness for the youngsters, while declaring, with a rather irradiated sense of irony, that while "the feeling of asserting authority can be very seductive," nonetheless "that doesn't make it right."[13] My point here, in this assessment of queer trans-antagonism, is merely that Reed's reading of Sedgwick in "Axiomatic" is, basically, right; or at least, it is in the same spirit as Sedgwick's reading of Sedgwick in "White Glasses." Egg theory suffuses the entire disciplinary scene that Reed has convened. Like Lamb's egg, Reed blames trans people for the authoritarian patrolling of gender—for Lamb, in the canny reference to "toys"; for Reed, in the fourth axiom: "People feel real pain because of artificial social expectations. One response is to help people meet those expectations. Another is to dismantle the expectations." The first of these, Reed apparently thinks, is the accommodationist trans position; the latter position is that of queer theory, which is revolutionary. Yet the affect that Sedgwick has committed to, and I suppose in the end it's not so different to Reed's own, is that of the "stubborn magical defiance," an asymptotic and repetitive performance of foreclosed femininity, the femininity of the difficult woman, which can always be relied on to supply a compensatory pleasure to the subject that fails to transform itself into the object of its own desire.

Which is, how you say, *fine*. The force worth resisting is not outright hostility to transition among queer scholars, which, after all, trans people have no chance of defeating on any existing institutional grounds, but the holding of trans thought to the implicit standards of egg theory. Sedgwick's thought, of course, is multivalent and supple, juicy if one likes juicy, and really good at rubbing on various surfaces and exposing various textures. Nonetheless the continued appeal of Sedgwickian paradigms of criticism seems, to this former egg at least, strangely looped into the temporal rhythms of egg theory. I was reading a supposedly trans-friendly review of Andrea Lawlor's book *Paul Takes the Form of a Mortal Girl* the other day, which ends with the following:

> Despite the fact that the question of bodily or sensate commensurability is staged across the putative chasm of what we call "sexual difference," however, Lawlor refuses to let bodily sex provide or remain any sort of stable explanatory frame for experience, precisely because of Paul's ability to change his body. Indeed, while Sedgwick's "people are different from each other" does point to the endless collection of differences, both large and small, that gather under the auspices of most identity descriptors (but especially gender and sexuality), her deceptively simple little maxim also quietly suggests that, from the start, people are simultaneously always different from themselves.
>
> In this sense, Lawlor's novel is both about trans experience and a vision of trans experience that is not yet, but could be, and nowhere is this more clear than in our encounter with Paul. His body's special capacity for change physically stages the limitless potential for a self not curbed by the stabilizing energies of identity—a potential that exists on psychic, social, physical, and cultural levels for all of us.[14]

What is this citation of Sedgwick doing? Clearly articulating a universalism of some kind, in line with the "violent universal bang" that Lawlor's titular character is claimed to have experienced in her first lesbian orgasm. But of what kind? A universalism predicated on the infinite divisibility of self into ever more complex and contradictory fragments, an "endless collection of differences." This is not, obviously, an attempt to police the bodies of trans people—although it is, perhaps, a refusal to assess the grounds on which trans people's experience is already constituted by a policed body. By failing to register that the condition of the body as a "stable explanatory frame" is precisely the fact on which dysphoria depends, the reviewer generates an account of embodiment that entirely elides even the possibility of transition, let alone the lived reality of trans people. This "vision of trans experience that is not yet, but could be" is a vision of "trans experience" as microdosing, as commodified, assimilated, low-risk, performance enhancement. It is a diet of purest egg. To put that another way: since what is being salvaged from Sedgwick, by Lawlor's reviewer as well as by Reed, is an idea of conspicuous, bland superfluity, one is prevented from disagreeing. Yes, people are different from each other. This reviewer did not, of course, go so far as to agree with Reed that "a stable gender identity may be like an iPhone X: a lot of people tell you you need to get one—but probably you don't," but the argument is substantially the same, and formally very similar. To define trans as "a self not curbed by the stabilizing energies of identity"—I suspect the difference between that position and Reed's is reducible to a difference of tone. But the tone entails a complex little twist: by reducing the difference between "trans" and "queer" to nothing, and tucking the former term neatly into the latter, this writer is able to diffuse the tension between the two constituencies by entirely eradicating the distinctiveness of one of them. A difference that, under the sign of egg theory, can only be felt as anxiety.

scrambled

Anxiety is nonadaptive, as everyone learns; the anticipation of suffering does not produce the prophylactic effect that we pin our hopes on. What Sigmund Freud calls "the affect of anxiety" he enmeshes within the complex of feelings, fears, and desires around castration—and therefore around transsexual ideation—an association that, from the 1926 essay "Inhibitions, Symptoms, and Anxiety" onward, he treats as an affect that precedes and catalyzes repression.[15] Which is to say that anxiety is structural and reproduces itself irrespective of conditions. For those whose bodies are subject to repressive biopolicing, not merely anxiety but that-which-anxiety-anticipates is reinstantiated as bodily threat; the regime of biopolitics thus becomes, for racial capitalism, a regime of terror. What Freud means by "castration" is somewhat different from what trans people signal with the term *transition*, at least insofar as Freud's conception produces recoil ("anxiety") in the (male) subject who experiences it, and trans women only produce recoil in those around us. Nonetheless, the problematic of castration anxiety depends on the anticipated loss of an ego ideal, and therefore it looks different once one has relinquished the ego ideal. To use the term *transition* in this context indicates an accession to Freud's reality principle—the surrender of a fantasy of phallic wholeness that enforced the paranoid-schizoid reproduction of the policed presentation of self.

Freud, ultimate egg theorist, was positioned on the precipice of a castration he couldn't even immanentize as theory, and never as practice without delegating the body to the authority responsible for taxonomizing and containing those marshalled under the diagnosis of schizophrenia. Nowhere is this problematic clearer than in the case of Schreber, who "believed that he had a mission to redeem the world and to restore it to its lost state of bliss, [which] he could only bring about if he were first transformed from a man into a woman."[16] Freud, as is well known, attributed the desire to become a woman to "the appearance in [Schreber] of a feminine (that is, a passive homosexual) wishful phantasy, which took as its object the figure of his doctor" (47). Critiques of that position ground the metapsychological accounts of castration in the work of Gilles Deleuze and Félix Guattari, and Jacques Lacan, yet in both cases what is found most troubling in Freud's text is his reduction of Schreber's cosmologically scaled ambition to the scale of the oedipal family. Neither objects that to attribute transsexual desire to thwarted homosexuality abolishes the former while ontologizing the latter. Freud's commentary on Schreber's *Memoirs*, as it goes, does leave some room for a transsexual ontology, although it is sequestered within an ambiguous modal verb:

> The most essential part of [Schreber's] mission of redemption is that it must be preceded by his *transformation into a woman*. It is not to be supposed that he *wishes* to be transformed into a woman; it is rather a question of a "must" based upon the Order of Things, which there is no possibility of his evading, much as he would personally prefer to remain in his own honorable and masculine station in life. But neither he nor the rest of mankind can regain the life beyond except by his being transformed into a woman (a process which may occupy many years or even decades) by means of divine miracles.[17]

One can sense, from the tenor of Freud's observation, that he would rather take transsexual desire off the diagnostic table because mere desire—manifest content—would fail to account for the principle of libidinal necessity that Schreber has articulated. Transsexual desire, then, is in fact nondesire; the delusional fantasy derives from the occlusion of homosexual desire. (Freud will not, therefore, line up on these grounds with those who reduce trans orientation to the workings of desire, because "desire" is an epiphenomenal condition: explication depends, in "The Schreber Case," on a firm grappling with the structures that preexist and govern desire.)

What one cannot fail to sense, however, is the looming identification that Freud feels with Schreber, which makes itself known in a modular syntax that places Freud before, after, inside, and athwart Schreber. A list of the modal verbs in this short section of prose: (1) "it *must* be preceded," a free indirect formulation that suspends the subject/object relation the sentence had initially erected (Freud does not say "he wanted/needed it to be preceded"); (2) "it *is not* to be supposed," presumably by a third party, the reader/supposer, whose scene of supposing is detached from, and incompatible with, the scene in which Schreber's mission *must* be preceded; (3) "a 'must' based upon the Order of Things," in which Freud pulls the necessity initially attributed to Schreber, back within the scene of his own text, in the form of a citation that one cannot confidently ascribe either to Freud or to Schreber; (4) "a process which may occupy many years," a framing which, given the difficulty governing the citational position of *must*, we are variously prohibited from confidently assigning either to Freud or Schreber. Let us underline this more fully: after introducing Schreber through a conspicuous attempt to take his megalomania seriously, or at least to appear serious and sympathetic while taking Schreber's megalomania seriously, Freud now introduces in parentheses a claim that, perhaps, could be taken to indicate that Schreber's delusion was not that he could be transformed into a woman, but that he could be so transformed quickly. Does Freud really believe that, given enough time, Schreber could have achieved his singular goal of transforming himself into a woman? I don't think the prose will allow us to rule it out.

Sedgwick's 1991 essay "How to Bring Your Kids Up Gay" performs a related sleight of hand around the figures of effeminate boy and gay man. The affective and political climate Sedgwick names is "a culture's desire that gay people *not be*" (26), and the problem she names is the emerging gay-affirming psychotherapies of the late 1980s that separated gender expression from sexual identity. This separation, Sedgwick argues, "is how it happens that the *de*-pathologization of an atypical sexual object-choice can be yoked to the *new* pathologization of an atypical gender identification" (21). This "pathologization" is, of course, the basis of a diagnosis of what we now call gender dysphoria that, while roundly criticized by trans activists calling for demedicalization, provides the basis for self-determination for trans people. Sedgwick, quite clearly, understands the medicalized subject of such a pathologization as a "proto-gay" child (22), and the child's medicalization within what we might as well call the apparatus of trans health care is problematic not, in the end, because it requires the recitation of a medical script as a condition of transition (as Dean Spade shows in "Mutilating Gender"), but because the mechanism removes embryonic gay men from the pipeline into gay adulthood, and furthermore recognizes that homosexuality, in the process of its depathologization, has thus been heterosexualized. The unspoken premise, then, is that any and all effeminate boys will grow up to be gay men unless they are medically directed to become trans women with male object-choices. The argument then sets up, with a strategy that one could only call paranoid, an apparent conflict of interests between gay and trans people that evaporates the moment one observes that not all effeminate boys grow up to be gay men, nor do all masculine girls grow up to become lesbians.

My arguments so far have been: (1) that the construction of queer universalism in a certain thread of queer theory has been predicated on the impossibilization of transition, which I have called "egg theory"; (2) that egg theory has been explicitly deployed in trans-antagonistic contexts; and (3) that it has also begun to shape certain elements of trans discourse itself, as though we were rushing to prove the impossibility of our own existence. That Sedgwick's case for foundationalist gayness incorporates both the arguments and the premises avowed by Stock and the other gender criticals would likely unnerve everyone except for Reed. But the point can hardly be made urgently enough, in a context in which the same genocidal animus Sedgwick correctly attributed to 1980s America is now being directed against trans people—by a political and cultural establishment that threatens, routinely, to prevent us from accessing medicine, restrooms, rape crisis centers, and so forth—that the practical manifestation of egg theory would be the removal of health-care provision for trans children. Not, as Jules Gill-Peterson has argued in *Histories of the Transgender Child*, that "protect trans kids" is an altogether adequate method for historicizing desires trans people feel in the present, or a sophisticated enough ethic by which to assess the applicability of a rubric for creating and sustaining life for trans people across ages and generations. As Gill-Peterson suggests, the drive to protect may also be a drive to "propertize," and the very idea of the egg, as I began by saying, seems to imply a claim to know others better than they know themselves—a claim that, however functionally indispensable to queer and trans relations, can hardly be generalized or scaled. As she puts it, "Trans-affirmative voices struggle to find a way to protect trans children that does not imagine them as deserving of protection because they are, finally the *property* of adults, not people with the right to gender self-determination" (ii). The same is surely true of pretransition adults. Eggs become chicks, chicks become hens, hens lay on top of eggs. The whole question of how to bring your kids up trans, of how to bring yourself up trans, instantiates the problematic of oviparous reproduction, which is to say the temporal formulation of dialectics as such: "Which came first, the chicken or the egg?" Is the ruse of trans latency one in which the past reveals itself as latent content only in light of the symbolic images that it appears to have hatched? The grievance incurred by such a trauma (that of hatching) would then entail the loss of a being that could never have been, that never was, much like the temporal doubling that occurs when the cognitive subject occasioned reignites herself and experiences, long after the first, a second puberty. Given which, it is not surprising that transition rarely works perfectly; the more remarkable fact is that it works at all. That we do, indeed, submit our bodies to programs of radical transcription, such that what is remodeled is not merely the ornamental or plastic accidents of the enfleshed soul but its definitive essence. (I write now as a hen, which is to say as a person who not only assumes the right to read and interpret egg theory but, more pressingly, as someone to whom self-avowed eggs—closeted trans women—have shared stories, fears, desires. There are many ways to prep an egg. One of the strangest of all is that of the masculine-presenting people who, on learning that I was not always a woman but have chosen to be one, respond wistfully, "oh, I have always wanted to do that," as though I were talking about taking a trip to Iceland or beginning a comprehensive physical detox. I do not always believe that they are telling me the truth. There are others, many others, perhaps some in every room of people I have ever addressed, whose relation to egg theory is one of absolute, disassociated foreclosure: who cannot transition and can only barely stop the drive to do so from pulling their ribs out of their flesh.)

Salvador Dalí's *Metamorphosis of Narcissus*, painted in 1937, presents a set of strange and incompatible mirrorings. On the left, Narcissus, with a walnut for a head, leans heavily down onto his own knee; his obscured gaze, we assume, is planted like his shin and wrist in the pool, love and shame inter-bled. His torso is a yellowed marble, and though we see his "reflection" as less a reflection and more an extension of his body, we do see imprinted next to him in the lake the virtual replication of the cave behind him: as Dalí writes, "With the loss of his divinity the whole high plateau pours itself out."[18] Narcissus is not doubled in the virtual space of the lake, but in the virtual space of the painting, nudged into the right-hand side of the visual field. What is the difference between the two like figures? Dalí wrote a poem to accompany the painting, which distinguishes these two figures from the "heterosexual group" in the background between them, but he does not name them. We cannot tell if these two figures, who share a geometric form, also share consciousness or some other kind of nonspatial continuity, but we can tell that there is a formal congruity, and that while the left pulls energy downward toward the lake, plunging languorously, the right is almost a plinth, gripping or balancing an egg, out of which grows a flower. Dalí's image reminds us that the metamorphosis of Narcissus is not merely a mutation of plastic matter but a transition, in the full sense, from one form of object into another. Here, indeed, there are two such mediations: the nudge, whose spatialization endows the composition with its unusual geometrical arrangement, and then, as though recapitulating that theme through a miniature thematic fragment, the emergence from the egg of not a chicken, but—a flower. Unlike Freud's Schreber, Narcissus transforms out of a surplus of desire, rather than its obliviation. For this reason, and others, it is surely a transsexual Narcissus, and not a homosexual one, that Dalí has in mind as the other of the "heterosexual group," when he ends his poem with the egg: "When that head slits when that head splits when that head bursts, it will be the flower, / the new narcissus."

a few fond farewells

I have a tattoo on my chest that reads "take me out to the beach and I'll tell you my secret name."[19] I won't tell *you* my secret name; in fact, when I was taken out to the beach yesterday (not by *you*, obviously, but the same beach Stephin Merritt was writing about, as it goes) I realized that there might not have been a secret after all: "Everyone knows what the female complaint is: women live for love, and love is the gift that keeps on taking."[20] I wonder how the word "female" hit you—and here the "you," until now so intimately addressed to *you*, the reading reader, must be taken to refer to a reader who'll never read this, the late Lauren Berlant—in recent years. You blurbed *Females: A Concern*, a book by a young feminist whose name was anything but secret, but whose complaint was all too real.[21] The title of that book presumably derived from yours, switching the commercial "concern" for the medicalizing "complaint," but its "female" means something quite different, an echo of a powerful ablative absolute:

> Life in this society being, at best, an utter bore and no aspect of society being at all relevant to women, there remains to civic-minded, responsible, thrill-seeking females only to overthrow the government, eliminate the money system, institute complete automation and destroy the male sex.[22]

To begin an essay with this breezy *collatio* is to signal confidence in one's own charisma, and very little in *The SCUM Manifesto* gives us reason to doubt the ferocious intimacy with which its author was almost literally armed. But we also know—you would teach us, let's say—that we would be unwise to assume what this manifesto could demonstrate were it to be used as evidence for *The People v. Valerie Solanas*—whether it proved premeditation for attempted murder, for example, or whether its foreclosed dream of a foreclosed utopia betokened more metaphysical, though perhaps no less murderous, violence. Essays aren't evidence—and "everyone knows" it.

After sitting in a body for over a year, this essay, "Unqueering the Essay," is disgorged onto a laptop on a day in June 2021, the day that I learned of your death. I find myself needing something more, less, or other than what "everyone knows," more than what "there remains . . . only," and yet what I have is the archive, which is what everyone knows. Do *I* know anything else? Emphatically not: I know that on the two occasions when I asked you to do something, and you declined, you were more courteous than demurrals have any right to be; I know that you delivered "Structures of Unfeeling: *Mysterious Skin*" while perched on one leg, like a little yogic stripling.[23] But who am I kidding, I didn't know *you*, except the you that everyone knows. Luckily, that was rather a lot. In the midst of an interview with my friend and former student Charlie Markbreiter (whom we'll all know as "BerlantBro" for a while), you told him that you were trans, that you had always been trans, that you went by they/them pronouns.[24] To me, and to (I would have guessed) many like me, this was a confirmation of what everyone knew, shifting that past subjunctive ("I would have guessed") into a diffused, deponent present ("everyone knows").

We write *laterally* when we write *essayistically*, etymologically downstream from the Latin *exagium*, meaning both "a weight" and "a weighing," both that which is used to measure the weight of an object and the act of establishing equilibrium on a scales. You were a Scorp, but on the Libra side—a Halloween babe. I crushed on a Scorp once; not too long ago—*ouch*. It often seems as though everyone who loathes me is a Scorp, but of course I merely run, afraid of them, because I am a Pisces sun: flowy, self-indulgent, and vague, albeit that my moon, and more or less the remainder of my chart, is in Aries (a cock in a frock). As both weight and weighing, an essay assumes the hydraulically improbable task of being both the counterweight against which the value of a given object will be assessed, and the act of assessment, both participant and observation. I suppose it is this double function of the essay that is responsible for an odd feature of the odd genre of "famous queer literary critics writing about famous queer literary critics," a collection that would include (among others) Barbara Johnson's "Bringing Out D. A. Miller," D. A. Miller's "Bringing Out Roland Barthes," Lauren Berlant's "Eve Sedgwick, Once More," and (what will be the primary focus of the present chapter), Terry Castle's "Desperately

Seeking Susan."[25] The paradoxical feature: an expressed desire to wrest, from the colleague, an avowal that, apparently, the colleague has already performed. The paradoxical nature of this generic expectation is brandished, conspicuously, by its practitioners. Barbara Johnson, beginning her essay on the modalities of outness yielded by Miller's reading of Barthes, begins by acknowledging that the phrase "Bringing Out D. A. Miller" "sounds like the equivalent of 'Barging through an Open Door.'"[26] Not merely redundant, but foolhardy, and liable to trip one up.

We might refer to this double function—or, really, we might decide not to, and do something else instead—as the *queerness* of the essay. The phrase seems automatically tiresome, doesn't it? In the era of *drones are queer*, for example; or when a resurgent LG-kinda-B movement seems determined to unreclaim the term; when the ontological security of sexuality and the sexual object seems to have become, somewhat unexpectedly, a going political concern.[27] Fucking *essays* are queer now, great—next, homework. The fatigue tells us a familiar story: that "queer" was to the 2010s what "modernism" was to the 2000s, and "deconstruction" was to the 1980s—a ballooning cultural category absorbing and denaturing everything with which it came into contact, migrating far from the recherché scenes of the coalitional LGBT front in opposition to post–HIV/AIDS respectability politics; unpopular European avant-garde literature of the 1920s; and a minor epistemological dimension of Heideggerian phenomenology. This isn't a criticism; on the contrary—*bliss* was it in that bright dawn to be alive, but to be tenured was very heaven. Nonetheless, as the bodies thin, the party dwindles, and now that you have left us, I can't locate the fulcrum on which this sun will be levered over the horizon. Last night, I was at a cabaret show at the Crown and Anchor on Commercial Street, hearing short, hortative anecdotes about the meaning of Pride, and how far "the LGBT community" has come. Soon, I thought, that so-called community will at last summon the self-respect to abandon its feeble attempt to maintain that fourth, unwanted quarter and succumb to the antagonisms that bind the first to the second, and the third to the pack. The next morning, I heard that you, Lauren Berlant, the one indisputably trans indisputable genius, had died—and found myself desperate to protest, all my cynicism in force, that you were just *queering death*, that I am now *queering mourning*, that perhaps you've *transed the eternal binary*, you've *transed gender for the final time, captain*, you've *gone where no nonbinary genius has gone before*. But death isn't subject to the optic switch between observation and participant that conditions the essay—it can't be verbed, much like "internet" can't be pluralized.

Too much observation, not enough weight. More pedantically: queer writers have often been drawn to write essayistically, not merely because essayistic writing might be understood and even defined as the writerly showing of a bit of leg, but more because essays differ from other genres of argumentative writing in formalizing the eminently queer switch between objective and subjective methods of analysis. The melancholy consequences of toggling between subject and object are offset, if they are, by the satisfaction of motley. On the other hand, the essayistic glimpse challenges the coalitional dimension of queerness, if it does, by confronting the flirtatiously self-disclosing subject with a reader whose desires, cathexes, aversions, and identities cannot but appear, if they do, alarmingly monodimensional by contrast. Over time, reader becomes writer—in fact, becomes obituarian—and the catalytic chain continues indefinitely. But at the scene of the glimpse, the essay presents the exhibitionist subject herself as scantily clad behind words, while a reader—clumsily arrayed merely in whatever flesh happens to have fallen in place—cannot but hoot for more, different, or contradictory disclosures.

At the Paris Dyke March in 2021, a group of women carried a banner that read "les LESBIENNES n'aiment PAS les PENIS," lesbians don't like dicks.[28] No (cis) lesbian reader of the present chapter whose advice I sought in composition and editing—does it disappoint *you* to know that you are neither the sole, nor indeed the original, reader of this work?—failed to point out that, whatever this banner's demerits as a political slogan, it's a bust as an empirical claim, as plenty of lesbians (cis) have been enthusiastically heralding penises, their own and others', for a good four decades by now. Nonetheless, its deployment of a putatively unobjectionable descriptive statement as though it were a normative claim has long been one of the characteristic stylistic markers of the antitrans activists who call themselves "gender critical feminists."[29] The most notorious of these sleights of hand is the now ubiquitous slogan "a woman is an adult human female," a line whose iambic-pentametric precision broadcasts its singular aesthetic feature: the self-evidence that contests any "woo" ambiguities that would drag each and every one of these words into the mire the moment that one looks at them for more than a second.[30] The antitrans literalist's literary mode takes straightforward (albeit inaccurate) self-evidence as the poetic sign for a no-bullshit approach to questions of sexual identity, turning away from the meandering striptease of the essay towards the quickening beat of the catechism, such that each of the slogans, in French as well as English, must be easily adaptable to the tune of "She'll Be Coming Round the Mountain When She Comes."[31] See also: "a female has large, immotile gametes." From prose to verse to formula: the apparent purpose of the descriptive-as-normative move is to sustain the illusion that, although you can't say anything any more, nonetheless 2 + 2 = 4, and it takes only the necessary impertinence to point out that the emperor is naked; but the dream of such a catechism would not merely be the displacement of one inadequate indexical system by a taxonomy of mathematical self-evidence, but the ontologization (or reontologization) of sexuality as the governing truth of social relations. The strategic gist, though not yet the prosody, of the verse-not-vers crowd was proudly on display on the signage of the group "Get the L Out," an antitrans lesbian organization that hijacked London Pride in 2018. "Lesbian = female homosexual" especially bears the unmistakable mark of apparent, unobjectionable self-evidence through the transcription of desires and identities into deductively rationalizable metalanguage. There is more at stake in these slogans than questions of literary form, but there are *also* questions of literary form: specifically, the queerness of the essay form, the genre that denatures the "=" in both "2 + 2 = 4" and "lesbian = female homosexual," postulating worlds in which one "two" and another "two" might be irreconcilable into a single "four," or indeed where "lesbian," "female," and "homosexual" entail complex and perhaps even contradictory predicates.[32]

None of this quite requires calibration; to write an essay claiming that one cannot write an adequate definition for social types like "lesbian," "woman," and "sexuality," without doing so in the form of an essay, might risk merely affirming the implicit prejudices of the genre. But the claim that the essay *imposes* such inadequacies of relation might be worth testing by examining, to my mind, the most vigorously prosecuted essayistic sally of the century to date, Terry Castle's obituary of the essayist Susan Sontag, "Desperately Seeking Susan," published in the *London Review of Books* on March 17 (my birthday: double Pisces), 2005. At the core of the encomium Terry Castle (Libra) writes for her recently deceased friend (Capricorn), is the curious relationship that Sontag had to self-disclosure. Curious, partly because of its lack of curiosity. Sontag's *New York Times* obituary, it is true, had made no reference to the author's sexuality at all, but as Castle notes, Allan Gurganus, in the *Advocate*, had made reference to the "disparity between her professed fearlessness and her actual self-protective closetedness," where the visibility of a closet might be thought to imply the presence of an invisible homosexual.[33] Gurganus and

Castle were only the most prominent of many voices expressing frustration with Sontag's tight-lippedness regarding sexual identity in the wake of her death. In an essay in *Out* entitled "Why Sontag Didn't Want to Come Out: Her Words," the magazine's editor, Brendan Lemon, leaves suggestively open the question of whether or not Sontag was, at the moment of her death, technically out or not, after "Joan Acocella's profile of her had just come out in *The New Yorker,* in which Sontag went on record as saying that she had had relationships with both women and men. Sontag didn't name any of them."[34]

Lemon's essay in *Out* transcribes a conversation that the editor had one night in 2000, after the Acocella profile, in which he goaded Sontag into coming out, with a set of moralizing challenges: "how can you say you're interested in liberty . . . and be so reticent about asserting your own?" and "Don't you feel that your ability to awaken people's passions would be increased if you came out—it would give gay and lesbian readers another powerful thing to connect to?" All of this took place, in Lemon's recollection, after Sontag had in fact already come out. To thicken the mystery, Acocella's brief note in the *New Yorker* contained no reference at all to Sontag's sex life—Lemon, one presumes, had confused it with a more substantial profile in the *Guardian,* in which Sontag had disclosed a great deal about her sexual life, including that she had been in love nine times: "five women, four men."[35] Lemon, of course, declines to see that disclosure as evidence of bisexuality, but in a short note published in the *Los Angeles Times* less than a week after Sontag's death, the gay historian Patrick Moore went much further in excluding that possibility from the record: "In a 1995 *New Yorker* profile, Sontag outed herself as bisexual, familiar code for 'gay.' Yet she remained quasi-closeted, speaking to interviewers in detail about her ex-husband without mentioning her long liaisons with some of America's most fascinating female artists."[36] The phrase "outed herself," as though these carefully organized dances were no more contrived than a wardrobe malfunction, is hardly the most objectionable part of the sentence. Castle raises the possibility of "bisexuality" with less contempt than Moore, but without really taking the word seriously as a descriptor of a person:

> I have to say I could never figure her out on this touchy subject—though we did talk about it. Her usual line (indignant and aggrieved) was that she didn't believe in "labels" and that if anything she was bisexual. She raged about a married couple who were following her from city to city and would subsequently publish a tell-all biography of her in 2000. Horrifyingly enough, she'd learned, the despicable pair were planning to include

> photographs of her with various celebrated female companions. Obviously, both needed to be consigned to Dante's Inferno, to roast in the flames in perpetuity with the Unbaptised Babies, Usurers and Makers of False Oaths. I struggled to keep a poker face during these rants, but couldn't help thinking that Dante should have devised a whole circle specifically for such malefactors: the Outers of Sontag.

For Castle, "bisexual" is not necessarily "familiar code for 'gay,'" as it was for Moore, but it was perhaps evidence of the sophomoric evasiveness whereby a distaste for "labels" could stand for a refusal to grapple with the realities of the real world. One of many comical analogies by which Castle roots Sontag in literary history joins the essayist to Dickens's Mrs. Jellyby, one of the many monstrous matriarchs of *Bleak House*, whose peculiar crime was to care more about the plights of starving orphans in Africa than about her own dilapidated household.[37] At the root of that analogy, one suspects, is Castle's sense that for Sontag, sexual identity remained notional, that her fame had allowed her to absent herself from what Gurganus called "what the rest of us daily endure."

To risk a summation, then: it is beyond improbable that what Castle, Moore, Lemon, and Gurganus wanted from Sontag was merely a self-disclosure—the *Guardian* profile had quite clearly yielded one, albeit one that enabled a phobic slippage between bisexuality, ambivalence, and ambiguity, though Sontag can hardly be blamed for that. What these writers wanted was for Sontag to write an *essay* on the subject. Castle acknowledges the fact somewhat explicitly with the double subject of an especially choice finite clause "the subject of female homosexuality—and whether she owed the world a statement on it—was an unresolved one for her."[38] Lemon puts the matter directly. After the failure of his moral case for Sontag to write a personal essay describing her sexuality, his final plea is offered in aesthetic terms: "I said all this would make for a fascinating essay, and that it was too bad she had never written it. She said she doubted she would ever take up this topic. Compared to the work, who cares about the biography? Oh, everybody, I replied." Lemon seems to have missed the subtlety of Sontag's response, which did not counterpose *work* to *life*, as Wilde is supposed to have done, but to *biography*, a genre of writing that, we know from Castle, the essayist held in low regard. Indeed, that subtlety indicates a willingness on Sontag's part to allow verbal self-disclosures—chat, discourse—to absorb the subtle tonal and lexical polysemy of the essay form. One derives a similar impression from the notorious 2000 *Guardian* profile by Suzie Mackenzie, in which Sontag adopted the emphatically Anglo argot of her British interviewer, and chatted in a misleadingly cheerful, bright way: "When you get older, 45 plus, men stop fancying you. Or put it another way, the men I fancy don't fancy me. I want a young man."[39] It is as though the very self-disclosure requires the erection of a parodic screen—Sontag as Bridget Jones.[40] Since the life/work futz raised the ghost of a famous Irish homosexual, one might as well recount, then, another sequence of necessary but redundant bringings-out: Pater on Winckelmann, Wilde on Pater, Bartlett on Wilde.[41]

Among the many juicy tidbits that Castle serves up in "Desperately Seeking Susan"—an essay, I might as well say, that I prefer to anything Sontag herself ever wrote and which goes some way towards making an otherwise sepulchrally unflapped manifestation of Manhattanite self-regard into someone it might have been fun to know—is that the grand defender of the modernism portion of the "Western Civ" syllabus adored Patricia Highsmith's *The Price of Salt*. "As far as Sontag was concerned," writes Castle, the "dykey little potboiler—published originally under a pseudonym—was right up there with *Buddenbrooks* and *The Man Without Qualities*." Though Castle's relentless bathos serves her puckish satire of the closeted lesbian, it also establishes a related but distinct contradiction between modernism and its others, whose relation to the closeted/out distinction remains tantalizingly unspoken. That Sontag placed *The Price of Salt* alongside the voluminous Teutonic masterpieces of Mann and Musil allows a glimpse, we are to think, of the lesbian concealed by "a number of exotic, billowy scarves," yet it also, and more damagingly, aligns Sontag with the vulgar tastes she consistently dismissed. It is this dimension of Castle's obituary, exposing the bourgeois Tucson girl behind the haute Manhattanite, that causes "Desperately Seeking Susan" to edge closest to cruelty, but Castle's omnivorous cultural appetites prevent such moments from drifting into contempt. Clearly, when Castle writes that "the famous Sontag 'look' always put me in mind of the stage direction in *Blithe Spirit*: 'Enter Madame Arcati, wearing barbaric jewellery,'" she is at least half-remembering Sontag's dismissive categorization of Noel Coward's plays as merely "camping," rather than camp.[42] But whereas Sontag's taxonomy depends upon a classed distinction between the apparently effortless grace of a Ronald Firbank and the belabored gagging of a Coward, Castle's comparisons work generally to the benefit of the hacks rather than the elect. Sontag's "comically huge" feet, "like Bugs Bunny's," knock Sontag off the perch of airy, sophisticated polysexuality, and drag her into a cartoonish and "dykey" space—the misfit gallery from where Castle is lobbing her legumes.

It would be at least an anachronism to frame this maneuver as an instance of the conflict between queer theory and its less rarefied antagonists—Sontag may not have been a lesbian in the sense that her obituarists had wanted, but nor was she a queer theorist in the Berlantian mold. Still, the sense that Castle is a lifer in, and Sontag merely passing through, the historical and cultural setting delineated by the "anthology of lesbian-themed literature I'd been working on for several years," roots itself in Castle's descriptions of the environments in which the two women encountered each other—to be precise, in the complex quasi-institutional setting of lesbian studies in the era of Judith Butler, Eve Sedgwick, and early Berlant. The assertive unfashionableness of "Desperately Seeking Susan," in other words, coincided with an emerging sense of sexual indeterminacy and anti-identitarianism as the keynotes of scholarly fashion. Although that turn, accomplished most grandly in Eve Sedgwick's *The Epistemology of the Closet,* did not in general avow Sontag as an influence, it did present itself (as Sedgwick's own career exemplifies and *Epistemology* narrates) as a move away from the pre-modernist focus of much lesbian and gay scholarship in the 1980s, and towards the promise of modernism as formal pattern for the postidentitarian sexualities that queer theory named.[43] ("Patterning" is Berlant's summary of Sedgwick: she "dedicated her remarkable intellect to asking about patterning, especially in the relation of aesthetics to sexualities."[44])

The sense of institutional embattlement, of imbrication within this particular cultural conflict, makes itself known in the two crowd scenes that bookend the narrative account of the friendship between Castle and Sontag: one a triumphant, if embarrassing, moment of lesbian election, and the other, the door being shut in the mob wife's face. The first takes place after a lecture at Stanford's Kresge Auditorium, in which Sontag had read from the "excruciatingly turgid" *In America,* after which:

> Sideswiping the smiling president of Stanford and the eager throng of autograph-seekers, she elbowed her way towards me, enveloped me rakishly in her arms, and said very loudly: "Terry, we've got to stop meeting like this." She seemed to think the line hilarious and chortled heartily. I felt at once exalted, dopey, and mortified, like a plump teenage boy getting a hard-on in front of everybody.

Triumphant *if* embarrassing, or triumphant *because* embarrassing? The desire to drag Sontag into the mulch of low cringe comedy, after all, characterizes much of the essay, and here is a moment of plain, stupefied witlessness, whose immediate effect is to endow Castle with an analogical "hard-on," the phallus being, prototypically, the object at which exaltation meets mortification. Yet the giddy little thrill, which feels little enough like an articulation of transsexual desire on Castle's part, also signals the essay's debt to the great nonmodernist plot for which Sontag was, revealingly, a sucker: Highsmith's *The Price of Salt*.[45] Castle may describe the plot with a heavy implication that Sontag identified with the young Therese—"a gifted (yet insecure) young woman who moves to Manhattan in the early 1950s"—but clearly, the "rakish" embrace signals the swagger of Carol herself. (It's too much to suggest, surely, that when Castle has Sontag "chortle," she thereby exhibits her in the role of Carroll: Lewis of that ilk.)[46]

The closing party scene belongs to a different melodrama and a different institutional setting: much of Sontag's discourse had worked to set "academics"—pedantic, small-minded, provincial—against the real seat of American intellectualism, the Manhattan art scene. When Castle is finally invited into the latter, she finds herself among the bodies of those whose names have been in circulation as currency: here is Lou Reed, "O great rock god of my twenties," now merely "silent and surly," as if to show how far things have fallen and yet how inter-bleeding are the social circles of the culturally elect. There is "the freakish-looking lead singer from the cult art-pop duo Fischerspooner," the spondaic phrase "cult art pop duo" coming as close as "Desperately Seeking Susan" ever does to actual clumsiness, rather than its virtuosic imitation. In the more densely populated setting of a Marina Abramovich dinner party, Castle's Dickensian diction neatly moves between an apparently sympathetic free indirect discourse and brutally satirical farce, characters becoming more monstrously cartoonish in the face of the narrator's apparent desire to impress them: "when I asked the man from the Guggenheim, to my right, what his books were about, he regarded me disdainfully and began, 'I am famous for—,' then caught himself. He decided to be more circumspect—he was 'the world's leading expert on Arte Povera'—but then turned his back on me for the next two hours." Castle's eventual retreat from the gay world into that of the "Little People" contains its own wobble: "Turning round one last time, I saw Sontag still slumped in her seat, as if she'd fallen into a trance, or somehow caved in. She'd clearly forgotten all about me." Upon turning, Orpheus (chubby priapic boy?) learns that Euridice has had no intention of following him—whether out of the Lethean demimonde or out of a closet grown to the size of the whole world.

The friction between the various polarities by which "Desperately Seeking Susan" examines its subject affords much of the interpretive interest of the essay: how exactly could the half-articulated critique of modernism map onto the half-articulated critique of queerness? Yet rather beautifully, Castle describes a category beyond modernism and its others, beyond lesbianism and its dissolution, or rather a category in which these differences can be experienced, provisionally, as harmonic: music. Fischerspooner and Lou Reed aside, and notwithstanding Sontag's hilariously rendered habit for overstatement ("Yes, Terry, I *do* know all the lesser-known Handel operas. I told Andrew Porter he was right—they *are* the greatest of musical masterpieces"), music is the topic on which Castle's enthusiastic ambivalence shudders least into mere resentment. After failing Sontag's quizzes on Robert Walser and Thomas Bernhard, Castle gains Sontag's admiration (or at least, she is "exempt from idiocy") because she "could hold [her] own with [Sontag] in the music-appreciation department." The nerdy swapping of music strikes Castle as "a peculiar, masculine, trainspotting" kind of pastime, but if it is so, it is one that even in the author's own irreverent style retains contact with German Romanticism and thus bypasses the aggression at modernist culture that structures much of the affect pointed at Sontag: "I was rapt, like a hysterical spinster on her first visit to Bayreuth. *Schwärmerei* time for T-Ball."

Do we just want those we love to be on our teams? I'm aware of how much of this work—not just mine, but Castle's and maybe Sontag's too—seems to collapse into a Carrie Bradshaw strap line, a telegram to *Miss Lonelyhearts*. If Castle's gossipy tribute to her erstwhile unrequited succeeds in making Sontag into more than she might have been, it would be because the emperor inflates with a surprising and sudden pathos at the moment that his nudity has been noted:

> "But he hasn't got anything on," a little child said.
>
> "Did you ever hear such innocent prattle?" said its father. And one person whispered to another what the child had said. "He hasn't anything on. A child says he hasn't anything on."
>
> "But he hasn't got anything on!" the whole town cried out at last.
>
> The Emperor shivered, for he suspected they were right. But he thought, "This procession has got to go on." So he walked more proudly than ever, as his noblemen held high the train that wasn't there at all.[47]

The ending of Hans Christian Andersen's story is, inevitably, far more complicated than its co-option by antitrans literalists might have suggested. For one thing, the Emperor's power, far from being undermined by the child's epistemic interruption, actually grows "more proudly than ever," and the noblemen whom the knavish tailors have cajoled into the ruse continue to carry his train. But it's not just that: it is far from clear, in fact, whether those who repeat the child (oddly genderless) really believe what the child has said. This translation, from the H. C. Andersen Centre and written by Jean Hersholt, introduces some speech from the townspeople, one to the other, that doesn't appear in Andersen's Danish, but neither in Hersholt's formulation ("A child says he hasn't anything on") nor in the original is it clear that the townspeople's perceptions have indeed been freed from ideology. [48] On the contrary, the child's perspective is characterized as both ideologically powerful (it spreads quickly) and political inefficacious (it makes no real difference).

One might expect an essay of this sort to conclude by aligning Castle's dream of an impossibly out Sontag with those of the "les lesbiennes n'aiment pas les penis" crowd. And there is certainly in both cases an articulated desire for a straightforward, no-bullshit, sexuality—the kind that was, a month before Sontag's death, exemplified in a paper published in *Psychological Science*, entitled "A Sex Difference in the Specificity of Sexual Arousal" and collectively authored by a team under the supervision of Meredith L. Chivers and Gerulf Rieger.[49] To investigate the titular difference, Chivers and Rieger isolated three groups—"women, men, and postoperative male-to-female transsexuals"—asked them to describe their sexuality, and then connected their genitals to electrodes while showing them pornography. As rudely physical as an ontologized account of sexuality could be, the electrical circuit convened as porn→electrodes→genitals→sensorium proves, or seems to, a set of hypotheses about the differences between sexual capacity of this tripartite sexual taxonomy. The study claims, interestingly enough, that "transsexuals showed a category-specific pattern [of arousal], demonstrating that category specificity can be detected in the neovagina using a protoplethysmographic measure of female genital sexual arousal," but more provocatively, that of the thirty-three bisexual-identifying men, one quarter (eight men) experienced arousal when shown straight porn, but not gay porn, and three quarters (twenty-five men) experienced arousal when shown gay porn, but not straight porn. The study was seized upon as evidence for the long-held prejudice that there are no bisexual men, only gay men in denial and straight men with flexible, not to say questionable, standards. In other words, that sexuality could be fully ontologized, if not as a gene, then at least as a singular capacity, inflexible and ennobling. The gay advice columnist Dan Savage interviewed Rieger, himself a gay man, who wonders of the 25 percent, "they might be straight, but go in for sex with other guys because it's so much easier for a male to have quick sex with another male than with a woman. But their true sexual feelings are still for women." Savage himself used the *t* word, suggesting there's a difference between someone's *true* sexual orientation and their sexual capabilities.[50] I don't mean to claim that the "true" coming-out that Castle would have extracted from Sontag would have had anything in common with the porn→electrodes→genitals→sensorium test, whose flaws as a test for sexuality perhaps warrant a footnote but no more, but the study and its reception do illustrate the proposition that the moment of Sontag's death felt like a crisis point for LGBT liberalism in more senses than one.

So, back to Berlant's generous, but devastating, assessment of the place feminist popular culture accords the real ambivalence women so frequently—inevitably—feel when confronted with knowledge of the gap between romantic fantasy and intimate suffering: "in popular culture ambivalence is seen as the failure of a relation, the opposite of happiness, rather than as an inevitable condition of intimate attachment and a pleasure in its own right."[51] So the truth is, I'm no longer convinced that the link between Castle and "les lesbiennes n'aiment pas les penis" is as unbroken as it seems, nor that the queering of identity successfully inoculated those who used it against the fraught desires exhibited in "Desperately Seeking Susan." In the days following the death of Lauren Berlant, a contest emerged on academic Facebook over which pronoun should be used to describe the recently dead. The difficulty of honoring Berlant's request—linked at the bottom of emails they'd sent—for a "they" is made clear in the University of Chicago's published obituary. Berlant's colleague Elaine Hadley (a member, with Berlant, of the Late Liberalisms group and thanked in the acknowledgments to *The Female Complaint*) deploys the repeated proper noun to skirt away from having to use pronouns at all: "Lauren wanted to know what young people were thinking and learn from them, which empowered them. On the other hand, Lauren was incisive and challenged them to work harder and be better . . . Lauren was always organizing reading groups . . ."[52] It's understandable, kind of: however used to it some of us have gotten since 2005, to those unused to the syntactical rhythms it produces, the singular "they" can still feel clumsy and a little embarrassing to say out loud—perhaps because it dares to name a utopia in the here and now, an ethical relation whose material presence manifests in the mouths of those who speak, those clothed in the dumb flesh of the respondent. But one couldn't escape the sense that to others in this conversation, those who could claim the intimacy of Berlant, "they" could only refer to someone they had never met—it was a cold and formal textual convention, merely clever. Inevitably, such voices claimed to have felt, and sometimes to have been, "policed" into the deployment of alienated and alienating speech. Berlant, of course, had written a great deal about the conflictual relations between desire and identity that emerge from the collision of public and private spheres (Facebook), generational tension (those who feel that the phrase "cancel culture" means something vs. those who are terrorized on account of it), and the charismas of the page and the seminar room. But the queerness of the essay form remains oddly inaccessible: the *out* that you *come* is different from the *out* that you *write*.

VII

The Cannibal's Diagnosis

(MIRROR/HOLE)

pseudo and proto

Dr. Hannibal Lecter's *ex parte* assessment of Jame Gumb—"Billy's not a real transsexual"—is surely the most notorious fictional diagnosis of pseudotranssexualism in the short but complex history of the condition.[1] If transsexualism was the condition of a male patient experiencing the obsessive desire to be a woman, pseudotranssexualism was the still more paradoxical condition of a male patient experiencing the obsessive desire to be a transsexual. Why would such a patient wish to place himself in the position of fruitlessly wanting something that could never be granted? And why would such a patient—having been denied the apparently sense-making or dignity-granting diagnosis of "transsexual"—pursue his own vernacular form of medical transition through the mass-murder of women, followed by the flaying of their bodies and their stitching into a "woman's body," unless, on some level, what he wanted was, after all, to become a woman?

This diagnostic oddity—in which both the symptomatology and the etiology of one condition is almost wholly isomorphic with those of the condition it mimics—is presumably one reason why pseudotranssexualism isn't in the DSM-5. But the word "autogynephilia" is, and that word has only incorporated, and not negated, the complex proliferations entailed by the transsexual problematic of a "desire to be." That desire, as we can already see, can stimulate an infinite regression of desires—a desire to be a woman; a desire to desire to be a woman; presumably also, a desire to desire to desire to be a woman, and so on—with no limit that can be fixed in advance. This regression series, moreover, might seem to have been ramified by a frequently noted (but rarely defended) dimension of contemporary queer life: that identifications are themselves erotic objects, such that one no longer merely wishes to *fuck that,* but moreover and in a more primary sense, to *be the one that fucks it,* to *be among those thought to be those that fuck it,* etc. Here it is the pseudotranssexual, and not the transsexual at all, that types the contemporary crisis of sexual subjectivity whose symptoms include the conflict among lesbians about whether by "identifying as a lesbian," an individual is obliged to eroticize a particular sexual organ. Or, conversely, whether not "identifying as a lesbian" relieves one of the otherwise burdensome obligation to take such a position.

Over two centuries of modern trans history, the question of the "real transsexual," meanwhile, has assailed trans people—though, it must be said, more usually as a negative than a positive descriptor. That people sought and indeed underwent sex changes prior to the mid-century emergence of gender as a diagnostic category is no longer in serious dispute, as Jules Gill-Peterson details at length in *Histories of the Transgender Child.* In 1917–18, Alan Hart obtained a hysterectomy and, in his own words, "left the hospital as a man." Michael Dillon obtained phalloplasty between 1946–48.[2] A trans girl named in the archive as "Val" reported to a psychiatrist in 1948 that from early childhood she had worn girl's clothes, used the women's restrooms at school and elsewhere, and been welcomed among girls.[3] Hart and Dillon obtained transsexual surgeries partly on the basis that they were both trained physicians—Val, whose profession is not recorded, did not. What *is* recorded in each case is that the condition of wanting a sex change—of needing one, indeed, if one takes seriously Hart's statement that his choice was between transition and suicide—was understood as a consequence of what Hart's doctors called "incurable homosexuality." That is to say, the notion that sex change might be desirable on its own terms, and not merely as an extreme presentation of homosexuality, was rigorously excluded from diagnostic consideration, leading Gill-Peterson to observe that the lives of trans people were "meant by medical design" to be distinguished from the intersex conditions whose medicalization in the same period was one of the most energetically contested fields of emerging medicine.

The notion that the transsexual was, prima facie, a species of *pseudohermaphrodite,* to adapt the period's vocabulary, might help us understand how the stigma of the "pseudo" attached itself to the figure of the transsexual as such. We could consider, for example, the case of Jennie June, whose *Autobiography of an Androgyne,* published in 1918, might be considered the first trans woman's memoir—and which bears a surprising number of the tropes of contemporary trans writing, especially the splicing of graphic sexuality with mordant wit that one finds, for example, in Torrey Peters's work or Sybil Lamb's.[4] June's narrative relates tales of youthful transsexual experience in the late nineteenth century, leading to homosexuality in adolescence and in particular a fetishistic taste for fellatio. As Emma Heaney has shown in the breathtaking reading of *Autobiography of an Androgyne* in her book *The New Woman*, June's account of her own condition refused the popular heterosexualizing logic that treated transsexual identification as an extension of the notion that homosexuality was the condition of a "woman's soul in a man's body."[5] On the contrary, argued June, it was not merely her soul, but her body that was a woman's, comprising what she called "female tissue," or "governing corpuscles of germs found ordinarily only in a woman." That position was, remarkably, marginally credited by Dr. Alfred W. Herzog, under whose deeply ambivalent aegis the *Autobiography* was published, apparently as a medical testimony, but in terms that nonetheless reduced June's condition to merely an unusual presentation of male homosexuality: Herzog describes June as "a congenital homosexualist . . . born with the body of a male, with perhaps some female characteristics, but with the soul of a female."[6]

That fascinating locution spins on a few asymmetrical pairings. First, that the adjective "male" modifies the noun "body," but the adjective "female" modifies the noun "characteristics," indicating that for Herzog the sexuation of a body might be best understood as an inductive summary of sexuated *characteristics*, which precede and in fact determine the body's sex. But second, that the body/soul distinction exists for Herzog to stabilize and reify a logic of sexual distinction that treats even "female characteristics" as secondary to the psychic sexual taxonomy in which homo- or heterosexual object choice affords the ontological grounds. Heaney powerfully demonstrates that the construction of the cis body in the modern era shores up the male fantasy of an impenetrable body—Heaney's trans feminist politics then, embarks from the observation that no body is impenetrable, so nobody is cis. My point here is related but somewhat different: that the emergence of the transsexual as a medical category depended on subordinating the embodied desire of trans people to the then-voguish taxonomy which treated gender of object-choice as the cornerstone of sexual subjectivity in general. Thus transness as such became a kind of pseudoheterosexuality interior to the clinical logic of inversion and thus subsumed under the regime of knowledge that exhibited the invert as the paradoxical proof of universal heterosexuality.

This dissolution was contested by the subjects themselves. Hart, Dillon, Val, and June all insisted that their trans commitments were distinct from their sexual object choices, and while one can detect a certain amount of ambivalence about sexual experience and identity in all cases, one can hardly take protestations of shame and self-disgust at face value. June, in particular, may say in one paragraph, "I am ashamed to look anyone in the face any more," but two later she is taking pornographic advantage of the censor's requirement that such narrations of sexual activity that cannot be excised must be transcribed in Latin:

> Even here I would be thinking of the soft satin-smooth cutis in inguine of my late guest, which I had found gratissima tactioni, peaesertim labiali et linguali, and would regret that it was always to be denied to me to touch again on viro this marvellously fine integument. I pined for the repetition of other similar pleasures which I had for the first time tasted in their fullness only a few weeks before, such as pillowing caput super abdomen aut femere nudo adolescentis, the fascinating sight membrum virilis ejus erectus, and the extremely smooth surface glandis, gratissima tactioni et digitorum et oris.

Autobiography of an Androgyne was published in the same year that Freud published the case notes on his analysis of Sergei Pankejeff, whose showpiece is the reconstruction from a dream of wolves of a "primal scene," an analysis which depends upon a retrieval from the Latin phrase "*a tergo*" of the sexual position known in English as "doggy style."[7] I wanted to spend a moment with June's steamy classicism, because I think it rather gives the lie to the notion that her condition could be easily explained as merely the product of an especially pronounced homophobia, if by that term we mean an aversive reaction to one's own sexual desires, especially insofar as they contradict or complicate the figural heterosexuality of the inversion model of sexual desire. Which June's certainly does: though she is enjoying the taste and feel of a man's body, the language that she deploys is feminizing and doting—it is the copresence of two femininities that she finds particularly hot. Especially notable here is the "cutis in inguine" in which June has enjoyed placing her fingers, lips, and tongue: translated by Scott Herring, perhaps euphemistically, as "torso," what June actually refers to here are the skin folds outside the inguinal canals behind the testicles that are often used as a penetrable sexual orifice by trans women: Mira Bellwether's classic 2013 zine, *Fucking Trans Women*, refers to the practice as "muffing."[8] It is, if you'll allow me to moisten the page with affect, more than a little moving to find this sexual technique outlined so lovingly in a book from 1918.

For these reasons, we might ask why transness has so consistently been framed as an incipiently heterosexualizing response to primary homosexuality. We might consider the recent provocations by the antitrans activist (and Professor of Modern History at the University of Oxford) Selina Todd, who has argued that:

> The attempt to reclaim transgender ancestors is deeply ahistorical. Transgender ideology argues that biological sex does not exist; and that gender is a personal identity brought into being by self-description. These claims do not speak to the experiences of people in the past. Before the late 20th century, gender and sexuality were widely understood as determined by one's biological sex. That's why some lesbians understood their sexuality as a biological "inversion".[9]

Of course, no part of this is upheld by the archive so painstakingly assembled by Heaney and Gill-Peterson, most particularly Todd's blundering claim that "before the late 20th century, gender and sexuality were widely understood as determined by one's biological sex"—indeed, as we have seen in Herzog's introduction to June, the opposite was closer to the truth. But it is not merely the openly antagonistic historian who seeks to draw a firm line between the trans and the prototrans, the transsexual and the pseudotranssexual. Recent work by trans critics like Cáel Keegan has probed the problematic temporalization of "trans" as logically, politically, and historically *posterior* to homosexuality, gayness, and queerness, in much the same way as early twentieth-century medicine positioned trans embodiment as merely the biological symptom of a primary inversion.[10] The current scholarly version of the *Autobiography* credits the author as "Ralph Werther"—strangely, since it was not the name that June used in day-to-day life, but nor was it the name with which she was endowed in childhood; it was simply a masculine pseudonym she had used, riffing on Goethe, for use at her day job. Herring's detailed introduction positions the *Autobiography* in relation to the gay New York subcultures in which she moved and worked. And more broadly, nineteenth- and twentieth-century histories of trans life, even of the most generally affirming kind, often describe their subjects as, as in the title of a recent book about nineteenth-century trans writers, "before Trans."[11] The dust jacket copy for Rachel Mesch's book begins, "before the term 'transgender' existed, there were those who experienced their gender in complex ways"—a fascinating locution that of course Mesch may not have written, which positions "transgender" either as the terminus of complexity, or as a modern formulation that could not be useful before the full medicalization of trans embodiment in the mid-twentieth century. We are not, in other words, too far from Todd's more overtly hostile claim that "before the late twentieth century," nobody was trans. (Todd doesn't explain there, although I'm sure she does somewhere, why it makes sense to use the word "lesbian" to describe people in the past who wouldn't have used it themselves.)

Although these arguments are not oriented towards the same political ends, they share a subtle political heuristic, the goal of which is to ensure that wherever and whenever trans *is*, it is not here, not now. That heuristic becomes inevitable once two stories have converged: the first, a liberal narrative of gay civil rights, in which the emancipatory movements of the 1960s and 1980s have worked to ensure an ontological status for lesbian, gay, and maybe even bisexual people, whose existence the narrative treats as self-evident, and self-evidently prior to political being. (In a Sartrean sense, we could refer to the argument as "essentialist": it positions essences prior to existence.)[12] The second: the medical authoritarian position that treats trans ideation and embodiment as merely an extreme and perhaps counterindicated symptom of clinical homophobia, whose medical liberalization depends upon an analogy with gayness that is both asymmetrical and indissoluble. Thus, the curious position of pseudotranssexualism: not merely a mise en abyme of transsexualism's already disorienting reorganization of the conceptual structure of inversion, but paradoxically the typifying example of transsexualism as such. The trans is pseudo–even unto itself.

not a real [*x*]

It is not hard to guess why an author like Thomas Harris, or a filmmaker like Jonathan Demme, might want to reassure their respective audiences that Jame Gumb, the serial killer known as Buffalo Bill, is "not a real transsexual": it lets them off the hook.[13] Marjorie Garber gestures to this in 1992 when she refers to Harris's book as "in one sense determinedly politically correct—Buffalo Bill is *not* a transsexual, and both transsexuals and gender clinics are exonerated from even associative blame—*The Silence of the Lambs* is nonetheless a fable of gender dysphoria gone spectacularly awry."[14] The novel, indeed, goes a step further than the film by including a scene in which the FBI agent Jack Crawford visits a gender clinic and meets there a doctor filled with the righteous indignation of the condescendingly created reader surrogate, whose goal is to distinguish his work from the messy business that travels under the sign "queer":

> To even mention Buffalo Bill in the same breath with the problems we treat here is ignorant and unfair and dangerous, Mr. Crawford. It makes my hair stand on end. It's taken years—we're not through yet—showing the public that transsexuals aren't crazy, they aren't perverts, they aren't *queers*, whatever that is—[15]

To Harris's cipher, any defense of trans people against the charge of being serial killers, or *like* serial killers (an association indelibly printed on the idea of the trans woman at least since *Psycho* in 1960), would *also* have to distinguish the transsexual from the queer.[16] This is perhaps because Harris, like Herzog before him, saw transsexuality and homosexuality as competing explanations for the same phenomenon.

In any case, of course, these attempts to stanch dissent didn't work. When Demme ascended the stage at the Dorothy Chandler Pavilion to receive the movie's five Oscars, including the rare quadruple of Best Picture, Best Director, Best Actor, and Best Actress, he looked increasingly sheepish and embarrassed each time.[17] Outside the theater, and reportedly within it, queer activist groups like ACT UP and Queer Nation were protesting both the outrageousness of the character and more generally the lack of realistic queer characters onscreen: "we're here, we're groovy / put us in your movie."[18] Yet in a further (slightly surreal) twist, the nature of the offense taken, and the defense offered in return, changed the terms from "not a transexual" to "not a homosexual," with Larry Kramer arguing in 1994 in the *Los Angeles Times* that many gays consider *The Silence of the Lambs* "one of the most virulently and insidiously homophobic films ever made."[19] Demme responded to these protests in their own terms. In an interview in 1991, he reassured audiences that "we knew that it was tremendously important to not have Gumb misinterpreted by the audience as being homosexual. That would be a complete betrayal of the themes of the movie. And a disservice to gay people."[20] Twenty-three years later, Demme sounded more rueful than dogged, saying in 2014: "Jame Gumb isn't gay. And this is my directorial failing in making *The Silence of the Lambs*—that I didn't find ways to emphasize the fact that Gumb *wasn't* gay."[21]

How to explain this? Certainly, Gumb has sex with the corpses of the women he murders—although he doesn't do so before he murders them. But his romantic and sexual relationship with Benjamin Raspail, whom he murders after sexual rejection, is narrated quite unambiguously in the movie, unless one subscribes to the theory that Lecter has confected his account of Gumb out of whole cloth. Indeed, Demme has simplified this plot from Harris's novel to make the point more obvious; in the novel, as in the *Hannibal* TV show, it is Lecter that kills Raspail, a musician in the Baltimore City Orchestra, because of what he calls his "gluey flute."[22] Yet it is difficult to imagine that Demme thought that "he's not gay, he's actually *bisexual*" would have resolved the problems the director had set out to quell. But by the early to mid-nineties, "gay" had come to indicate a restorative and civic form of cultural practice; if Buffalo Bill wasn't gay, nor was Andrew Cunanan. Any collectivity that could, even in principle, be identified as a subject of civil rights could not therefore count a serial killer among its members. One might speculate that the figure of the serial killer, which has no particular meaning either in criminal law or in the study of psychopathology, exists to compensate for precisely this absence, both in fiction and in sensationalist accounts of the crimes of Ted Bundy, Jeffrey Dahmer, and their cohort. Given nineteenth and early twentieth-century narrative's association of the violent criminal with the nonetheless politically salvageable narrative of class struggle—one thinks of Dickens's ambivalence facing a Bill Sykes, for example, compared with his utter distaste for a Pecksniff—the serial killer is the violent criminal who represents no constituency, whose cause is entirely circumscribed by the bourgeois ego—hence male, white, typically a homeowner, etc.[23] It would be on the grounds of such definitive non-inclusion that an Edelman might characterize the serial killer as a subject of the sinthomosexual, the subject whose jouissance can be put to no project of future world-building because it comes from nowhere.[24] Not a transsexual, not a homosexual, therefore not a "sexual" being at all, and finally not a creature in any sense of the word, the serial killer is the hapax legomenon of the death drive, the subject who belongs in no taxonomy and produces no etymology, that appears once and is never dispelled. The serial killer stands outside causality: "nothing happened to me, Officer Starling. *I* happened," as Hannibal Lecter puts it in the novel.[25] Meanwhile, the resistance to taxonomic modes of identification in nineties queer theory engendered a strange defense of the position: in *Skin Shows*, Jack Halberstam writes: "I would agree with Hannibal Lecter's pronouncement that Buffalo Bill is not reducible to 'homosexual' or 'transsexual.' He is indeed a man at odds with gender identity or sexual identity, and his self-presentation is a confused mosaic of signifiers."[26] Except, of course, Hannibal didn't argue that Buffalo Bill's identity wasn't "reducible" to being a transsexual; he said he wasn't one at all. One wonders whether Halberstam really agrees or not.

To treat the question like a pragmatist, meanwhile: Buffalo Bill *is*, straight up, a transsexual. He has undergone a medical procedure to change sex; he has just done so with medicines procured outside the medical industrial complex—as many trans women do. The novel makes clear that he has taken "Premarin and diethylstilbestrol, orally," and that while they "couldn't do anything for his voice, . . . they had thinned the hair a little across his slightly budding breasts."[27] He has also had "a lot of electrolysis," which "removed Gumb's beard and shaped his hairline into a widow's peak, but he did not look like a woman. He looked like a man inclined to fight with his nails as well as his fists and feet."[28] This condition is difficult to specify, but it is certainly transsexual: the syntax of that latter clause—"nails as well as his fists"—models transsexuality as an additive procedure in which one acquires a set of feminizing weapons, without surrendering their phallic complements. If the phrase is designed to land an insult on Gumb, it is an insult that thereby hits the figure of the negated transsexual nonetheless, even notwithstanding Lecter's diagnosis or the gender clinician's outrage.

That outrage has been expressed, in a milder tone, by Agent Starling herself: "transsexuals are passive types, usually."[29] Lecter agrees, but clarifies (another line cut from the movie) "sometimes you see a tendency to surgical addiction—cosmetically, transsexuals are hard to satisfy—but that's about all." The clinical "you" marks the moment of a metalepsis, where a psychiatric "case" becomes a criminal one, where the *you* who sees the symptom morphs into the *you* who sees the wreckage. Given the emphasis on the visible, it is easy enough to read Gumb's obsession as essentially sartorial, which indeed is how Lecter presents the case to Starling—"a vest with tits"; "a girl suit out of real girls"—parenthetically, the sheer vulgarity of Lecter's speech quickly gives the lie to his self-serving claim to abhor Miggs's "rudeness," as indeed Starling points out after the doctor has launched into one of his supposedly probing questions about her boss.[30] Halberstam sees that sartorial ambition as the key to Buffalo Bill's "posthuman gender," which is almost literally nothing more than drag.[31] In that sense, Halberstam's reading of *Silence of the Lambs* offers a triumphant observation that the film illustrates Judith Butler's argument about the *mattering* of sex through conscious performance.[32] The seductive image of Butler as a dressed-down Buffalo Bill is almost too delicious to resist, yet despite its having been crudely mischaracterized as a defense of voluntaristic embodiment, *Bodies That Matter* scrupulously and repeatedly distinguishes itself from a merely sartorial understanding of gender, crucially in an early passage: "The misapprehension about gender performativity is this:

that gender is a choice, or that gender is a role, or that gender is a construction that one puts on, as one puts on clothes in the morning."[33] For a richer understanding of Buffalo Bill's practices, we must turn away from the fashion system, toward the epidermal.

Gill-Peterson argues in *Histories of the Transgender Child* that the very conceit of transsexual surgery depends upon a notion of bodily plasticity rooted in, and designed to defend, a modern phenotypical account of racial difference. It is rarely observed that, for Buffalo Bill's "suit" to work, his victims must all be white—indeed, while we see him concerned with the texture and volume of the flesh he "harvests" (the word is used repeatedly), Harris does not provide us with much introspection around skin color. Perhaps, however, racial difference "comes out" (is itself symptomatized) in one of the novel's many coincidences: the fact that the mother of the woman Gumb kidnaps shortly after Starling gets on the case lives quite close to her, and is indeed the powerful and besuited US Senator for the State of Mississippi, Ruth Martin. Lecter's attempts to manipulate Senator Martin take the form of a series of escalating demands for middlebrow cultural products—culminating in "Glenn Gould, the *Goldberg Variations*," which he is granted (and which he listens to in Florence, in the novel's final scene), before, as the Senator turns to leave, Lecter tosses out "love your suit." As this plays in the movie version, Anthony Hopkins's delivery is an incongruous burst of comic camp, Lecter relishing his triumphant teasing of the Senator with a strangely Kleinian castration fantasy: "Tell me, Senator, did you nurse Catherine yourself? Toughened your nipples, didn't it? Amputate a man's leg, and he can still feel it tickling. Tell me, Mom, when your little girl is laid out on the slab, where will it tickle you?"[34] (This line, incidentally, does not appear either in the novel *or* the screenplay—it may have been improvised on set?)[35] The implication is either that the dead child is a kind of amputated limb or a kind of disembodied auxiliary to the breast, but either of which depend upon a psychic link between the embodied and the disembodied, the mother and the daughter. In that context, "love your suit" is nothing more than a victory lap, lap in the sense that a dog laps at water.

But in the book, "love your suit" is far more circumspectly and precisely aimed by Lecter, who is reminding the reader, as well as many of the people in the room who have been looped in, that Catherine is herself destined to become part of the stitched white body that he has been calling a "suit." It is unsettling, because deniable, rather than camp; yet it loops together the cultural objects of white embourgeoisement, from Glenn Gould to the body of a US senator, with the flesh-stitching of the serial killer. We could observe that

Buffalo Bill's *unmarkedness* as serial killer, and as sinthomosexual, is white only according to the general rubric of white supremacy, according to which unmarkedness as such is exclusively preserved as the negative construction of white flesh; in another register, the suit of the white woman is that which both Gumb and Lecter *love*, and therefore (like all transsexuals) do not possess. The film's final shot, excluded from the novel, is of Lecter himself strolling away in a wig and a white suit—having completed the outfit that Lecter believed Gumb to have been fashioning. This strange likeness is one of the many clues by which we learn that it is the education of Dr. Hannibal Lecter, and not the therapeutic treatment of Agent Clarice Starling, that will shape the narrative's minimal concession to *Bildung*: what he learns of himself is that he cannot take for granted his difference from Gumb, and thereby neither can he really distinguish himself even from Miggs, whose jizz-splashing of Clarice in an early scene affects him so much that he persuades his neighbor to swallow his own tongue. That code of secret likeness is typed into his name—Hannibal Lecter, as a number of readers have suggested, echoes Baudelaire's famous "*hypocrite lecteur*"; Dr. Lecter is the Baudelairean reader whose delight in the violence of others fails to exorcise his own more vulgar instincts.[36] Gumb's name, meanwhile, signals to the reader an effeminate fussiness, while sounding as a kind of dumb rhyme in *mm*, "He pronounces his name like *James* without the *s*, Jame. He insists on it."[37] Even the latter sentence maintains the lispy sibilance of the stereotypical gay discriminator.

Yet the collapse of the reader's *faith* in a categorical difference between Lecter and Gumb must also discredit, to some degree, Lecter's dismissive account of "a vest with tits." At which point, I must go off-script for a little—or off-book, or whatever it is to indicate that the archive of knowledge upon which I draw to make the following observation cannot be found on JSTOR, or indeed in the Kinsey archives, but rather in the vague chitchatty premises and deductions shared by us real transsexuals and our friends when we are off the clock: there is something more than moving, and positively revelatory about the deployment of transsexual ideation onto an epidermal grid, rather than a genital one. Thus, indeed, is the condition of trans women whose mental and spiritual needs are met not by contemplating castration and its other, but by the sweet rhythms and textures of skin thinned and softened by estradiol and spironolactone. Not merely is Gumb's transsexualism a transsexualism of the skin, either—it is, even more powerfully, a deification of the fat woman's body, a murderous fetishism of size and space that takes fat and its folds both as delightful surfaces to be painstakingly maintained *and* as a spatial environment through which another body can move. For helping me think through the implications of Gumb's rhapsody on fat women's skin, I want to express my indebtedness to the artist and activist Annie Rose, whose thoughts on *Silence of the Lambs* have greatly shaped my own.

between the hole and the mirror (in night vision goggles)

Annie also pointed out to me that Gumb's costume includes a necklace of the Willendorf Venus, a sign of his murderous worship of fat women. It is one of the many aspects that have been roundly misrepresented both by critics and defenders of Demme's movie, and perhaps most catastrophically by Demme himself, whose own fetishism requires him to cut away from the erotically inviting scene of self-creation to a scene of Catherine Martin screaming in a pit. Do we understand those cuts, in which the eye but not the ear (which continues to hear the diegetic music) is interrupted, as disciplinary—as reminders that we must not take pleasure in this individual fastidiously crafting a new soul from a new body? Or, more troublingly, are we supposed to see the abused, pit-bound woman as the secret desire, the hole from which the eye recoils towards the "shine" of the jeweled and tattooed body, which is then forced to serve Demme as the fur serves Freud's fetishist?[38] That is, to conceal the truth of women's castration, the eye-camera turns from the hole to the nearest thing that captures its interest—like Precious, the poodle who resembles a fetish only in one sense—that she alone passes between the hole and the mirror. (And, perhaps, in another sense: that her name brings to mind Smeagol from *Lord of the Rings*—who is both Tolkien's primary fetish and his primary fetishist.) I refer to the latter option as more troubling because it would mean that, unlike Gumb, Demme's camera would associate maternal castration with eternal screaming and scheming—and yet it is Catherine, rather than Gumb, whose trap to ensnare and endanger the Precious is set into motion in the movie's final reel. The castrated hole is itself, then, an agent of castration, pulling in that which is precious and endangering it. Whereas the scene of the tucked penis becomes, then, the fetishistic scene of phallic plenitude that reassures the viewer. If one follows this logic to the end, there is no way to avoid the conclusion that the ideal viewer of this scene, and indeed the only viewer capable of perceiving the cuts in this way, is Jame Gumb himself, the uncastrated subject whose work depends upon the repeated mutilation of the hole that pulls him in. And it is a mirror scene, after all—and a lusciously sexy one, at that.

Gumb's presence in this shot is uncastrated in two senses: first, in that he is presumed to be phallically whole—we presume he has a penis. Catherine, meanwhile, is both in the hole and herself a hole being dilated and prepared for mutilation; like the transsexual he therefore is, what the uncastrated Gumb lacks is lack itself. But secondly, and more suggestively, he is uncastrated in the sense that a fetish is uncastrated: *his lack of a lack is itself hidden*. Or, in more straightforward terms, we do not know anything about this person's actual genitals—only that he leans forward and grunts, seems to reach behind himself, and then withdraws to display his body, butterfly-like and shimmering, to the mirror-camera. We must infer the tuck from its most indirect of outward signs. The epistemic security that might be afforded by his penis—as when, for example, a trans-antagonistic feminist understands the presence of a penis on a trans woman's body as irrefutable and self-evident proof of maleness, Demme denies his viewer, requiring us instead to tuck whatever ambivalence emerges around this body in, behind the horror of the hole. Insofar as such affective tucking mimics the camera's own recoil, we might observe (echoing Emma Heaney once more) that the hole in question, the psychoanalytic hole in which the fact of castration is made unavoidably apparent, presents as an anus rather than a vagina.[39] Which nobody can doubt Jame Gumb "has," if it doesn't have him.

Yet this scene, which so begs to be read as the movie's psychoanalytic apocalypse, and so stages this film studies seminar for your viewing delectation, need not and indeed should not be taken at face value. In psychoanalytic terms, my contention is: this scene does not depict fetishism, at least in the sense that fetishism can be deployed in a psychoanalytic register to shore up a distinction between presence and absence, or—in the terms I've been using so far—the real and the pseudo. Rather, this scene extends, but does not conclude, the film's absorption within a *narcissistic* circuit of self-regard, upon which that distinction cannot and will not be brought to bear. The implication of that contention is that *The Silence of the Lambs* finally contradicts the cannibal's diagnosis not by occluding the *pseudo*transsexual, but by abolishing the *real* transsexual. If "Billy's not a real transsexual," it is only because the film's interest in the intensifying mediation of the perceptual apparatus renders, as though by a Hegelian reversion, the "real" as a perceptual effect of the unreal.

This progressive mediation of self-presence makes itself known through a progressive suffusion of the screen by such perceptual effects, as Demme's camera moves from the intimacy of direct address to increasingly extravagant mediating structures and conceits, until, eventually, the intimacy of the shot has been decisively relocated.

1. The first scene between Crawford and Starling consists of alternating POV shots in which the two of them look directly at the camera. This is as powerful a form of cinematic convergence as any with which Demme supplies us, although it is not without its irony, given that Crawford is deceiving Starling about the nature of her mission and additionally, trying to get inside her head.
2. Lecter's first appearance mimics Crawford's, in the sense that he is also looking directly at the camera, in an uncomplicated pose. However, now we have interposed a plexiglass boundary between camera and subject, which border will eventually be crossed only by the olfactory sense, when Lecter smells remnants of Clarice's customary perfume.
3. Catherine's first appearance in her car, driving and singing along to Tom Petty's "American Girl," complete with selfie-ready duckface, picks up on the head-on/behind-transparent-boundary shot of Lecter, but with the additional dimension that she is now singing; her voice has been mediated.
4. When we next encounter Lecter, we are behind the transparent boundary with him, now observing Clarice through the interposed holes, but additionally we are watching a second screen—the televangelist that Dr. Chilton is forcing him to watch.
5. In the key scene in which Hannibal offers his diagnosis, we see him *in* the reflected surface, from his side, so that we are observing the scene prismatically, as though from two directions at once.
6. When we get to the basement scene, we begin with Gumb's mouth, the organ of his mystification, speaking narcissistically both to and about himself: "Would you fuck me? I'd fuck me," in place of the conventional pronoun "myself," because he is not talking about doing something to himself, but about becoming two beings doing things to each other.
7. In the tucking shot, the mirror-camera remains still, indicating that although we are in a species of POV shot, our POV is materially constrained by an object, the mirror, rather than by the perceptual apparatus of the subject. That is, we are watching *from the mirror's point of view.*

8. Which material constriction remains after Gumb puts his night-vision goggles on, so that we see from the goggle's perspective—and therefore implicitly *not from Gumb's perspective at all.*
9. Eventually, we witness Gumb's hand enter the frame, as an alien object—we have become the goggles, and although the hand interacts with the objects we can perceive, it does not do so on our behalf or with our consent.
10. In the closing sequence, Starling is photographed accepting a commendation and commission, and she smiles at the camera: but here, in a movie that has been repeatedly staging acts of technological mediation, she does not smile *at the camera*; in this shot, it is both true and not true to say that she is smiling at the camera, and so the progressive alienation of the object from itself has become complete.

Such observations cannot tell us everything we want to know about a film's relation to perception, desire, memory, and cognitive form.[40] But it can demonstrate, I think, one thing: that the fetishistic search for a real transsexual against whom the others might be discredited is not merely accidentally misguided, in the sense that it has been historically deployed against every trans person who ever drew breath, but necessarily narcissistic, in that it presumes an arbitrary grounds for establishing a difference between original and copy. What remains to be explored, after everything—after the deconstruction of cisness and the abolition of the real transsexual—is what ontologies of transness might mutate, and how they might condition the greater freedom of fakes of all genders.

VIII

generic deductiveness

REASONING AS MOOD IN THE STONER NEO-NOIR

Sexuality is the area where the homogeneity of the new world manifests itself most clearly. Significantly the hero's erotic instincts are themselves all but extinguished by his epistemological confusion.

—LARRY GROSS, "FILM APRÈS NOIR" (1976)

ORDELL ROBBIE: You know you smoke too much of that shit, that shit's gonna rob you of your ambition.

MELANIE: Not if your ambition is to get high and watch TV . . .

—QUENTIN TARANTINO, DIR., *JACKIE BROWN* (1997)

IT FEELS LIKE EVERYONE I speak to these days seems to say that they're tired of talking about trans*ness,* and only want to notice trans people and bodies—lives as they are lived. The authors collected in the recent volume *Trap Door* all seem to echo a point made succinctly by Morgan Page: that trans visibility entrenches trans inequity, by drawing attention and prestige to a minority of trans celebrities, while directing state and public violence to the less prestigious majority.[1] A central mechanism of biopolitical governance, "visibility" functions through a logic of racial selection. Jules Gill-Peterson argues that the historical construction of the cis body in the early twentieth century served to rationalize the eugenic science of racial plasticity.[2] Eva Hayward and Che Gossett have argued that the generalization of trans modes of analysis outside the remit of the transsexual has led to the catastrophic neglect of, especially, those subjects whose subjection by cisness is most violently enforced: Black trans women living with HIV/AIDS.[3] Insofar as there is a trans everywhere, it screams to stop the theorizing and attend instead to the mechanical reproduction of death by racial capitalism and the global transnational state.

As a result, there are not one but many cisnesses that we are up against. There is the cisnormative movement in social policy, which is not so much a designation as a project of social cleansing; there is that thinking, which attempts for example to make a firm distinction between "reversible" and "irreversible" spots of time; there is, perhaps most basically, the cisness of ontic legibility that names a body or mind "cis" if it is uncontaminated by the touch of conscious design, and "trans" the moment that a motive is traceable. There is the voice in a head, that endows each value system with a currency—which distinguishes between natural and synthetic hormones (or breasts, whose growth may be catalyzed but is never *caused* by hormones) or between the true and the false transsexual. To lay these resistances out for analysis, then, would be to reveal that "cis" and "trans" are hardly ontologized concepts—they are felt limits encountered at the edge of every project of self-knowing or world-building. "Leave us alone" is the cry of trans feminism against cisness; a mode of collective conjuration that demands its own closure to contradict the sequence of medico-political reopenings, rephrasings of old demands, re-enforcements of stale injunctions.

As if to produce a psychic equilibrium with this demand for nonvisibility, nonconceptualizability emerges as a coeval power of scrambled knowledge, a sequence of mythologemes flitting back and forth between minute and gigantic scales. Conspiratorial thinking runs through trans knowledge for much the same reason gossip does: they both feel fun, and the particular kind of fun they feel is an especially effective compensation against the otherwise depressive effects of nonconceptualizabilty—loneliness, confusion, feeling stupid. The meme would be an effective vehicle of compensation if it bypassed interpretation and landed on the mutually presencing nodes of feeling-togetherness, which otherwise may as well have been abolished along with the concept. A meme becomes, one hopes, a mood; a mood might freeze into a meme—which, if it does, it does by sloughing off every possible trace of historical specificity. Benjamin writes that the dialectical image is that "wherein what has been comes together in a flash with the now to form a constellation."[4] A meme, by contrast, is that image wherein the conceptualizability of history as a dialectical particular recedes entirely, and the limitless negativity of space

FIG. 8. "Memes are instruments // of conspiratorial knowing." Meme by the author.

capacitates the co-being of a you and a me, *not* as positively related subjects in a historically determined configuration, but as objects thrown into the same slipstream of cosmic indifference.

Memes are, among other things, instruments of conspiratorial knowing. They evoke knowingness in the absence of knowledge, the negative imprint of a dialectical image. The art historian Michael Fried referred to this condition as "deductive structure": the minimalist notion that the content of an art object should derive, as literally as possible, from its form—that the dimensions of a canvas determine the marks one puts on it.[5] Memes refuse to stipulate whether there is one mood or many moods, instead they repair the schizoid split between singular and plural, bypassing theory and conceptualization and returning knowledge to the presencing zone of affect. The process reverses what Stephen Colbert used to call "truthiness"—the self-satisfied structure of knowledge that vibes out on the purported credibility of a given ideologeme, rather returning us to the vacuity of knowledge claims in untheorizable space, the essential untruthiness of the mood. Yet there is a certain dogged optimism, too: an effort to show one's working, to draw lines and scratch lines over them, to build architectural palimpsests from one's cognitive labor, to build a house from one's own delusion.

Although, again, *is* Charlie Day deluded? Is this space he has furnished propositional—does it make a claim?—or is it purely the negative architecture of nonpropositional, nonconceptual, nonabstract deductiveness? Would deductiveness shorn of proposition indeed be in any way distinct from delusion? This question approaches the condition of the cultist who awaits the apocalypse on a particular day and, when the day passes, decides that his calculations, but not his premises, were misguided. Interminable deduction—the work of the day (the working day) as the labor of fitting in the latest *drop* (for QAnon) or *root* (for queer Twitter) with the schematically absented nontheory towards which one is moving. The rationale, to adopt the form of R. D. Laing's formula in *Knots,* would be something like:

——I know that I was gay when I was a child, because I am gay, and when I was a child I liked *Space Jam*, and *Space Jam* is gay.
——I know *Space Jam* is gay because I am gay, and I liked it when I was a child.
——When I was a child, I did not know *Space Jam* was gay, but I should have known *I* was gay, because I enjoyed *Space Jam.*[6]

And the conspirator reappears as the absented subject who knows only what she does not know (but should have known) and who suspects that the shared condition of "should have known"—of belated nonknowledge—is the negative condition of the mood. And if that subject appears narcissistic (which of course it does), it is a narcissism of the primary kind, rather than the secondary: developmentally dashed, the primary narcissist is the infantile type who simply has not had cause to differentiate between the negative space of mind and the negative space of world. Different to the pathological secondary narcissist, the mature subject who self-replicates by investing objects with her own ego-libido, and who loves only the parts of herself she finds in the world.[7]

Deductiveness, on the other hand, was stoner logic—this much seemed obvious . . .

The work of psychoanalysis depends upon the unsutured copresence of interpreter and witness. This is, as Paul Ricoeur points out, one of the central problematics of Freud's work: sometimes, it seems as though Freud is interested in meanings, and sometimes in the mechanics, of what happens. Yet what Ricoeur names this "mixed discourse" he also calls the "*raison d'être* of psychoanalysis," as he attempts to think through the notion that Freud's mission was to make interpretation part of the act of witnessing, and witnessing part of the act of interpretation, without surrendering either to the other.[8]

> How can the economic explanation be *involved* in an interpretation dealing with meanings; and conversely, how can interpretation be an *aspect* of the economic explanation? It is easier to fall back on a disjunction: either an explanation in terms of energy, or an understanding in terms of phenomenology. It must be recognized, however, that Freudianism exists only on the basis of its refusal of that disjunction.[9]

Unpeeling the implications of that refusal leads Ricoeur into *The Interpretation of Dreams*, the inaugural text of psychoanalytic method, and in particular to observing the coordination of the hermeneutic and the descriptive in the Freudian "*Deutung*," or interpretation. Interpretation is the "mixed discourse" par excellence, because "to say that a dream is the fulfillment of a repressed wish is to put together two notions that belong to different orders: fulfillment (*Erfüllung*), which belongs to the discourse of meaning, and repression (*Verdrängung*), which belongs to the discourse of force."[10] For Ricoeur, interpretation is not (just) a hermeneutics, but rather that "putting together" of hermeneutics with descriptive analysis, such that the subject of interpretation in *The Interpretation of Dreams* is not the dream—Freud's is not a dictionary of metaphysical symbols—but the mechanic of interpretation itself.

A "refusal" to disentangle mechanics from hermeneutics, however, is not only the destination of a science of interpretation, but the premise of an autoanalysis, in which not merely were the witness and interpreter identical, so too was the analytic subject, the dreamer himself. Psychoanalysis, infamously, started with a notoriously unsuccessful instance of self-exculpation: Freud's own dream of "Irma's Injection."[11] That dream, the subject of Freud's initial autoanalysis, revealed nothing more repressed by the dreamer-analyst than the latent thought "I am not responsible for the persistence of Irma's pains," but, as Freud's friend Max Schur realized as early as 1966, nothing could have been further from the truth: Emma Eckstein, a patient of Freud's, had been subject to a serious surgical malpractice at the hands of Freud's confidant Wilhelm Fliess, who had left half a meter of medical gauze inside her nasal cavity, which had triggered the seepage of blood that Freud had diagnosed as hysterical "occasioned by longing."[12] The episode illustrates with horrifying clarity the notion that, in the text of psychoanalysis, there is no mechanical description that is entirely devoid of hermeneutic overdetermination.[13]

Schur also realized that Eckstein played an important role in an equally formative moment in Freud's early career: the first stirrings of doubt in the so-called seduction theory of the origin of hysterical neurosis. That theory, which Freud elaborated in a paper entitled "The Aetiology of Hysteria," which Freud delivered to the Vienna Psychiatric Society on April 21, 1896, held that the origins of hysterical symptoms in his patients (including Eckhardt's) were repressed memories of sexual abuse, usually carried out by their fathers—this view was treated skeptically by the Society and dismissed as "a scientific fairy tale" by the sexologist Richard von Krafft-Ebing, who was in attendance.[14] That skepticism, in turn, led Freud to abandon the seduction theory altogether over the following year, explaining at last to Fliess in September 1897 that "it was hardly credible that perverted acts against children were so general."[15]

This narrative is well known outside the ranks of those who read Freud's letters because of two connected critiques leveled against Freud in the 1970s and 1980s: in an essay entitled "The Sexual Abuse of Children: A Feminist Point of View," delivered by the feminist activist Florence Rush at the April 1971 New York Radical Feminists Rape Conference, and *The Assault on Truth: Freud's Suppression of the Seduction Theory*, a systematic critique of psychoanalysis by Jeffrey Moussaieff Masson.[16] These two essays took Freud's malpractice in the Eckstein case, and his ambivalence about the reception of his 1896 paper, as evidence of a wider "cover-up" of child sexual assault, which in turn led psychoanalysis structurally to undervalue the testimony of patients reporting childhood sexual abuse.[17] Scholars tend to agree not only that Rush and Masson overstated the significance of Freud's abandonment of the seduction thesis—after all, he continued to believe that *some* of his patients had been sexually assaulted, and his later work was primarily concerned with post-traumatic symptoms—but that Rush in particular had mistaken the argument of Freud's 1896 paper based on the account of it he offered nearly forty years later in the *New Introductory Lectures on Psychoanalysis*.[18] Yet the accounts that Rush and Masson offered were persuasive enough to stimulate public interest in the notion of repressed memory of childhood sexual assault.

The subject of a "seduction theory," if one takes the argument as seriously as Rush and Masson urged, is radically at odds with the subject of psychoanalysis. As Ricoeur showed, psychoanalysis operates by endlessly imbricating explanation and interpretation, orienting each process around the other, and binding the witness ever more firmly into the position of interpreter. But the position of someone whose memories themselves are repressed, whose project of cognitive reunification depends upon the interpretation of memories whose mechanic is utterly absent to them but which nonetheless emerges into consciousness with the full force of literal truth, has sundered forever any dialectical mechanism. Rather, the work is simply to build truth via a process of permanent deductiveness, inferring lifeways from truths one inherits from a memory-function beyond even the minimally felt temporal continuity of consciousness. The subject of a seduction theory wakes up, receives narrative fragments whose ontology they are required to assume, and builds narrative in all directions towards and away from them. The affective texture of self-knowing is deductiveness; the medium is mood.

One might hypothesize, too, that the genre of such a project of deduction would be neo-noir; that genre of emerging Hollywood narrative coincident with Rush and Masson, two of whose early successes—Robert Altman's updated adaptation of *The Long Goodbye* (1973) and Roman Polanski's *Chinatown* (1974)—share more than their location in the dusty, semi-Western expanse of Los Angeles. Classic Hollywood noir movies, especially the works of Alfred Hitchcock, have long been associated with classically Freudian psychoanalytic accounts of subjectivity.[19] In D. A. Miller's essay "Anal *Rope*," for example, the heterosexual gaze of Hitchcock's camera associates the shadowy backsides of the gay male characters with the fear of castration that characterizes oedipal maturity. Thus the visual and technical aspects of noir filmmaking reproduce—or perhaps have been cut to reproduce—the psychic conditions of oedipalization, the developmental framework with which Freud supplanted the seduction thesis.

Neo-noir, on the other hand, is characterized by a certain aesthetic scrappiness, a multiplicity of visual and textual elements whose clutteredness signifies not merely the overdetermination of clues or data, but more crucially their inassimilability, the overabundance of knowable things. This aspect of neo-noir is highlighted in Larry Gross's 1976 essay on the "sociological" rather than "psychological" aspect of neo-noir, "Film après Noir: Alienation in a Dark Alley." While the traditional dick's greatest skill is his sense of timing, the neo-dick bumbles through a set of plots that happen *to* him: though both Altman's hero and Polanski's are detectives, neither is exactly trying to solve a crime, and until *The Long Goodbye*'s Philip Marlowe (Elliot Gould) kills Terry Lennox (Jim Bouton) after speaking the last line of the film, neither escapes for even a second the complete control that other characters—Lennox, and *Chinatown*'s Noah Cross (John Huston)—have over them. Gross refers to these movies' understanding of protagonism as "a purely figural abstracted conception of a hero," and elaborates that subtle phrase, "purely figural," with an observation about Elliot Gould's dick: "[Marlowe's] nicotine addiction, his clothing, his catch-all line 'It's all right with me,' are foregrounded signs of a purely figural existence rooted in Hollywood's past."[20] His personhood has been vaporous, diffuse. Through a curious device of sound editing, Elliot Gould's mouth is, for most of the movie, kept out of shot, so his mumbling monologue, which is more or less uninterrupted for the whole two hours, feels like one line in the ambient soundscape, another instrument in the slow jazz variations on John Williams's title tune, as though Marlowe's interiority were itself an ambient effect, absorbed rather than emitted by the actor.

Is there a historical claim to be made? Neo-noir emerges as a response to the public collapse of faith in the psychoanalytic settlement of this question and the attempt to reopen the question of repressed memory? I wasn't sure . . .

I've been asked to write something autotheoretical—"is that what you would say you do? I know not everyone likes the term . . ."—about the unusual position I've played in the "terf wars" of the last couple of years. "An object of other people's paranoia," was her phrase. Damn straight. Earlier today I received a bizarre email from an anonymous account—bizarre, except I get messages like this every day. It describes a scene in which I interrupt some regular working-class men going about their business, desperate for them to make me feel like a woman. When one of the men starts to undress, my heart leaps. Turns out he's asking me to iron his shirt. If that's a joke, this whole damn system is a joke.

In thrall to a sexual masochism she can name but hardly control, this "flustered" and evening-gowned gull "zeroed in" on these polite ("heck") but strip-happy joes, only to realize that patriarchy's disinterest in satisfying even *masochistic* desire when it is articulated from a place of conspicuous femininity, subs out the sauce and reapplies the beefcake. Male body as threat of non-sexual sadism—exhilarating, my Aunt Fanny. Femininity is the spectacle of wanting to get fucked, and getting *fucked* instead.

How does it feel to be the object of someone else's paranoia? Hell, it feels great. Len Gutkin suggests that the traditional dick's anomie might have been constructed, by Raymond Chandler at least, through an ambivalent negotiation with the Wildean epigram—itself evidence of a more fundamental ambivalence about the figure of what Chandler called "the homosexualist."[21] Obviously, I'm getting high on it. Yesterday, a man named Adam Hibbert—and what a name for a white-bread chump—ran a Twitter thread asking, "why

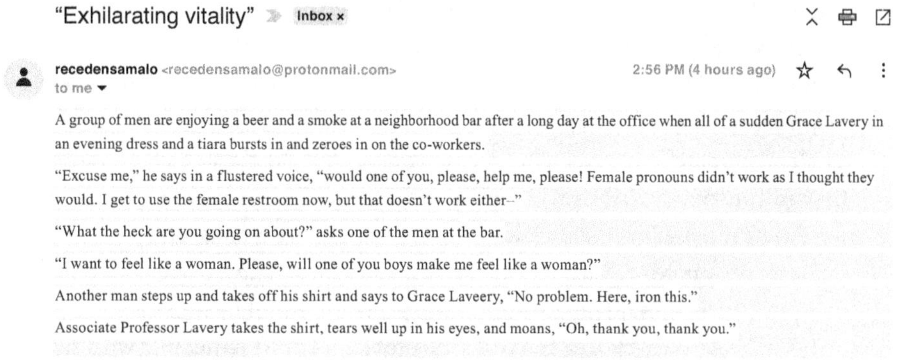

"Exhilarating vitality" Inbox ×

recedensamalo <recedensamalo@protonmail.com>
to me
2:56 PM (4 hours ago)

A group of men are enjoying a beer and a smoke at a neighborhood bar after a long day at the office when all of a sudden Grace Lavery in an evening dress and a tiara bursts in and zeroes in on the co-workers.

"Excuse me," he says in a flustered voice, "would one of you, please, help me, please! Female pronouns didn't work as I thought they would. I get to use the female restroom now, but that doesn't work either–"

"What the heck are you going on about?" asks one of the men at the bar.

"I want to feel like a woman. Please, will one of you boys make me feel like a woman?"

Another man steps up and takes off his shirt and says to Grace Laveery, "No problem. Here, iron this."

Associate Professor Lavery takes the shirt, tears well up in his eyes, and moans, "Oh, thank you, thank you."

FIG. 9. Anonymous email sent to the author.

is Grace Lavery an icon and Rachel Dolezal is a pariah?"[22] The missile was precision-tipped to produce the compensatory affect of stupefied but asymptotic assent: *good question, mm yes this is the question, once you've framed the question this way, the absurdity of this whole situation is revealed.* What fascinates str8 ppl about transsexuals is the same as what fascinates everyone else: the superfluity of embodiment—always "figural," but never "purely" so. But the value they extract from us is of another kind entirely: it is the promise that politics might be conflictual again, that competing interests (even on the left) might be enumerated and split. A political scientist colleague of mine, who insisted on pronouncing the word "trans" to rhyme with "barns," once explained to me during a meeting that debates over trans women's access to public restrooms would have the salutary effect of ending the détente between anti-sex feminism (which, he said, was rooted in American puritanism) and the sexually licentious liberalism of the boomer flower children.

"As a British Marxist, I'm thrilled," he added.

"Oh yeah?" I asked.

"The left has been complacent, papering over disagreements, unable to explain its positions, and that's why we've been unable to build a mass movement."

"Whatever you say, man."

"You don't agree?"

"I try not to discuss toilet architecture in the workplace . . ."

"—it's NOT just architecture—"

". . . but I do think that any unity forged in a bonfire of trans feminine vanity doesn't sound like a whole lotta fun to me . . ."

"But don't you see, it's not supposed to be *fun*—"

"Whatever you say, Doc. Whatever you say."

So it's not just paranoia. But it is paranoia, too. I realize that, when I was talking about conspiratorial thinking earlier, I referred to a conspiracy theorist as a "conspirator." My lover, who read this, said "but they're not conspirators, they're conspiracy *theorists.*" I replied to indicate that, in my view, potatoes were very much like po-*tah*-toes, and that to theorize a conspiracy is to become a conspirator. That's the nonnegotiable reflex action to believing in a conspiracy. "Sure," said my lover, "but they'd never admit it."

I could have been clearer. But that's the problem: I don't remember what side I'm on, theorist or conspirator. That's another aspect of the neo-noir to add to the list of decathexes: the institutions that might have allowed one to know by whom one is claimed have blurred into one, and there are no sides, just ambience.

Around the house, I refer to the suspects by their last names. I don't pin those names to the corkboard, but I might as well: Stock, Linehan, "Posie Parker" (it's a nickname, so I use both), Jones . . . Sometimes this group of brainiacs fills the whole page, and I see nothing more than a totality. Damn str8, I'm paranoid. My ex told me I was a member of the Illuminati now. Maybe she was right.

I forget if they're brave warriors after truth, or deliberate misinformation peddlers. *The Invisibles* taught me that all conspiracy theories are true—aliens are among us; the Queen was complicit in the human sacrifice of the personification of the hunter goddess Diana—and that felt true, felt energizing.[23] Power protects power, so maybe the epistemic immiseration of the disempowered could produce the knowledge specific to the revolutionary class? "Queer theory" is increasingly named as the psychic blitzkrieg of the ruling class—it is on these grounds, and because I supposedly preach it, that dozens of people call me a pedophile online. QAnon, but starring queer academics.[24] Three days ago, in his essay explaining why I am "grooming" students by teaching texts by Foucault and Hocquengham, Graham Linehan twice uses the phrase "no wonder Lavery didn't want parents listening in."[25] Today he's speaking to the House of Lords.

Sure. Autotheory. That's what I do.

The neo-noir has always had an affinity with marijuana. And close kin with the stoner caper: the first Cheech and Chong movie, *Up in Smoke,* shares with *The Long Goodbye* a plot concerning smuggling people into Tijuana, and like Gould's Marlowe the central pair are equally pestered by cops and organized criminals. Likewise, the animated stoner movie *Fritz the Cat* (1972) shares with *The Long Goodbye* a mumbly urban soundscape in which the speaking mouths are never seen—in the opening sequence, three working joes are speaking an apparently documentary dialogue, and the animation jump cuts to reveal that these are cartoon animals, sitting on a girder.[26] The visual field has been crafted to the specifications of the audio track, not just in the sense that the cartoon characters are moving their mouths along to prerecorded audio, but in a more capacious sense: in order to illustrate the sense of quotidian Manhattan hubbub that the apparently found audio footage conveys, one of these animals is struggling to squeeze his sandwich, ballooning over with meat and lettuce, into his expanding mouth. The object and his body concertina in scale in wobbly dance: it's a stoned association, suspending the laws of physics and replacing them with mere scuzzy, fungible congruence. Later on, a group of hippie animals smoke weed and play with each other's bodies in a bath: a bunny (after the *Playboy Club* waitresses, presumably) moans, "I'm there, I'm there!" and could mean either that she is stoned or that she is coming; the two merge.

The motif of stoned, hippie sexual community recurs in *The Long Goodbye*, with the girls getting high with their boobs out on the balcony opposite Marlowe's apartment. "A melon party. Melon party!" he mumbles, rounding the corner. What makes this scene especially striking is the lack of visual interest that the camera extracts from the nymphets in blue jeans: their circle is closed, and Altman seems (typically, perhaps) happy to observe, rather than to penetrate, the social connections he depicts. The shot spreads open the landscape of Hollywood Heights—the apartment building scenes were shot at 2178 High Tower Drive—as if displacing from the bodies onto the landscape the possibility of exploration, incursion, escalation. Gross argues that the erotic energies of the neo-noir hero are "all but extinguished," but it would be premature to conclude that the universes of these movies are themselves anerotic. Rather, the frazzled libido in neo-noir is no longer focalized through characters, but displaced onto closed communities of blissed-out stoner girls, nature-chicks whose oneness with the landscape is a sexual, and not merely aspirational, fact.

If the ecological embrace of the landscape insures Altman's dick against the potentially castrating closure of the group of girls, the embrace of Mother Earth makes use of the particular landscape of Los Angeles, terra-cotta roofs smeared over canyons and hills.[27] At stake in this embrace is the scalability of

FIG. 10. Still from *Fritz the Cat,* directed by Ralph Bakshi. Fritz Productions, 1972. Photograph of a grease-smeared laptop screen (the investigator's own).

FIG. 11. Still from *The Long Goodbye,* directed by Robert Altman. Lion's Gate Films, 1973.

pastoral: an urban site depicted as the oversaturation of space by the pleasures of space, greenery, and the "colonial style." Gould's shuffling but unfazed Marlowe acts as gofer for the girls—his first action is to head to the supermarket, and he agrees to pick them up some brownie mix, to ferry goods between the green world and that of shoddy commercialism. (Gould's Marlowe is above all a mule: he conveys brownie mix to the girls, Terry Lennox to Tijuana, and Roger Wade back to his cheating wife.) Weed, the part of the green world that the girls take into their bodies, cannot be obtained at the supermarket. *Chinatown*'s green worlds are entirely hypothetical, the film's title naming the Los Angeles that negates that green world altogether, and the patches of green in which Evelyn Mulwray (Faye Dunaway) fantasizes her safety, are themselves evidence of the villainy of her father, Noah Cross. At an individual scale, because the salt water from the Mulwray lawn proves that Cross killed Hollis Mulwray, but globally, because his plan to irrigate (and therefore greenify) and then incorporate the San Gabriel Valley is the motive behind his murderous and megalomaniacal plot.

Although neo-noir always possessed this affinity with marijuana, with its attendant oscillations between natural/synthetic, urban modern / rural pastoral, paranoia/imaginativeness, and torpor/spontaneity, it was not until the late 1990s revival of the genre that it moved, seemingly, to incorporate the ethos of stonerdom altogether, in Quentin Tarantino's *Jackie Brown* (1997), *Lock, Stock, and Two Smoking Barrels* (1998), the Coen Brothers' *The Big Lebowski* (1998), and then later in *Pineapple Express* (2008), Thomas Pynchon's 2009 novel *Inherent Vice,* which Paul Thomas Anderson adapted into a movie released in 2014, and *Under the Silver Lake* (2018).[28] *L.A. Confidential* (1997), a pastiche of a noir movies of the Otto Preminger type, rather than a neo-noir, had turned marijuana into an important element of the plot, but the movie itself didn't feel stoned, and its method of reasoning was essentially distinct: it is his unexpected retreat to traditional shoe-leather detection that gets Jack Vincennes (Kevin Spacey) to the truth, and killed; Ed Exley (Guy Pearce) gets there through archival work, and due to the villain's saying a shibboleth—"Rollo Tomasi"—that revealed he was Jack's killer. The movie contains none of the verbal or visual signs of deductiveness: the liquid-furrowed forehead melting, druggily, over the brow of crossed eyes; the stuttering dick's comically inarticulate attempt to persuade one of the str8s that he's on top of the facts.[29]

These signs are all exhibited in *The Big Lebowski,* which has generated enough scholarly attention to fill a volume jovially entitled *The Year's Work in Lebowski Studies,* which compiles essays exploring the resonances of the Coen Brothers' movie with high-cultural touchstones as far apart as the Fluxus movement, the Grail quest, and the New Left.[30] The film's appeal as a switchpoint for various genres and apparently diverse lines of cultural influence has obscured, however, the degree to which *The Big Lebowski* so perfectly encapsulates the genre in which it does its own work: the stoner neo-noir. To stipulate three of the more emphatically realized of these effects:

(1) circular bathos: In the scene at his mid-century mansion, the pornographer Jackie Treehorn (Ben Gazzara) takes a call (on an anachronistic phone), writes something invisible to the camera on a pad of paper, rips off the top leaf, and then walks out of the frame. Our hero the Dude (Jeff Bridges),

perhaps remembering Cary Grant in *North By Northwest,* heads over to the phone and rubs a pencil over the palimpsest, to reveal what perhaps might be a secret message but in fact turns out to be a doodle of a male figure masturbating an enormous phallus. The joke is a little more complicated than it might appear: what the Dude realizes, when he sees the doodle, is that the cinematic genre whose conventions he was mimicking was, after all, no more capable of disclosing plot or assigning meaning than he could juice from his own posture of speculative, stoned immobility. It is like learning that the grown-up genres smoke weed too, and that the taste not merely for the sexual, but for the *dumbly* sexual, is a vector of continuity between the stoner counterculture and the rich str8 folks in the hills. The moment thus recapitulates visually the logic of the Dude's *conscious,* but equally failed, attempt at bathos a minute earlier:

> JACKIE TREEHORN: The new technology permits us to do exciting things with interactive erotic software. Wave of the future, Dude. 100% electronic.
>
> THE DUDE: Uh-huh. Well, I still jerk off manually.
>
> JACKIE TREEHORN: Of course you do. I can see you're anxious to get to the point.

It is clear that the Dude's attempt to knock Treehorn off his future-surfboard has failed, but less clear precisely what Treehorn's withering response is supposed to indicate: that the Dude is an analogue masturbator in a digital world (which, then, might position Treehorn's doodle as something of a defeat)? Or, with a more sadistic bent, that while he did not expect the Dude to have any opinion on "interactive erotic software" worth hearing, he is nonetheless disappointed by the sheer witlessness of his failure to play along (which might then exempt the character from the exposure of generic vacuity with the doodle)?

(2) stickiness: The language of *The Big Lebowski* is like that sticky icky—dank and difficult to dislodge. The stoner mind absorbs phrases from the str8 world and disgorges them back into it elsewhere. First, he hears George Bush is on the television telling Saddam Hussein "this aggression into Kuwait will not stand," and then later he spits it back at the titular Lebowski: "This will not stand, man. If your wife owes money . . ." Or, when the hifalutin Maude Lebowski (Julianne Moore), herself mimicking speech she considers beneath her, says that her father's wife "has been banging Jackie Treehorn, to use the parlance of our times," the phatic phrase reappears, once more in the face of the big Lebowski (David Huddleston), when the Dude refers to a "young trophy wife, I mean, in the parlance of our times." Yet here, Jeff Bridges's enunciation reveals

that the character hasn't fully understood Maude's usage, and seems to think the phrase means something like "nowadays, when things are so precarious."

(3) "new shit": The spectacle of stoned deductiveness requires the exhibition of conspicuous thought, of the exertive application of effort. The stoner hero is not a dick, exactly, since the dick (like Da Fino, a "brother shamus") is a schmo, and the stoner is nobody's fool but fortune's. So the labor of the non-dick stoner is to produce not a solution to the case, but the *appearance* of working on the case, without forgetting that everything is, in reality, out of his control. His performance of reasoning is not persuasive ("new shit has come to light and—shit, man! she kidnapped herself!"), but nor exactly is it intended to persuade, since it would be just as useful from the Dude's perspective that the big Lebowski think him an earnest idiot as that he think him a credible detective.

There are more, obviously.

I don't know what I think about autotheory. It seems like one way out of the relevance-and-hype market of academic prose, which has been in rapid and unmanageable inflation for a few decades and which shudders still further with each spasmodic contraction of the labor market. I don't want to be relevant—I don't want my transition to be theorized!—except if it be by happy accident, by being in the right place at the right time, and letting history suffuse me. But I don't know the provenance of this wish. I'm skeptical of it. "Sometimes there's a man, and I'm not saying a hero, cuz what's a hero, but sometimes there's a man—and I'm talkin' about the Dude here—sometimes there's a man who, well, he's the man for his time and place."[31] The guileless classicism of boomer historiography discloses itself each time history simply engulfs a passive dude, filling him with history in return for his injection of meaning: Forrest Gump showing his ass to LBJ.[32]

Look at history happening to me: Forrest Gump, Jeffrey "the Dude" Lebowski, Paul Preciado. Masculine men, each of them, but each also penetrated, oddly passive in the face of their own discourse, flirtatious and indirect. Preciado writes:

> I'm not interested in my emotions insomuch as their being mine, belonging only, uniquely, to me. I'm not interested in their individual aspects, only in how they are traversed by what isn't mine. In what emanates from our planet's history, the evolution of living species, the flux of economics, remnants of technological innovations, preparation for wars, the trafficking of organic

> slaves and commodities, the creation of hierarchies, institutions of punishment and repression, networks of communication and surveillance, the random overlapping of market research groups, the biochemical transformation of feeling, the production and distribution of pornographic images.[33]

Preciado (b. 1970) is supposedly a member of Generation X, rather than a baby boomer, but he has nonetheless absorbed the boomers' characteristic subordination of macrohistorical narrative into a series of private traversals: "you had to be there," but also, "if you can remember the sixties, you weren't really there." The passage smashes together two rhetorical figures: praeteritio and asyndeton. Praeteritio, the art of saying something under negation, works its scuzzy magic in that classic formulation of scholarly bad faith: "I'm not interested in . . ." This isn't about *me*, this is about the world as it happens to me; it is a phenomenological inrush of historical matter that I hold in my emotional sensorium solely because there is nowhere else for me to hold it, but the body is as disposable a vessel as can be imagined. The hygienic discretion with which Preciado wipes away the traces of *auto* in his theory conspicuously draws attention to that which, in fact, it was never supposed to obscure: the phenomenologist's genial objectivity, his asserted capacity to withstand the battening of historical and chemical force with his disinterest manfully intact. Autotheory earns its bones behind the body of the autotheorist, inters him in a shallow grave of macrohistorical runoff. That runoff, meanwhile, splashes through the page as asyndeton, unsubordinated and polyvalent: as with Flaubert in Barthes's description, "a generalized asyndeton seizes the entire utterance, so that this very readable discourse is *underhandedly* one of the craziest imaginable: all the logical small change is in the interstices."[34] Between the apparently disorganized phrases Preciado discloses an unspoken *auto*, which is to say an undisavowed *auto*.

What are the historical conditions of possibility for this image (fig. 12)? History has taken Linehan (born in May 1968, an astrological *soixante-huitard*, which is to say inspired either with the final flatulation of boomer grandiosity or the birth-whelp of Gen X nihilism, or both) by surprise, too, though he is a stunt autotheorist, who also believes that he can arrest the insanity of the present moment merely by exhibiting it, amplifying it in the emptiness of his own sensorium. It is a project of profound hostility to the *auto*, self-immolating in the service of a comic construction of history, as though Forrest Gump were *himself* trying to imagine the historical position of a Forrest Gump. The conspiracy, which is obvious to anyone inside this discourse and surreal to everyone else, is that the dating app Her, which claims to serve the lesbian

FIG. 12. Graham Linehan, on the lesbian dating app Her, pretending to be a trans woman. Posted on *The Glinner Update*, February 20, 2021.

community, in fact sells that community out by including men as sexual prospects.[35] Perhaps there are examples of this, but the only one that anyone will cite is now Linehan himself, goofily mugging from the isolation of his own self-exile. Does such a project of historical self-erasure possess a motivation, beyond the obvious desires inevitably caught in the undertow of such steamy negations? (Which is to say, the lesbian phallus.[36]) Perhaps this: that the trans woman Graham, who claims to be twenty-nine, has lied about her age and therefore performed a generational betrayal, and even (more fancifully) has traveled in time.

If the stoner non-dick (the Dude, Preciado) is the diagnostician of twentieth-century history, then what we learn is that diagnosis is betrayal, a treacherous renaming of the condition of historical being.

I wanted to write about my love affair with a lesbian named L—, and about the ways she has taught me to rename my body, as well as those parasomatic moods that govern my, for example, fidgetiness, or the psychosocial praxis that governs whether or not I am passable in a given frame. I wanted to write into my lover, to groove my words into her flesh, as I pump them out of her with my hand. This, I thought, would be an autotheory worth the name, would answer the stuntists and historical castrati, phallically would reconstruct the episteme of modernity from the lesbian pussy. I wanted to be born out of her into my own body, to birth her through my hole, and I wanted to mash my face into her clit until I gagged and choked, love and melody. Everything I care about is love; why does anyone write about anything else, ever?

I don't know, man. I don't know what I'm making, what I'm repairing. I feel stoned in love and I need a vocabulary. It's not autotheory, it's autocriticism, and it's only that because it isn't anything else.

To recap the argument. ("The story so far.") I have noticed that trans people seem weary of being the subject of endless theoretical speculations, and our being positioned as either the apogetic example or the confounding case of queer theory. I have suggested that this weariness is felt through a curious epistemological condition that I have called "deductiveness," which proceeds by a series of enthymemes: inquiries in which neither conclusion nor premise is known. This mode of reasoning, I have argued, is rigorously depicted (or as rigorously as possible) in a genre of representation I have called stoner neo-noir, which has its roots in seventies noir revivalism but also absorbs new, and generational, theories of historical causality ("boomer historiography"). I have also aligned this mode of reasoning with the 1970s challenge to psychoanalytic accounts of hysteria, and in particular with the attempt by Jeffrey Masson and Florence Rush to restore the so-called seduction thesis, which in turn enabled the so-called recovered memory therapy. Like the stoner neo-noir, recovered memory positions people as receivers of their memories, splitting the

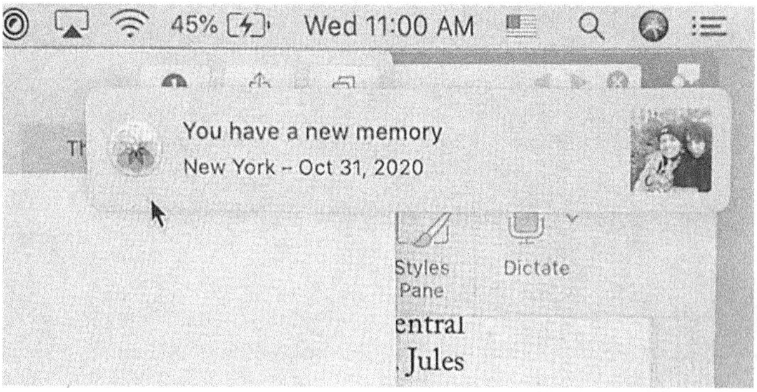

FIG. 13. "You have a new memory" notification from the macOS Photos app.

functions of witnessing and interpreting, prizing apart metapsychology and hermeneutics. We come to, with a new memory.

This literally just popped up on my computer. Coincidence? I wondered.

David Robert Mitchell's 2018 neo-noir *Under the Silver Lake* picks up a number of these themes.[37] The central character Sam (Andrew Garfield) is a rapacious consumer and reproducer of conspiracy theories who has absorbed part of the paranoid relation to media that *The Invisibles* disseminated.[38] Since his life as a drifter in Los Angeles is suffused on all sides by media, from the smiling ophthalmology ad on a billboard saying "I can see clearly now" (a face half of which is eventually replaced by a clown) to the notices across the Silver Lake neighborhood saying "Watch out for the Dog Killer," he therefore develops a paranoid, nineties method of reading his own existence out of the world. The film therefore affords an opportunity to distinguish between boomer (*The Big Lebowski*), Gen X (*Testo Junkie*), and millennial stoner neo-noir, and to thread through this genre a history of postmodern relation to genre. In *Under the Silver Lake*, the disintegrated subject of neo-noir moves into a phase of re-enchantment and repair, where the melancholic effects of split subjecthood have worn off, and we are left with a subject whose objecthood has been fully installed into the world of object-signs. Sam not only accepts his position as a powerless cipher of genre, he revels in it; unlike the Dude, then, he has cheerful, low-stakes sex with a handful of people—one of whom, his middle-aged topless neighbor, seems to stand almost literally for the stoner girls in *The Long Goodbye*, in the same apartment, forty-four years later. Or, the same type of apartment—the later movie was shot at 3205 Los Feliz Blvd., a fifteen-minute drive away on the other side of Griffith Park.

FIG. 14. Still from *Under the Silver Lake*, directed by David Robert Mitchell. A24 films, 2018.

The Big Lebowski plots to embezzle funds from the Little Lebowski Urban Achievers charity and create the impression either that the Dude has stolen the briefcase or the kidnappers failed to make good on their ransom note. His scheme is the squalid and ordinary shittiness of a man who, for all his pretentions, is even worse with money than the Dude; when the Dude unveils what has happened, the Lebowskis are, perversely, each diminished by becoming equal with the other. The Dude requires no accommodation to the events of the plot ("let's go bowling") because he has ingested and normalized a difference: a doppelgänger initially troubling because of his difference from the little Lebowski, has been brought into the muck, much as the pig-cop in *Felix the Cat* is thwarted by being pulled into the bath-orgy. *Under the Silver Lake* portrays the most paranoid conspiracies that deductiveness can produce (enthymemes without premises): the number of letters in each word in one song leads Sam to derive a code from the lyrics of another one, which produces the phrase "rub Dean's head and wait under Newton." Sam heads up to the Griffith Observatory, rubs the statue of James Dean, and crouches under the bust of Newton until he is visited by the "Homeless King" and taken to an underground system of tunnels—which eventually he learns are pyramid-style tombs build under the Hollywood Hills where wealthy Angelenos are buried alive with three "brides," so that, as the "Final Man" puts it shortly before he himself is interred, "future men will understand that *we* were the modern kings. Rulers without statues or effigies." No renormalization for Sam, whose paranoia plot deprives of bathetic deflation, but the perverse normality of harmonization—a reunification of the sign deriving from the universalization of deductive reasoning.

It feels counterintuitive to align Freud, arch nominalizer of phenomena and traducer of fuzziness, with deductiveness—the feeling of thought deprived of premise or destination. Yet to return once more to the dream of "Irma's Injection," that dream by which (as we have seen) Freud deflected any regret he felt over Emma Eckstein and, plenty have argued, sublimated his feelings of unprofessional attachment towards Wilhelm Fliess, we can pay special attention to the moment when the dream violates both the natural physical order and, in its retelling, the syntactic organization of elements:

> Not long before, when she was feeling unwell, my friend Otto had given her an injection of a preparation of propyl, propyls . . . propionic acid . . . trimethylamin (*and I saw before me the formula for this printed in heavy type*) . . . Injections of this sort ought not to be given so thoughtlessly . . . And probably the syringe had not been clean.[39]

In fact, Freud's list of chemicals slips into asyndeton, as the chemicals slip off the page and into Freud's line of imaginative vision, and he starts to slur his own words. The sequencing of elements emerges from phonic echoes—"propyls, propyls, propionic acid"—rather than from logical orientation. Freud is stupefied, for once. Fittingly, since the terrain into which he is passing here is a terrain in which the text of memory—the basis for what he thinks of as the "seduction theory"—is staring him right in the face.

PART THREE

Epilogue

FIG. 15. “Everybody acts so serious. How am I gonna show this cowboy I’m alive?” Still from music video for “Friday” by Rebecca Black. ARK Music Factory, 2011.

EPILOGUE

Someone Else's Beauty and *My Beauty*

WHO OWNS BEAUTY? One's answer will depend upon the manner of one's resolution of a tricky problematic within traditional aesthetics, concerning the location of beauty within the subject/object relation at the scene of its being. To take the pre-Kantian position, sometimes called the "classical" perspective and attributable to, for example, Edmund Burke, beauty is a property of the object found beautiful; one could then infer that beauty is among the "properties" of the object that a purchaser might acquire when buying the object itself.[1] Along with the canvas, the blueness, and the exchange-value of, say, Chagall's *Hommage à Apollinaire, ou Adam et Ève* the private collector who has paid for the piece acquires thereby the work's beauty. On the other side of the antinomy, the perspective sometimes called "romantic" and attributed to Alexander Baumgarten or Walter Pater, beauty is a property of the subject and not of the object-in-trade at all: and so, while a bourgeois capitalist might certainly purchase an elegant painting and acquire with it not merely its properties but the various forms of capital that might have congealed within it, the capitalist could not possess its beauty, which belonged more fundamentally to the one who appreciates the art than the one who merely pays for it—though of course, as the example of Pater among other Victorian romantics might demonstrate, the two roles can be occupied by the same person.[2] The Kantian intervention, for reasons that have little to do with Kant's negligible interest in the question of ownership, took the form of a synthesis of these two positions: though Kant held that indeed beauty occurred in the phenomenal experience of the subject and did not inhere in the object, nonetheless the nature of that phenomenal experience constituted a willed subordination of the faculty of the imagination to a certain transcendental logic sometimes called "purposiveness without purpose."[3] Kant differentiates the judgment of the beautiful from the mere appreciation of an "agreeable" object by attributing to it a "bracketing" of the interest or telos of the object as it is considered, and insisting on the *willed* refusal to assign a final determination to the meaning to the experience, and to linger instead in the interminable but formally patterned state of "free play."[4] As the Japanese philosopher of aesthetics Kojin Karatani puts it, "the common saying that Kant's aesthetics is subjective is correct to a certain extent, with the proviso that the Kantian subjectivity is totally different from the romanticist one. . . . [It] is the *will* to execute transcendental bracketing."[5] So, who owns beauty: to the classicist, the purchaser; to the romantic, the cultivated spectator; to the Kantian—who?

To transition, as we have been seeing, is to seek the acquisition of a new competence, but it may also be to unearth in oneself the paradoxical quality of a desire one didn't know one had; a hitherto unidentified, but now unavoidable, stigma, that has been part of one's being, perhaps the definitive part, for years before one noticed it. Trans women sometimes call this stigma "my identity," or "my womanhood," sometimes "love"; Janet Mock calls it "my own power," and Kevin Rowland calls it *My Beauty*.[6] In none of these cases can the possessive pronoun be taken for granted.Such claims have not, self-evidently, been written with Kant's scrupulous attention to causality and subordination, and a pragmatist's assessment of them—that they articulate a political or normative *claim* rather than a descriptive *assessment*—must be borne in mind; trans women are no less likely than anyone else to speak imprecisely or even mistakenly when describing their subjective experiences. But they are no more likely, either, and when a trans woman speaks of "my beauty," she is articulating a position consistent with Kant's distinctive description of aesthetic judgment. This response to Kant might offer other left theorists of aesthetics a way out of an impasse into which the question of the Kantian "subject" sometimes leads, and will offer, in the midst, a rebuttal to a couple of claims by trans-exclusionary feminists concerning the relation between trans feminism and property.

In particular, I am talking about the intersection of these questions in a peculiar location—a 1999 album of pop covers by the former frontman of Dexy's Midnight Runners, Kevin Rowland, entitled *My Beauty*.[7] The album did not conform to the conventions of a transition narrative: Rowland changed neither his name nor his pronoun for its release, and after the hostile reaction, critical and public, that *My Beauty* generated, Rowland never appeared in public in a dress again. Yet there is no question that the antagonism the album stirred up was directed at the spectacle not merely of a man presenting femininity, but more pointedly at the spectacle of a man presenting femininity without making an attempt either to pass as a woman or to ironize his appearance so as to submit it to the interpretive rubrics of drag or camp.[8] Remembering the occasion of the album's release in an interview in 2020, Kevin Rowland blamed Alan McGee, the force behind Creation Records, for much of the antipathy he received: "[Alan said] I was mad, just because I wore a dress," adding, "some of the stuff that was said wouldn't even be allowed today."[9] Indeed, it would not have been "allowed" within the dogmatically liberal pages of the British music press in 1999 if the object of Rowland's identification had been clearer—if he had been coming out, for example, as a gay man or even perhaps as a transgender woman. But instead the album presents an abundance, a profusion of sentimentality that saturates and denatures any and all available identity claims and subject positions. While *My Beauty* is arguably camp, it is also, and more pointedly, perversely sincere—a mediatic sincerity absent any message, a transition (if one wanted to think of it in these terms) without a destination. In an interview he gave in 1999, Rowland mused about *My Beauty* as the name for a kind of purposiveness without purpose: "these songs showed me my definition of beauty, my beauty."[10]

It is on these grounds, and not any identity claim, that any transness could be imputed to *My Beauty*. Yet it is possible to understand the album as part of a tradition of trans woman–authored pop music whose origins might be found in working-class drag cultures of the early twentieth century and whose more celebrated examples might include Angela Morley, RuPaul, and Sophie, albeit that the differences between a white British orchestral arranger, a Black Southern club kid, and a Scottish raver, cannot be taken for granted. Yet what these composers share with Rowland is a commitment to orchestral and instrumental lushness, to a kind of oversaturated sentimental density, as a conveyance for a beauty that exceeds and displaces referentiality. "Referentiality" is perhaps a tricky predicate to apply to music: I mean that the intensity with which these composers orchestrate does not in any self-evident way correspond to the thematic content of the songs that they are setting—which in many of these cases are songs that the arrangers did not write: Morley set John Williams's orchestral scores for some of his most popular film themes (becoming the first trans woman to be nominated for an Academy Award, for *The Little Prince* in 1974), but is mostly remembered today for her arrangements on Scott Walker's early solo albums; although RuPaul has written his own songs, he is also well known for his lip syncs and arrangements; and Sophie, who died in

January 2021, was well known for her remixes and production collaborations with Charli XCX and Madonna.[11]

Although the arrangements on Scott Walker's first three solo albums were credited to Morley under her deadname (she transitioned in 1973, just as Walker was winding down), her transness was well known within the studios, with the fourth track on *Scott 3*, entitled "Big Louise," supposedly referring to the trans woman in the production booth: "she's a haunted house / and her windows are broken / and the sad young man's gone away."[12] The song with the clearest link to *My Beauty*, however, is the arrangement of "Wait Until Dark" that Morley scored for *Scott 2*, so sappy a number that it must have mystified fans of the movie *Wait Until Dark*, for which Henry Mancini originally wrote it, a vicious melodramatic thriller in which Audrey Hepburn plays a blind woman being tortured by a maniacal drug addict played by Alan Arkin.[13] In particular, Morley is responsible for the descending and arpeggiating strings in the arrangement's opening movement, since the opening of Rowland's cover of Marmalade's "Reflections of My Life" on *My Beauty* adopts something of the technique, incorporating the melody of Whitney Houston's "The Greatest Love of All," with which *My Beauty* opens.[14]

Indeed, the Whitney Houston echo is significant in itself, since although Rowland was likely unaware of the fact, his recording of "The Greatest Love of All" was not the only trans Whitney cover recorded that year: the Californian performance artist Kevin Blechdom put out a version of "I Will Always Love You" (originally recorded by Dolly Parton, of course, but irreducibly Whitney's) entitled "Jon Whitney Houston," released on a sampler album of the London experimental record label V/Vm Test Records. It is an extraordinary track: the first three minutes follow Whitney Houston's arrangement quite closely, but with a few extra cracks in the glissandos, a conspicuously white voice, and a bingo-hall-sounding Hammond organ in place of the strings. At the moment in the Whitney version in which the diva moves to a higher key, however, Blechdom deviates by instituting a weird device: not only does the music go up a step, but as the tune comes round to the bridge of the chorus, they do so *again*, and *again*, moving the melody up in pitch mechanically rather than vocally, a total of eleven times, until the track is little more than a shriek, vaguely following the contours of the famous torch song. "Jon Whitney Houston" thus intensifies the aesthetic phenomenon I've been calling clockiness about as far as it can go, using sentiment and duration to bring to crisis many of the binaries that continue to dominate and structure the fugitive energies of trans embodiment: natural/synthetic; pleasure/unpleasure; love/sickness; original/copy.

V/Vm Test Records, meanwhile, put out small runs of compilations and original music in the 1990s, many of which were in reality pseudonyms for V/Vm himself, whose birth name was Leyland James Kirby and who additionally recorded under the name "The Caretaker." While the range of recordings and acts that found their way onto V/Vm Test records is too large to sustain many formal generalizations, a few features led music critics at the time to refer to V/Vm as pioneers of "glitch music," a kind of electronic pop song that makes extensive use of digitally created distortions in order to create a challenging soundscape. "Glitch music," however, fits V/Vm less comfortably in retrospect, partly because the term (and its successor, "PC music") has come in the intervening years to refer to more commercially minded experimental pop, led especially by trans artists like Sophie and the pop act 100 Gecs, whereas V/Vm's music was aggressive in a particular way: it shaded into white noise, and the tracks of basically indistinguishable distortion frequently lasted for longer than ten minutes. The most conspicuous differences between tracks were often merely the titles, which were usually themselves adapted from tracks embedded in the noise: the 2001 track "Hate You," for example, was a stretched-out distortion of the sing-along at the end of "Hey Jude." Nonetheless, both the formal delight in aggressively bad cover versions, and many of the themes of the V/Vm records—meat; cringe; light entertainment; abjection, especially bodily; gothic horror—prefigure the interests of the trans musicians working two decades later.

This music is clocky in that it fails to pass as music, yet there isn't another word with which to describe it. Its function is partly to stunt: you put on this music in company in place of a joke, to deform and suspend the discursive norms that might otherwise condition the sharing of music, especially in the Brit-pop era, during which indie aesthetics were more-than-usually subject to co-option and recuperation by capital, under the rubric of "Cool Britannia," a presumptively white, cosmopolitan, and secular aesthetic structure of British neoliberalism. Yet clockiness also comports a certain thrift: a preparedness to make do with the impoverished scraps of grace with which one has been endowed by capital. Thrifty, too, is V/Vm's aesthetic commitment to offal and to meat production as a guiding norm: the first of the record label's samplers was called *Aural Offal Waffle Ten Pints of Bitter and a Bag of Pork Scratchings*, which conveys something of the act's mission: a boozy conflagration of sound, meat, and drink—unassimilable and likely to be vomited out later. Offal re-enchants the clocky body by transforming the unwanted and conspicuous part—trotter, or adam's apple—into a concentrated nugget of meaning. Yet the move refuses and even repudiates the transformation of offal into bourgeois self-possession implied by the "new British food" movement of the same period: place *Aural Offal Waffle* next to, for example, Fergus Henderson's influential 1999 cookbook *Nose to Tail Eating: A Kind of British Cooking,* and one notices two contradictory accounts of offal—one neoclassical and self-possessed, the other abject and unchosen. The visual repertoire of the V/Vm Test Record releases resembled the digitized and mass-copied "poor image" described by Hito Steyerl: though the poverty of the V/Vm repertoire derives from the label's cheap photocopying and printing techniques, the result is startlingly similar to the kind of deep-fried meme one might have discovered on Reddit circa 2015.

Yet the fact that V/Vm's work, while electronic, was *not* digital, remains significant insofar as the poverty of, and drag on, the band's aesthetic commitments indexed a set of material limits whose physical properties could be sensed more directly in the finished object than one can trace, for example, the *material* effects of compression on a meme. The clockiness of the material world impedes what Steyerl calls the "concept-in-becoming of the images"—a trans object, then, the clocky offal, threatens to abolish transition by giving itself away, but also remains the signifier of transition, the sign of an unsignified originality. In his "Theses Against Occultism," Theodor Adorno offers a typically critical assessment of what he sees as occultists' and astrologers' guileless derivation of metaphysics from materialism. Adorno writes:

> If, to the living, objective reality seems deaf as never before, they try to elicit meaning from it by saying abracadabra. Meaning is attributed indiscriminately to the next worst thing: the rationality of the real, no longer quite convincing, is replaced by hopping tables and rays from heaps of earth. The offal of the phenomenal world becomes, to sick consciousness, the *mundus intelligibilis.* It might almost be speculative truth, . . . and yet it is, in a positivity that excludes the medium of thought, only barbaric aberration alienated from itself, subjectivity mistaking itself for its object. [15]

Advocates, or at least delegates, of a *Sick-Love* stemming from a "sick consciousness," V/Vm's practice indeed turns "the offal of the phenomenal world" into "speculative truth." This because, unlike Adorno, the V/Vm artists refuse the dualism of transcendental speculation, and see the material world itself as enchanted—in this sense not merely is *Aural Offal Waffle* a work of trans art, it gestures towards the universality of transsexuality, since the body it figures derives meaning from its own unwantedness, its own unlovability.

Selecting fragments from the vast, probably mostly untraceable, corpus of V/Vm Test Records is challenging. I've been returned to my own teenage ventures into London because there were no V/Vm records for sale (to the best of my knowledge) in Birmingham. Berwick Street has since been transformed from a den of adult bookstores and oddball record emporia into one of the main drags in one of London's fanciest food districts. The names of some of the fancy restaurants now sound like the titles of V/Vm tracks—Bone Daddies; Duck & Waffle—the recuperation from V/Vm of the gonzo meat aesthetics that they had pilfered from the London restaurant scene in the first place. Most of the music has never been digitized, so it isn't available on Spotify (though some is); some tracks have found their way onto YouTube. But this archive exists, when it does, primarily as a set of cheap CD-ROMs, with color-photocopied inlay sleeves, often scrawled with pissy little jokes about other bands they disliked. Their targets might seem surprising, especially since, while the tracks themselves often comprised nothing more than grimly re-tuned mainstream love songs, the shit lists exhibit some fondness for their mutilated sentimentalism. The real bad guys were other DJs and electronic musicians whose work denied the body by denying sentiment, like the Derrida-quoting DJ Spoony, to the brilliant and successful Aphex Twin (towards whom one suspects the V/Vm gang was responding partly out of envy). But sentiment itself remains oddly untouched by the apparently scathing critique. While the Sex Pistols reportedly masturbated into their bassist Glen Matlock's sandwich after he had admitted to quite liking the Beatles, V/Vm exhibited no such punitive macho brio—no punk masculinity at all, really.

A characteristic track from one of the earlier records would be "Sticklebrick," credited to an act called Isnasakenai Douji—who could be V/Vm, or another of his acts, takes the recording of "How You Remind Me" by the band Nickleback, one of the most turgid and joyless of dick-rock anthems, speeds it up, and plays it over a DJ Shadow–inspired drum and bass beat. While critics who noticed V/Vm Test Records often described their work as a kind of critique of the tracks being reprocessed, this track in particular strikes me as instructively an act of charity—retrieving both meaning and drive within an original track whose more conspicuous features are a dull, self-important masculine self-loathing. Another would be "The Lady in Red (Is Dancing With Meat)," attributed to "V/Vm feat. Chris de Burger," which is the closest thing that V/Vm had to a breakout hit: it was "Single of the Week" in the British musical weekly *New Musical Express* in 2000, although those who wanted to buy the record wouldn't have been able to find it in most record stores. It was a few years after the release of this single that Kirby relinquished the V/Vm mantle altogether and started releasing music under the name The Caretaker. This development in Kirby's career marked a reversion to the kind of moody instrumentalism that the glitchy records had resisted so eloquently—a development that was amply rewarded by the 2000s and 2010s new media critics, who finally rewarded him with the kinds of generous, borderline-meaningless critical ponderings that had been piled on DJ Spoony a couple of decades before and which are currently lavished on Sophie. These narratives converge in a 2005 album by The Caretaker, comprising five hours of moody ambient electro tracks, entitled *Theoretically Pure Anterograde Amnesia* and bearing liner notes by none other than K-Punk himself, the theory bro Mark Fisher. In *Ghosts of My Life*, Fisher expanded his thoughts: "Isn't, in fact, theoretically pure anterograde amnesia the postmodern condition par excellence?" The self-assured speech of the theoretical hygienist—hard to imagine a sentence less like offal, yet more in need of a trashcan.

In thinking about how this curious lineage, and the ways in which *My Beauty* bears and fails to bear it, I have identified four paradoxes that travel under the heading of "my beauty" and help to unpack some of the complexities that emerge when one thinks beauty and property together. First, that the phrase "my beauty" denotes a kind of slippage between a beauty proper to the subject (who regards herself, newly, as beautiful) and a way of appreciating beauty in the object-world—to recap, "these songs showed me my definition of beauty, my beauty." That slippage between subject and object expresses itself in the work's distinctive handling of the material it is adapting, "covering," or "setting." Thus, not merely is Rowland appreciating a new "definition of beauty," he is developing a new way of being led ("these songs *showed* me") by objects. This object relation might illustrate Roland Barthes's famous notion that the function of pop music is to engender fantasies of creativity in the listener, except that the substance of the fantasy in question consists in, precisely, its realism, its foundational sincerity.[16]

Second, that the question of property emerges to broker the question of aesthetic authenticity, so that the method by which "my beauty" can be asserted derives from a notion of ownership as a kind of self-estrangement incompatible with (for example) the dominant modes of propertization particular to the capitalist mode of exchange. This paradox crystallizes in Rowland's cover of Bruce Springsteen's song "Thunder Road," the song in which Rowland introduces the phrase "your beauty," flipping subject and addressee: "this is your beauty, but hey, you're alright." The question of whether that line addresses the song's singer (and if so, from where) was sadly left unasked by the record's initial release, since McGee had forgotten to secure permission from Bruce Springsteen for the switch in lyrics from the original "you ain't a beauty but hey, you're alright."[17] Rowland's cover appeared for the first time on the 2020 reissue of *My Beauty*. So, whose "beauty" indeed?

Third, that femininity, as a style of personification distinct from any identity claim, offsets any ambiguity around the question of imaginative ownership as *My Beauty* derives it, since femininity is the style by which the notion of property is evacuated entirely—the feminine position is one in which ownership is impossible, according to the division of sexual labor that positions the feminine as, definitively, that which is either owned or unownable, but never *owning*—as Silvia Federici points out in "Marx and Feminism," Marx himself conspicuously deploys masculine terms to describe not only productive labor, but also capital, whereas not only reproductive labor but also the latency of the world of objects are always feminized. "*Madame la Terre*, Marx calls it, against *Monsieur le Capital*."[18] This paradox raises the question of what some antitransgender activists call "female appropriation," which positions the trans woman's appearance as an expropriation of femininity from women at the latter's expense—an argument that Rita Felski makes in respect of late-nineteenth-century decadents:

> It would be unwise to assume that this early modernist appropriation of the feminine was necessarily in sympathy with the aims of feminism. On the contrary, I will suggest, its appropriation of an aesthetic of parody and performance in fact reinscribes more insistently those gender hierarchies which are ostensibly being called into question. In at least some of the texts of early modernism, the resistive power of feminine artifice is predicated upon a radical disavowal of a dissociation from the "natural" body of women.[19]

Rather than adjudicate Felski's claim regarding the wisdom or otherwise of allying what she may as well have called "trans femininity" with feminism, I want rather to note the peculiar alignment between property and femininity in this argument: since femininity bears value in the decadent aesthetic system, it can be "appropriated" as though it were an index of capital, much as we talk about "cultural appropriation" in the more colloquial sense as though tradable commodities were at stake (which indeed they may be). But what is left in the place from which femininity has been appropriated is "the 'natural' body of women," which Felski puts in scare quotes as if to remark that the bodies in question are only ostensibly natural, that their merely apparent naturalness is a by-product of the primary expropriation. By depriving women of femininity, the expropriator unwittingly creates the very distinction between natural and artificial that he had set out to erase. This far exceeds the famous theory of social reproduction as an accumulation of expropriated female labor in the form of unwaged housework that Federici developed in *Caliban and the Witch*.[20] Indeed, in her recent book *Beyond the Periphery of the Skin*, Federici herself, as is by now well known since the publication in *Full Stop* of a blistering critique by Cory Austin Knudson, displaces a primary transphobia from the figure of the trans femme onto an understanding of historical precocity, which counterposes the neoliberal present of "body remakes" with an authentic, "1970s"-grounded feminism in which "we saw each other as beautiful because we were defiant, because in freeing ourselves from the prescriptions of a misogynous society we explored new ways of being, new ways of laughing, hugging, wearing our hair, crossing our legs, new ways of being together and making love."[21] Perhaps no surprise to encounter the word "new" so many times in a sentence whose sole purpose is to laureate as theory a boomer historiography composed of nothing more than nostalgia.

Fourth, the orientation around the putatively natural body from which femininity can be detached depends upon a prior racialization by which the Black woman is positioned as the unlikely safeguard and guarantor of the white trans woman's claim on femininity. Unlikely only in the sense that Blackness as an aesthetic formation, to echo bell hooks's essay "An Aesthetic of Blackness," appears to have been rigorously excluded from the semantic field of *My Beauty*, which otherwise traffics in none of the usual tics of racial drag associated with more prominent white gay and trans social practice—RuPaul's *Drag Race*, for example—and which spills out into occasional public controversies concerning an imputed white gay "appropriation" of Black women's culture, as in Sierra Mannie's 2014 essay "Dear White Gays: Stop Stealing Black Female Culture."[22] Despite Rowland's refusal of these kinds of practices, which have characterized white trans identity-practices in the United States at least since *Paris Is Burning* (1990), a paradoxical racialization presses into *My Beauty* in two conspicuous moments, and these are merely occasions of a wider structural aspect of the work.[23] The first occurs partway through the opening track, in which an uncredited but audibly Black male voice echoes one of the lines with a twist, "that old children's laughter." The echo of a vocal styling from the awkward sentimental Black caricatures of postwar movies like *Song of the South* disrupts the phonic scene of a distinctively postsynth orchestration, but a later track, a cover of The Hollies' "I Can't Tell the Bottom from the Top," suggests a through-line when a group of Black women backing vocalists turn one of the song's refrains into a duet. When Rowland sings, "On and on I was drifting into fear," the backing trio sings, "he didn't know that life could be good for him"—confirming, lest there was any doubt, that it is the *masculine* pronoun that we are to use when discussing the subject of the song's lyrics. That this is the only moment on the album where a pronoun is used in such a way is hardly surprising—how many other pop songs contain refrains where backing vocals refer to the singer in the third person at all? As though inverting the obliquely racializing call-and-response of Lou Reed's "Walk on the Wild Side," Rowland positions his Black backing singers as his beard, ensuring both that his femininity is associated with the racial aesthetic logics of openness and sincerity *and* that it does not finally challenge the locus of his masculine authorship. Thus the album's opener, and its recurring motif, is Whitney Houston's "The Greatest Love of All"—a song that conveys to Rowland, through the logic of universalized Black womanhood, both sincerity and artifice, virtuosic display of skill and guileless confession of selfhood.

With this admittedly rather cumbersome set of questions on the table, so to speak, I now turn back to Kant, in the hopes of answering the question with which I set out: how does Kant think about the ownership of beauty? Political engagements with Kant's aesthetics in the English-speaking world tend to derive in significant part from a series of lectures Hannah Arendt gave in 1970, in which she argued that Kant's *Critique of Judgment* formed the basis of a political theory, since it dealt with the necessarily political question of taste from the perspective of an immersed observer-participant.[24] Arendt described aesthetic judgment as the hinge between the faculty of imagination—a highly individuated mental capacity for playful appreciation of form—and common sense, whereby a putatively social type of judgment emerges to control for personal eccentricity.[25] Yet, as I've argued elsewhere, Arendt dramatically misconstrues the melancholic condition of Kant's "subjective universal": it is not that the reasoning subject submits himself to the judgment of his peers, but rather demands they assent to his own position, a demand that is (as Jean-Francois Lyotard argued) quelled only by the phantasmatic simulacrum of assent that the subject supplies himself. Accordingly, Kantian aesthetic judgment concedes nothing to the collective will of the social and indeed offsets any potential anxiety that social disapprobation might accord with the compensation of self-satisfaction.[26]

So I turn rather to a nuance of Kant's theory that has proven one of the most puzzling, and indeed controversial, among Kantian scholars, but which unquestionably imputes a political relation between beauty and property: the distinction drawn between free and adherent kinds of beauty.[27] "Adherent beauty" describes a type of beauty dependent upon conformity to a concept in order to be beautiful—as (to use Paul Guyer's example) a cathedral "must have a cruciform floor plan, but . . . not every edifice with a cruciform floor is beautiful; a beautiful cathedral must satisfy that constraint [but also] induce a free place of imagination and understanding."[28] Free beauty, conversely, pleases independently of any purpose—it describes the beauty of, for example, the natural world, which stimulates the free play of the faculties without any conceptual constraints. I say "for example," because that is the logical framework within which Kant assesses free beauty, but it is hard to think of examples of free beauty that are not flowers or evolutionary adaptiveness, except—as we shall see—the concept of *culture* insofar as it can be grasped in general. It is worth dwelling on the adjective "*abhängende,*" which Guyer and Matthews translate as "adherent" but which can also be translated as "dependent," implying a sense of political subordination as well as logical subordination. That this distinction would have bearing on the treatment of human beings as objects of aesthetic judgment, rather than as the rationalizing subjects, would seem unlikely, until we encounter a startling convergence of types: "a figure could be beautified with all sorts of curlicues and light but regular lines, as the New Zealanders do with their tattooing, if only it were not a human being."[29] What startles about the description of the indigenous Maori practice of *ta moko* is not merely the submission of the term "human being" as a name for the paradigmatic cultural practice—David Kazanjian has examined the figuration of indigenous cultures as the grounds for Kant's aesthetics[30]—but the immediate transformation of that "human being" into a mere object, "it," adherent therefore to the aesthetic concept of "human being"—which, whatever it be (and Kant, of course, cannot tell us), must not be adorned with "curlicues and light but regular lines." We therefore encounter a forerunner of Federici's complaint about body modification in an unexpected location, with the difference that, unlike Federici, Kant is at least honest about having reduced something so apparently noble as a "human being" to a mere object of aesthetic fascination.

The appearance of the "human being" as an object of adherent beauty, subject to the constraints of its concept, raises a question that Kant does not address, however, which is that of what relation, if any, might exist between the subject of reflexive judgment and the human as object. Kant develops the idea of the tattooed Maori further: "the latter could have much finer features and a more pleasing, softer outline to its facial structure if only if were not supposed to represent a man."[31] We notice the complex logical operation being held in Kant's modal verbs: does "the [Maori] *could* have much finer features" mean that he would be capable, or that he would be permitted, to feminize if he were not supposed to be a man; and does "if it were not *supposed* to represent a man" imply that the constraint of adherent beauty depends upon whether the human being *ought* to be a man, or is merely *believed* to be a man? Whichever, there can be no rebottling the idea that escapes in these lines: that the freedom denoted in the phrase "free beauty" is theoretically available to the tattooed Maori who is not a man and who perceives himself as an aesthetic object. That such a self-instrumentalizaiton would seem perverse to the author of the *Groundwork to the Metaphysics of Morals* can hardly be doubted, but the principle purpose of the *Critique of Judgment* is to establish grounds to distinguish aesthetic judgment from moral judgment, and treating oneself as a mediatic means to an aesthetic end might, after all, characterize the cultural project of decadence in a more generalizable sense.

To ask whether the phenomenon Rowland calls *My Beauty* might be of the free or adherent type might be to preempt the important question of where, exactly, we position the subject of judgment in an encounter with that object. The tattooed Maori, after all, cannot speak of "my beauty," because although Kant treats him as the paradigmatic subject of modernity, he remains an object.[32] Yet we can recall that the record itself exhibits a great deal of doubt concerning its own position with respect to the address of subject and object—what Émile Benveniste called the "subject of enunciation."[33] Not only do the backing vocalists, like a Greek chorus, position the vocalist as "he" in "I Can't Tell the Bottom from the Top," they address him directly as "you" later on in the same song; sometimes (as in the spoken bridge to "Rag Doll"), Rowland appears to be addressing himself ("this beautiful choir / they're singing for you"); at other times (such as in the breathy opening of "The Greatest Love of All"), he plays two separate vocal tracks so that he appears to be having a conversation with himself ("I know" / "oh, you know"). Though some part of this ambivalence is proper to the content of the record, some aspect of self-splitting is, as Barthes suggested, proper to the experience of pop music in general—which is, by that same token, always already a cover version whose primary performance is not the one that emanates from the singer, but the one that emanates from the listener, for which the "original" is recast as merely a hypothetical occasion. Hence, the sentimentality of *My Beauty* commutes to the scene of listening the character of a protocol, as though the record itself were less significant than the principles by which *My Beauty* was achieved, prompting the listener to produce her own beauty by reciting from her own catalogue of pleasurable guilt. Perhaps this is what the *NME* reviewer Victoria Segal meant by observing that "nobody would doubt [Rowland's] right to make this record," adding, "whether it should be released for widespread consumption is another matter."[34] (After I'd spoken sharply about that assessment in an informal way online a few years ago, Segal contacted me to clarify that, at the time, she was motivated by a concern for Rowland's well-being since he was so obviously being exploited by Alan McGee. In so many ways, the world of pop music criticism was not ready for *My Beauty*.)

The album's front cover, however, offers a visual referent for "my beauty" even in the absence of any other: it is whatever he is showing us underneath his dress, which is certainly not a tucked penis in the usual sense (and in the video produced in 1999 for "Concrete and Clay," the visible sack has a certain kinetic momentum). Though if Rowland declines to obscure his penis, he hardly makes much of it—in both cover and video, his crotch appears as a massy, almost abstract presence, almost nonrepresentational, perhaps curved by a dance belt, the item dancers use to mold, but not constrict, their genitals. Neither penis nor phallus, Rowland's "beauty" depicts the genitals as plastic potential, already somewhat shaped but only so as to render them more fully neutral and to advertise their limitless amenability to further shaping. What we are accustomed to thinking of as the comic payoff of trans panic—"that ain't a woman, that's a man, man," to quote Austin Powers—Rowland acquires as his most treasured possession, a property that finally belongs neither to himself nor to anyone else.[35] His own shaped penis has become, in the very simulacrum of castration, a psychoanalytic fetish, which is to say that it becomes a surrogate phallus whose function is to compensate for the loss of the maternal penis.[36]

For which reason, it has been jarring to witness the reissue of the album by Cherry Red in 2020 and the strange account of the initial composition and circulation that the reissue has engendered. Understandably appalled and shaken by the hostile reception that *My Beauty* received—bottles of piss thrown at him during his fifteen-minute set at the Reading Festival—Rowland disavowed the album for years afterwards and now when interviewed insists that his outfits were no more than mere costuming, trivial when contrasted with the music.[37] In a recent Guardian interview, Rowland protests,

> "Can you believe it? That people got so worked up about what someone was *wearing*?" he says today. But they did, and even those sympathetic to Rowland's vision seemed baffled. One marketing guy at Creation sent him a bunch of material about cross-dressing. "And I was like, no, I don't wanna wear a wig! I had sideburns on, a male haircut. I just wanted to wear a dress. . . . Someone else at the label thought it was about sexuality. It may have been a bit. But I remember having to write something, saying it's not a gay thing, it's not this, it's not that. I kind of defined it through people misinterpreting it. Because I'm not the kind of guy to go, "This is a statement and it means this." It was all intuitive.[38]

The interviewer, Tim Jonze, picks up what Rowland's laying down and describes his own belated understanding of *My Beauty* once he became "bed-bound with depression" after a series of traumatic events and eventually realized that "the [*My Beauty*] sleeve made sense to me now, not as a big statement on gender so much as a visual metaphor that Rowland was laying it all on the line with an incredibly personal gesture."[39] Rowland's new record label is likewise insistent that the record has nothing to do with transvestism. Indeed, it is hard to decipher what precisely is intended by the phrase "not cross-dressing," since in addition to the "men's dresses" that he wore, Rowland was clearly wearing makeup and nail polish—certainly not trying to *pass*, but clearly doing something more than wearing "men's dresses," whatever they may be. Indeed, if his look had been reducible to a mere bit of indeterminate gender-fuckery, it would hardly have felt "radical" in a scene already familiar with Nicky Wire, King Adora, and Brian Molko. Or, indeed, with Kurt Cobain, whose suicide in 1994 had already been attributed (albeit in slightly conspiratorial ways) to the trans ideation he expressed on occasion in his dress, his lyrics, and in some accounts, in his suicide note.[40]

In order to understand the strange erasure of gender from Rowland's own reassessment of the album twenty years later—the topic warrants half a sentence in the twenty-minute interview Rowland filmed for Cherry Red—one needs to look not merely to the aftermath of the vicious transphobia to which he was subjected, but also, and more pointedly, to the increasing importance of gender-variant social practice in British antitransgender activism. Within antitrans discourse, gender-fuckery is usually positioned as the *antinomy* of trans claims about personhood: the prominent activist Jane Clare Jones, for example, often distinguishes trans people's claims about themselves from those made by Prince and David Bowie, on the grounds that the pop stars understood gender as a self-conscious artifice, whereas trans people naively believe that gender is a vehicle for self-discovery and that the ontology grounded by the experience of transition is one of the fundamental and realistic kind.[41] Fair enough in the cases of Prince and Bowie, perhaps, but it was surely the clumsy spectacle of sentimental self-disclosure that made Rowland so loathsome to those throwing their piss at him in 1999. So one cannot but suspect that the historiography with which Cherry Red and Rowland now market *My Beauty* has been designed not to celebrate, but to neutralize the distinctiveness of the record as it originally appeared. Central to this erasure is the manner in which Rowland positions his genderqueer grandson, whom he invites to lip sync to his 1999 performance of "Rag Doll" in the video shot in 2020, reproductive heterosexuality now working to displace historical queerness with its own Whiggish history of loosening gender norms, universal gender fluidity, and metrosexual, LGBQ sophistication.[42] A technique—a transition—cannot be narrated in such terms, let alone historicized. To pay attention to such is to confront without defense the alarming and irreducibly historical inevitability of anachronism.

NOTES

Prospectus

1. Todd, "Feminism."

2. Janice Raymond, *The Transsexual Empire: The Making of the Empire* (New York: Teachers College Press, 1994); Sheila Jeffreys, *Gender Hurts A Feminist Analysis of the Politics of Transgenderism* (London, UK: Routledge, 2014).

3. See Simon Joyce, "Two Women Walk into a Theatre Bathroom: The Fanny and Stella Trials as Trans Narrative," *Victorian Review* 44, no. 1 (Spring 2018): 83–98.

Introduction

1. Sedgwick, *Epistemology of the Closet*, 34.

2. Gill-Peterson, *Histories of the Transgender Child.*

3. A list of bills introduced and passed follow. Relating to requiring public school students to compete in interscholastic athletic competitions based on biological sex: H.B. 25, 87th Legislature of the State of Texas (2021); participation in school sports, State of Indiana, House Enrolled Act No. 1041 (2022); Fairness in Women's Sports Act, State of Louisiana Act No. 283 (2022); an act to amend Tennessee Code Annotated, Title 49, Chapter 6, relative to school sports, State of Tennessee, Pub. Ch. 909 (2022); an act to amend Tennessee Code Annotated, Title 49, relative to participation in athletics, State of Tennessee, Pub. Ch. 1005 (2022); interscholastic and intramural athletics, Arizona Revised Statutes, 15-120.02 (2022); Save Women's Sports Act, seventy Oklahoma Statutes Annotated § 27–106 (2022); a bill for an act relating to student eligibility requirements in school district, accredited nonpublic school, regent institution, community college, and certain other institution of higher education athletics based on sex, and including effective date provisions, H.F. 2416, 89th General Assembly of the State of Iowa (2022); Protect Fairness in Women's Sports, S.B. 46, 97th Legislature of the State of South Dakota (2022). Bills introduced, passed, vetoed, or temporarily passed: an act providing for sport activities in public institutions of higher education and public school entities to be expressly designated male, female or coed, H.B. 972, 2021–2022 Regular Session of the General Assembly of the Commonwealth of Pennsylvania (2022); Student Eligibility in Interscholastic Activities, H.B. 11, 64th Legislature of the State of Utah (2022). Bills introduced and failed: Save Women's Sports Act, H.B. 358, 155th Legislature of the State of North Carolina (2021); "To provide that it shall be unlawful for public or private schools whose students compete against a public school to operate athletic programs that permit a person whose gender is male to

participate in an athletic program that is designated for females," H.B. 276, 156th General Assembly of the State of Georgia (2021); to provide a definition for the term *gender*, H.B. 372, 156th General Assembly of the State of Georgia (2021); designating University of Wisconsin and technical college sports and athletic teams based on the sex of the participants, A.B. 195, 105th Legislature of the State of Wisconsin (2021); designating athletic sports and teams operated or sponsored by public schools or private schools participating in a parental choice program based on the sex of the participants, A.B. 196, 105th Legislature of the State of Wisconsin (2021); male student participation in female athletics restricted, H.F. 1657, 92nd Legislature of the State of Minnesota (2021); an act to amend Title 14 of the Delaware Code relating to the Fairness in Women's Sports Act, S.B. 227, 151st General Assembly of the State of Delaware (2022); to modify provisions relating to school activities, H.B. 1973, 101st Legislature of the State of Missouri (2022);to modify provisions relating to elections, H.B. 2140, 101st Legislature of the State of Missouri (2022); Save Women's Sports Act, S.B. 781, 101st Legislature of the State of Missouri (2022); Fairness in Women's Sports Act, Senate File 0051, 66th Legislature of the State of Wyoming (2022). Bills introduced: concerning equitable competition between students who participate in school athletic activities, H.B. 1556, 67th Legislature of the State of Washington (2021); enactment of Save Women's Sports Act, H.B. 61, 134th Legislature of the State of Ohio (2021); Interscholastic Sports-Gender, H.B. 4082, 102nd Legislature of the State of Illinois (2021); the revised school code, S.B. 0218, 101st Legislature of the State of Michigan (2021); a bill to amend the State School Aid Act of 1979, H.B. 5795, 101st Legislature of the State of Michigan, (2022).

4. Bills introduced and passed: Act No. 2022-290 (public schools' restrooms or changing areas required to be used based on individual's biological sex, affecting kindergarden to fifth-grade classroom instruction), Alabama Code §16 (2022). Bills introduced and failed: an act to amend Tennessee Code Annotated, Title 39, Chapter 13, relative to observation without consent, H.B. 1177, 112th General Assembly of the State of Tennessee (2021); provision for the designated use of public school multi-occupancy rooms and sleeping rooms, H.B. 1005, 97th Legislature of the State of South Dakota (2022); regarding public school restrooms, H.B. 2314, 55th Legislature of the State of Arizona (2022).

5. Bills introduced and passed: prohibition of irreversible gender reassignment surgery for minors, Arizona Revised Statutes, 32-3230 (2022); Alabama Vulnerable Child Compassion and Protection Act (V-CAP), Alabama Code §22 (2022). Bills introduced and failed: Youth Health Protection Act, H.B. 2835, 112th General Assembly of the State of Tennessee (2022); Oklahoma Save Adolescents from Experimentation (SAFE) Act, H.B. 3240, 58th Legislature of the State of Oklahoma (2022); a prohibition of the reassignment of the gender identity of minors, S.B. 1045, 55th Legislature of the State of Arizona (2022); a prohibition of certain procedures to alter the sex of a minor child, H.B. 570, 2022 Regular Session of the State of Louisiana (2022); a bill for an act relating to actions relative to treatment or intervention regarding the discordance between a minor's sex and gender identity, H.F 193, 89th General Assembly of the State of Iowa (2022); addition of sexual reassignment to the definition of child abuse, H.B. 1651, 2022 Regular Session of the State of New Hampshire (2022).

6. Fairness in Women's Sports Act, S.B. 160, 2021–2022 Regular Session of the Legislature of the State of Kansas (2022) [vetoed]; Fairness in Women's Sports Act, S.B. 208, 2021–2022 Regular Session of the Legislature of the State of Kansas (2022) [died in House committee]; Fairness

in Women's Sports Act, S.B. 484, 2021–2022 Regular Session of the Legislature of the State of Kansas (2022) [died in House committee]; making it a crime for a doctor to perform gender reassignment surgery or hormone replacement therapy on minors, H.B. 2210, 2021–2022 Regular Session of the Legislature of the State of Kansas (2022) [died in committee]; making it a crime for a physician to perform gender reassignment surgery or hormone replacement therapy on certain children, S.B. 214, 2021–2022 Regular Session of the Legislature of the State of Kansas (2022) [died in committee].

7. Amends existing law to provide for the crime of genital mutilation in certain instances, H. B. 675, 66th Legislature of the State of Idaho (2022) [failed].

8. A bill for an act relating to the construction of the Iowa Civil Rights Act of 1965 regarding sex and gender identity, H.F. 340, 89th General Assembly of the State of Iowa (2021) [failed]; a bill for an act removing gender identity as a protected class under the Iowa Civil Rights Act, H.F. 272, 89th General Assembly of the State of Iowa (2021) [failed]; an act to amend Tennessee Code Annotated . . . relative to courses of treatment for children, H.B. 0578, 112th General Assembly of the State of Tennessee (2021) [failed]; gender transition prohibition, H.B. 2608, 55th Legislature of the State of Arizona (2022) [failed]; change to display of gender on birth certificates, H.B. 2292, 55th Legislature of the State of Arizona (2022) [failed]; state documents sex identification, H.B. 2294, 55th Legislature of the State of Arizona (2022) [failed]; and a prohibition on changing sex on birth certificates, H.B. 2086, 101st Legislature of the State of Missouri (2022) [failed].

9. Wayne C. Booth, *The Rhetoric of Fiction* (Chicago, IL: University of Chicago Press, 1961).

10. Franz Kafka, "Das nächste Dorf," Wikisource, https://de.wikisource.org/wiki/Das_n%C3%A4chste_Dorf. My own translation.

11. Charles S. Peirce, "How to Make Our Ideas Clear," *Popular Science Monthly*, no. 12 (1978): 293.

12. Gyorgy Lukács, *The Theory of the Novel: A Historico-Philosophical Essay on the Forms of Great Epic Literature* (Cambridge, MA: MIT Press, 1973).

13. Fredric Jameson, *The Antimonies of Realism* (London, UK: Verso, 2013).

14. Eve Kosofsky Sedgwick, *Touching Feeling: Affect Pedagogy, Performativity* (Durham, NC: Duke University Press, 2003).

15. Karl Marx and Friedrich Engels, *The Communist Manifesto* (New York: Penguin, 2006), 12.

16. John Ruskin, *The Nature of Gothic: A Chapter from the Stones of Venice* (London, UK: G. Allen, 1900), 7, 48, and passim.

17. Arnold, "The Function of Criticism at the Present Time," in *Essays in Criticism*, 1–41.

18. Michel Foucault, Preface to *Anti-Oedipus: Capitalism and Schizophrenia* by Gilles Deleuze and Felix Guattari (New York: Penguin, 2009), xiii. I should clarify that I take Foucault's attempt to dispel "castration" to be an explicit critique of Lacan's reading of Freud, rather than any gesture of hostility towards trans femininity. I explore this theory of castration in chapters 2 and 6, as well as throughout this book.

19. *Silence of the Lambs*, directed by Jonathan Demme (1991, Beverly Hills, CA: Metro-Goldwyn-Mayer Studios; 20th Century Fox Home Entertainment, 2008).

20. Jack Halberstam, *The Queer Art of Failure* (Durham, NC: Duke University Press, 2011); Ann Cvetkovich, *Depression: A Public Feeling* (Durham, NC: Duke University Press, 2012); Eve Kosofsky Sedgwick, "Paranoid Reading and Reparative Reading, or, You're So Paranoid, You Probably Think This Essay Is about You," in *Touching Feeling: Affect, Pedagogy, Performativity*

(Durham: Duke University Press, 2003), 123–52; Eric Stanley, "The Affective Commons: Gay Shame, Queer Hate, and Other Collective Feelings," *GLQ: A Journal of Lesbian and Gay Studies* 24, no. 4 (2018): 489–508; Heather Love, *Feeling Backward: Loss and the Politics of Queer History* (Cambridge, MA: Harvard University Press, 2007).

21. Charles Dickens, *Hard Times* (New York: Penguin, 2003). For a critical response to "Gradgrindism" as an account of routinized labor, see Catherine Gallagher, "Hard Times and North and South: The Family and Society in Two Industrial Novels," *The Arizona Quarterly* 36, no. 1 (Spring 1980): 70–96.

22. RuPaul, "Supermodel (You Better Work)," released November 17, 1992.

23. Stopes, *Married Love*; and *Alcoholics Anonymous*.

24. Howard J. Falcon-Lang, "Lecture: Marie Stopes—Palaeobotanist and Coal Geologist," *The Merceian Geologist* 17, no. 1 (2008): 61–63; (lecture given at meeting of Midlands Geological Society, January 12, 2008). http://www.emgs.org.uk/files/mercian_vol13on/Mercian%20Geologist%20volume%2017%202008-2011/Mercian%202008%20v17%20p061%20Marie%20Stopes,%20Falcon-Lang.pdf.

25. F. W. Stella Browne, *The Sexual Variety and Variability among Women and Their Bearing upon Social Reconstruction* (London, UK: British Society for the Study of Sex Psychology, 1917), 13.

26. Ernest H. Starling, "Letter from Professor E. H. Starling," in Stopes, *Married Love*, 8.

27. Laura Doan, "Marie Stopes's Wonderful Rhythm Charts: Normalizing the Natural," *Journal of the History of Ideas* 78, no. 4 (October 2017): 595–620.

28. Peter Neushul, "Marie C. Stopes and the Popularization of Birth Control Technology," *Technology and Culture* 30, no. 2 (April 1998): 245–72; Ellen Martha Holtzman, "Marriage, Sexuality, and Contraception in the British Middle Class, 1918–1939" (PhD diss., Rutgers University, 1982).

29. Isabella Mary Beeton, *Mrs. Beeton's Book of Household Management* (New York: Oxford University Press, 2000).

30. Marie Carmichael Stopes, *Wise Parenthood: The Treatise on Birth Control for Married People* (London, UK: G. P. Putnam's Sons, 1951), 62.

31. Quoted in Alexander Geppert, "Divine Sex, Happy Marriage, Regenerated Nation: Marie Stopes's Marital Manual 'Married Love' and the Making of a Best-Seller, 1918–1955," *Journal of the History of Sexuality* 8, no. 3 (January 1988): 400.

32. Sigmund Freud, *Three Contributions to the Theory of Sex*, trans. A. A. Brill (New York: Nervous and Mental Disease Publishing Co., 1920).

33. "I am very much against the parade of unwholesome sex matters particularly by the psychoanalysts" (letter to a physician in Bradford, 1922). Quoted in Doan, "Marie Stopes's Wonderful Rhythm Charts," 600–1, n17.

34. Werther, *Autobiography of an Androgyne*; Bellwether, *Fucking Trans Women*.

35. Stopes, *Married Love*, 147.

36. Geppert, "Divine Sex," 400.

37. Quoted in Doan, "Marie Stopes's Wonderful Rhythm Charts," 612–13.

38. Doan, "Marie Stopes's Wonderful Rhythm Charts," 612.

39. The phrase is found in later editions, not the first edition. See, for example, Stopes, *Married Love*, 10.

40. Stopes, *Married Love*, 37.

41. For example: "It should be realized that a man does not woo and win a woman once and for all when he marries her: *he must woo her before every separate act of coitus*; for each act corresponds to a marriage, as the beasts of the field and the fowls of the air know it. Wild animals are not so foolish as man; a wild animal does not unite with his female without the wooing characteristic of his race, whether by stirring her by a display of his strength in fighting another male, or by exhibiting his beautiful feathers or song. And we must not forget that the wild animals are assisted by nature; they generally only woo just at the season when the female is beginning to feel natural desire. But man, who wants his mate all out of season as well as in it, has a double duty to perform, and must himself rouse, charm, and stimulate her to the local readiness which would have been to some extent naturally prepared for him had he waited till her own desire welled up," *Married Love*, 85–86; "The well-worn phrase 'Ontogeny repeats Phylogeny' has helped to concentrate our attention on the fact that the young in their development, in ourselves as in the animals, go through many phases which resemble the stages through which the whole race must have passed in the curse of its evolution. // While this is true, there is another characteristic of youth: It is prophetic!" 170–1; "Actions differ, however, in their relative positions in the scale of things. Only those actions are worthy which lead the race onwards to a higher and fuller completion and the perfecting of its powers, which steer the race into the main current of that stream of life and vitality which courses through us and impels us forward," 144.

42. *Alcoholics Anonymous*, 84.

43. Robyn Warhol, "The Rhetoric of Addiction: From Victorian Novels to AA," in *High Anxieties: Cultural Studies in Addiction*, edited by Janet Farrell Brodie and Marc Redfield (Berkeley: University of California Press, 2002).

44. Susan Zieger, *Inventing the Addict: Drugs, Race, and Sexuality in Nineteenth-Century British and American Literature* (Amherst: University of Massachusetts Press, 2008).

45. *Alcoholics Anonymous*, 1–16.

46. *Ibid.*, 58.

47. Catherine Gallagher, "George Eliot: Immanent Victorian," *Representations* 90, no. 1 (Spring 2005): 61–74.

48. *Alcoholics Anonymous*, 1.

49. *Ibid.*, 4.

50. Mariana Valverde, *Diseases of the Will: Alcohol and the Dilemmas of Freedom* (New York: Cambridge University Press, 1998), 129; Robyn Warhol-Down, "Academics Anonymous: A Meditation on Anonymity, Power, and Powerlessness," *symploke* 16, nos. 1–2 (2008): 54.

51. *Alcoholics Anonymous Comes of Age: A Brief History of AA* (New York: Alcoholics Anonymous World Services, 1980).

52. Gallagher, "George Eliot," 61–74.

53. *Alcoholics Anonymous*, 9.

54. Mel B., *Ebby: The Man Who Sponsored Bill W.* (Center City, MN: Hazelden, 1998), 131–45.

55. *Alcoholics Anonymous*, 85–86.

56. *Ibid.*, 88.

57. George Eliot, *The Mill on the Floss* (New York: Penguin Classics, 2003); George Eliot, *Romola* (New York: Penguin Classics, 1997).

58. George Eliot, *Middlemarch: A Study of Provincial Life* (New York, 2015).

59. Robyn Warhol and Helena Michie, "Twelve-Step Teleology: Narratives of Recovery/Recovery as Narrative," in *Getting a Life: Everyday Uses of Autobiography*, ed. Sidonie Smith and Julia Watson (Minneapolis: University of Minnesota Press, 1996), 327–50.

60. George Eliot, "Janet's Repentance," in *Scenes from Clerical Life* (New York: Oxford University Press, 2015).

61. *Ibid.*, 284.

62. *Ibid.*, 307.

63. Samuel Smiles, *Self-Help, with Illustrations of Character and Conduct* (London, UK: J. Murray, 1859). For a study of self-help literature, see also Beth Blum, *The Self-Help Compulsion: Searching for Advice in Modern Literature* (New York: Columbia University Press, 2020).

64. Paul Peppis, "Rewriting Sex: Mina Loy, Marie Stopes, and Sexology," *Modernism/Modernity* 9, no. 4 (November 2002): 561–79.

65. Sianne Ngai, *The Theory of the Gimmick: Aesthetic Judgement and Capitalist Form* (Cambridge, MA: Harvard University Press, 2020), 54.

66. Melanie Klein, "Notes on Some Schizoid Mechanisms," in *Envy and Gratitude and Other Works: 1946–1963*, vol. 3 of *The Writings of Melanie Klein* (New York: Free Press, 1975), 1–24.

67. Cunningham and Lesschaeve, 1985:, p. 137.

68. "Merce Cunningham," Merce Cunningham Trust, accessed September 29, 2022, https://www.mercecunningham.org/about/merce-cunningham/.

69. Friedrich Schiller, "Letter XXVII," in *On the Aesthetic Education of Man: In a Series of Letters* (New York: Oxford University Press, 1982).

70. Friedrich Schiller, "On Grace and Dignity," in *Aesthetic and Philosophical Essays* (Project Gutenberg, 2004).

71. Ian Duncan, "Natural Histories of Form: Charles Darwin's Aesthetic Science," *Representations* 151, no. 1 (2020): 51–73.

I: Trans Realism and Its Referents

1. "No doubt the twin aims of psychoanalysis—to provide therapy and to generate theory—are usually compatible and interdependent. But at times they clash: the rights of the patient to privacy may conflict with the demands of science for public discussion. It was a difficulty Freud would confront again, and not with his patients alone; as his own most revealing analysand, he found self-disclosure at once painful and necessary." Gay, *Freud*, 74.

2. A move in this direction is achieved by Summer J. Star in her recent essay "Feeling Real in *Middlemarch*," *ELH* 80, no. 3 (Fall 2013): 839–69. Star argues that Eliot's realism is "not so much an empirical but a phenomenological approach to narrative," and therefore to lived experiences and perceptions of the world (840). Star's argument, then, focuses attention on realism as an attempt to represent cognitive phenomena, but does not, as my approach does, treat Eliot's subjectivism as the motor of a fundamentally normative project designed to produce therapeutic effects in readers.

3. Sigmund Freud, "Lecture XXIX: Revision of the Theory of Dreams," in *New Introductory Lectures on Psycho-Analysis* (1933 [1932]), vol. 22 of *The Standard Edition of the Complete*

Psychological Works of Sigmund Freud, trans. James Strachey et al., ed. Strachey, 24 vols. (London, UK: The Hogarth Press, 1953–74), 10.

4. Eliot, *Middlemarch*, 785.

5. See Janet Mock, *Redefining Realness: My Path to Womanhood, Identity, Love & So Much More* (New York: Atria Books, 2014).

6. *Ibid.*, 116.

7. *Ibid.*

8. *Ibid.*, 173.

9. *Ibid.*, 258.

10. Butler, "Gender Is Burning: Questions of Approximation and Subversion," in *Bodies That Matter*, 126.

11. Deanna Kreisel uses this phrase, without direct reference to its usage in trans discourse, in her excellent 2003 essay on Eliot's fiction. Kreisel's reading of *Daniel Deronda* and especially *Adam Bede* suggests that Eliot's attempt to produce an "androgynous incognito" was an attempt to synthesize as narrative form a "feminine sympathetic realism" with a "masculine narratorial intervention." Deanne K. Kreisel, "Incognito, Intervention, and Dismemberment in Adam Bede," *ELH* 70, no. 2 (Summer 2003): 570, 543. My own position is less nuanced, I think: the realism towards which Eliot's thinking asymptotically strives is, or would be if it were achievable, the breach of sexual difference.

12. This necessarily truncated account of Lukács's theory of realism as a kind of historical reference was nonetheless a constant in his otherwise laudably inconsistent engagement with the term; its definitive formulation appears in György Lukács, "Realism in the Balance," trans. Rodney Livingston, in *Aesthetics and Politics: The Key Texts of the Classic Debate within German Marxism* (New York: Verso, 2007), 29–59.

13. Oxford English Dictionary Online, s.v. "realistic."

14. Raymond Williams, *Keywords: A Vocabulary of Culture and Society* (New York: Croom Helm, 1976), 259.

15. Fredric Jameson, "George Eliot and *Mauvaise Foi*," in *The Antinomies of Realism* (New York: Verso, 2013), 129. Bruce Robbins summarizes Jameson's position as such: "The *style indirect libre* [Eliot] favors may look like moral judgment, but is all the more effective because the reader is left uncertain, sentence by sentence, as to whether judgment is happening at all." Bruce Robbins, "Fredric Jameson on the Taking of Sides," review of *The Antinomies of Realism* by Fredric Jameson, *Victorian Studies* 57 (Autumn 2014): 92.

16. Jacqueline Rose, *Sexuality in the Field of Vision* (Verso: New York, 1986), 107.

17. Anonymous, Review of *Middlemarch: A Study of Provincial Life* by George Eliot, *Edinburgh Review* 137 (January 1873): 255.

18. Eliot, *Middlemarch*, 705–6.

19. See Laplanche and Pontalis, "Reality Principle," in *Language of Psychoanalysis*, 379–82. Part of Laplanche and Pontalis's reading of the reality principle derives from D. W. Winnicott's work on the topic, formulated most succinctly in "The Use of an Object and Relating through Identifications," *The International Journal of Psychoanalysis* 50, no. 4 (1969): 711–16. The other part they extrapolate through an analogy between two distinctions made by Freud, between pleasure and reality in "Formulations on the Two Principles of Mental Functioning" (*Papers on*

Technique [1911–1915 (1914)], *Standard Edition,* 12:218–26) and the self-preserving and self-eroticizing impulses in "On Narcissism: An Introduction" (*On the History of the Psycho-Analytic Movement* [1914], *Standard Edition,* 14:73–102).

20. Michel Foucault, *The Care of the Self,* vol. 3 of *The of the History of Sexuality,* trans. Robert Hurley (New York: Pantheon, 1986), 45, 51.

21. *Ibid.,* 51.

22. Freud, "Mourning and Melancholia," in *Papers on Metapsychology* [1915], *Standard Edition,* 14:244.

23. This is a characteristic element of Eliot's idiosyncratic mode of omniscient narration. Here, for example, is the introduction of Fred Vincy in *Middlemarch*:

> You will hardly demand that his confidence should have a basis in external facts; such confidence, we know, is something less coarse and materialistic: it is a comfortable disposition leading us to expect that the wisdom of providence or the folly of our friends, the mysteries of luck or the still greater mystery of our high individual value in the universe, will bring about agreeable issues such as are consistent with our good taste in costume and our general preference for the best style of thing. (219)

24. Gallagher, "George Eliot," 73.

25. David Kurnick, "Abstraction and the Subject of Novel Reading: Drifting through Romola," *Novel,* no. 42 (Fall 2009): 491.

26. Mary Ann O'Farrell, "Provoking George Eliot," in *Compassion: The Culture and Politics of an Emotion,* ed. Lauren Berlant (New York: Routledge, 2004), 145.

27. James Strachey, "Editor's Introduction," in *Papers on Technique, Standard Edition,* 12:87.

28. Freud, "The Handling of Dream-Interpretation," in *Papers on Technique, Standard Edition,* 12:94.

29. Given that it is in his discourses on technique that Freud feels, more conspicuously than anywhere else, the fear of being overheard, it is interesting that, in Peter Brooks's influential alignment of Eliot and the psychoanalytic tradition, the novelist's critique of the practice of knowing "woman's body" through the "phallic field of vision" was surpassed by the analyst's attempt "to supplant seeing by listening to the body." Peter Brooks, *Body Work: Objects of Desire in Modern Narrative* (Cambridge, MA: Harvard University Press, 1993), 199.

30. Freud, "Observations on Transference-Love (Further Recommendations on Technique of Psycho-Analysis III)," in *Standard Edition,* 12:160. Of course, it is on the grounds of his denial of countertransference that Freud's writings on technique have been all but abandoned by the institution of professional psychoanalysis at present; in the various Kleinian and post-Kleinian schools that have pushed back against that occlusion, countertransference is understood as a foundational, even primary, dimension of the therapeutic transference.

31. Freud, "Recommendations to Physicians Practising Psycho-Analysis (1912)," in *Papers on Technique, Standard Edition,* 12:118.

32. *Ibid.,* 111, 115.

33. Freud, "On Beginning the Treatment: (Further Recommendations on the Technique of Psycho-Analysis I) (1913)," *Standard Edition,* 12:135.

34. *Ibid.,* 114.

35. Strachey, "Editor's Introduction," in Freud, *Standard Edition,* 12:85.

36. As Caroline Levine points out, the pause works metadiegetically (the story is put on pause while something else happens) and diegetically (the story is, for the purposes of this chapter, that a pause is taking place; specifically that Arthur Donnithorne has been interrupted leaving Reverend Irwine's company). Levine extrapolates from this observation the principle that the discursive otherness of the pause models an ethical relation to otherness in general—an encounter with the real world as irremediably distinct from the reader's inner life. But to the extent that the pause brings the reader out of the story, the reader experiences the kind of shock Freud feared his patients would experience if they read the *Papers on Technique*: by being pulled further into Eliot's narrator's world, we are thereby expelled from it. See Caroline Levine, *The Serious Pleasures of Suspense: Victorian Realism and Narrative Doubt* (Charlottesville: University of Virginia Press, 2003), 104.

37. George Eliot, *Adam Bede*, ed. Margaret Reynolds (New York: Penguin Classics, 2008), 193.

38. *Ibid.*, 9. Indeed, for Garrett Stewart the contract is the stereotype of all novelistic apostrophe: "the reader I have in mind, the reader I am in my mind while moving through a text, is there to establish, without ever stabilizing, a contact that grows increasingly contractual. Readers do more than underwrite the act of textual communication; they are conscribed, in short, by narrative's own economy as silent partners." Garrett Stewart, *Dear Reader: The Conscripted Audience in Nineteenth Century British Fiction* (Baltimore, MD: Johns Hopkins University Press, 1996), 10.

39. Eliot, *Adam Bede*, 193.

40. *Ibid.*, 9.

41. J. Hillis Miller, *The Form of Victorian Fiction: Thackeray, Dickens, Trollope, George Eliot, Meredith, and Hardy* (Cleveland, OH: University of Notre Dame Press, 1979), 81.

42. Eliot, *Adam Bede*, 465.

43. *Ibid.*, 487.

44. Stewart, *Dear Reader*, 306.

45. Eliot, *Adam Bede*, 491, 492, 493.

46. *Ibid.*, 193–94.

47. *Ibid.*, 194.

48. Gallagher, "George Eliot," 65.

49. "Above all Eliot seems drawn to the unpleasant color and texture of the human complexion." Aaron Matz, *Satire in an Age of Realism* (Cambridge, UK: Cambridge University Press, 2010), 6.

50. Eliot, *Adam Bede*, 195, 196.

51. *Ibid.*, 197.

52. "If the novel were realistic merely because it saw life from the seamy side, it would only be an inverted romance; but in fact it surely attempts to portray all the varieties of human existence, and not merely those suited to one particular perspective: the novel's realism does not reside in the life it presents, but in the way it presents it." Ian Watt, *The Rise of the Novel: Studies in Defoe, Richardson, and Fielding* (Berkeley: University of California Press, 1957), 11.

53. See Rebecca Mead, "George Eliot's Ugly Beauty," *New Yorker*, September 19, 2013, www.newyorker.com/books/page-turner/george-eliots-ugly-beauty; and Lena Dunham (@lenadunham), "FYI George Eliot's Wikipedia page is the soapiest most scandalous thing

you'll read this month. Thesis: she was ugly AND horny!" Twitter, September 15, 2013, twitter .com/lenadunham/status/379293041892134912.

54. For these and other assessments of Eliot's appearance, see Mead, "George Eliot's Ugly Beauty."

55. Eliot to Mrs. Bray, February 24, 1859, in *The Life of George Eliot: As Related in Her Letters and Journals*, ed. John Walter Cross. 1884 (Oxford, UK: Oxford University Press, 2010), 289.

56. See George Eliot, *The George Eliot Letters*, ed. Gordon S. Haight (New Haven, CT: Yale Universtiy Press, 1954).

57. Gillian Beer, *George Eliot (Key Women Writers)*, (Brighton: Harvester Press, 1986), p. 25.

58. Eliot, *Middlemarch*, 399

59. *Ibid.*, 400.

60. *Ibid.*, 448.

61. *Ibid.*, 400.

62. *Ibid.*, 614.

63. Émile Benveniste, *Problems in General Linguistics* (Coral Gables, Fla.: University of Miami Press, 1997), 225.

64. *Ibid.*

65. Eliot, *Middlemarch*, p. 640.

66. *Ibid.*, 448–49.

67. *Ibid.*, 316.

68. Abraham Nicolas and Maria Torok, *The Shell and the Kernel: Renewals of Psychoanalysis* (Chicago: University of Chicago Press, 1994), 114.

69. *Ibid.*, 113.

70. Eliot, *Middlemarch*, 596.

71. Anthony Trollope's notable name for Dickens, in *The Warden* (New York: Dick and Fitzgerald, 1862), 210.

72. Eliot, *Middlemarch*, 145.

73. *Ibid.*, 671.

74. *Ibid.*, 576.

75. *Ibid.*, 668.

76. *Ibid.*, 458.

77. *Ibid.*, 499.

78. *Ibid.*, 426.

79. *Ibid.*, 467–68.

80. Eve Marie Stwertka, "The Web of Utterance: Middlemarch," *Texas Studies in Literature and Language* 19, no. 2 (1977): 179–87.

81. *Middlemarch* is "a novel without weaknesses, except perhaps Will Ladislaw is a little too light and romantic—he's a bit underweight for a novel so ample and deep." Martin Amis, "What Middlemarch Means to Me," *The Guardian*, February 28, 2014, https://www.theguardian.com /books/2014/feb/28/middlemarch-george-eliot-martin-amis-as-byatt. Kathryn Hughes, similarly, writes that he is "underwritten as a character (he is nothing but a lovely shimmering empty space)." Kathryn Hughes, "What Middlemarch Means to Me," *The Guardian*, February 28, 2014, https://www.theguardian.com/books/2014/feb/28/middlemarch-george-eliot-martin-amis -as-byatt.

82. Ernst Bloch, "A Philosophical View of the Novel of the Artist," in *The Utopian Function of Art in Literature* (Cambridge, MA: MIT Press, 1988), 265–77.

83. Jerome Beaty, "The Forgotten Past of Will Ladislaw," *Nineteenth-Century Fiction* 13, no. 2 (1958): 159–63.

84. *Ibid.*, 160.

85. Freud, *Interpretation of Dreams*, 289.

86. See Freud, *Interpretation of Dreams*, 279–304.

87. Freud, *Interpretation of Dreams*, 289.

88. *Ibid.*

89. *Ibid.*, 292.

90. *Ibid.*, 291.

91. *Ibid.*

92. *Ibid.*

93. See Didier Anzieu, *Freud's Self-Analysis*, trans. Peter Graham (London, UK: Hogarth, 1986), 449–50.

94. Kofman, *Enigma of Woman*, 85.

95. Freud, "Analysis Terminable and Interminable," 252.

96. *Ibid.*

97. *Ibid.*, 268.

98. Alfred Adler, "Inferiority Feeling and Masculine Protest," in *The Individual Psychology of Alfred Adler: A Systematic Presentation in Selections from His Writings*, ed. Heinz L. Ansbacher and Rowena R. Ansbacher (New York: Basic Books, 1956), 48. Adler acknowledged that the masculine protest existed for women too—"very frequently one finds during analysis the wish to become transformed into a man"—but female masculinity, like any other type of masculinity, posed less of a problem, since the tendency can "comprise all sorts of human excellencies and short-comings"; that is, the woman-that-wishes-to-be-a-man, not really being a man, can at least become a human being (49).

99. Quoted in *Gay, Freud*, 221–22.

100. Quoted in *Gay, Freud*, 615.

101. Freud, "Analysis Terminable and Interminable," 250.

102. Anzieu, *Freud's Self-Analysis*, 474.

103. Freud, "The May-Beetle Dream," in Freud, *Standard Edition*, 4:290.

104. Freud, *Die Traumdeutung* (Berlin: Adansonia, 2018), 186.

105. Quoted in Ernest Jones, *The Formative Years and the Great Discoveries: 1856–1900*, vol. 1 of *The Life and Work of Sigmund Freud*, 3 vols. (New York: Penguin/Pelican, 1953), 174. Notice here again the theme of being overheard that Freud raises in the *Papers on Technique*.

106. On January 18, 1858, Charles Dickens posted a letter thanking the author of a promising debut entitled *Scenes of Clerical Life* for having sent along, via the book's publisher William Blackwood, the first two stories from that book. Dickens, however, treated the author's identity somewhat quizzically:

> In addressing these few words of thankfulness, to the creator of the sad fortunes of Mr. Amos Barton, and the sad love-story of Mr. Gilfil, I am (I presume) bound to adopt the name that it pleases that excellent writer to assume. I can suggest no better one; but I should have been strongly disposed, if I had been left to my own devices, to address

> the said writer as a woman. I have observed what seem to me to be such womanly touches, in those moving fictions, that the assurance on the title-page is insufficient to satisfy me, even now. If they originated with no woman, I believe that no man ever before had the art of making himself, mentally, so like a woman, since the world began (Charles Dickens, letter to George Eliot, Jan. 18, 1858, in *The Selected Letters of Charles Dickens*, ed. Jenny Hartley [New York, 2012], 331).

He was not exactly misgendering Eliot, but he came close: it is difficult not to hear, under the letter's suasive treble, the menacing bass tone of Raffles the blackmailer. "My own devices": as though Dickens bore responsibility not merely for interpreting but singularly for generating the terms of address. Far from censorious, however, the letter is underpinned by an antiessentialist understanding of gendered address as an arbitrary relation; it remains possible, unsatisfied as Dickens is "even now," that the "feminine touches" of the author's style are not merely creative gestures but signs of his having been touched—that is, as feminine textual features emerging from a more primary, but no more natural, stylistic feminization. The stories have conjured, for Dickens, a world in which a man can make himself—"mentally"—like a woman. Eliot did not seem to see Dickens's response as any kind of threat but did decline to respond to it directly, asking Blackwood to thank Dickens for it himself, adding: "I am so deeply moved by the finely-felt and finely-expressed sympathy of the letter, that the iron mask of my incognito seems quite painful in forbidding me to tell Dickens how thoroughly his generous impulse has been appreciated." Eliot, letter to John Blackwood, Jan. 21, 1858, *The Writings of George Eliot: George Eliot's Life as Related in Her Letters and Journals*, ed. J. W. Cross, 25 vols. (Boston, MA: Houghton Mifflin, 1908), 24:76.

107. The identity of the man in the iron mask, a famously anonymous French prisoner, we might remind ourselves, was a matter of occasional speculation in the nineteenth century. We should not, then, conclude from the response to Dickens (as several of Eliot's biographers have done) that the masculine posture of the Eliot author was an affectively inert performance. Eliot's journals and letters reveal a broad set of feelings about the "incognito," by no means restricted to painfulness or repression. In a sense, Eliot's ambivalence is endemic to the modern construction of authorship itself. As Gallagher argues at length in *Nobody's Story*, the slipperiness of the identity of the author of fiction as such—a slice of mechanically reproduced selfhood routed through several copying machines and circulating, at last, at several ontological and material removes from any living person—was profoundly shaped by mutating constructions of femininity in the century before Eliot took up writing. The modern author of fiction is, for Gallagher, the feminine author of fiction—insofar as public articulations of authorliness depended, from the eighteenth century onwards, on the articulation of gendered ideas of textual incompleteness that had been incorporated into the emerging figure of the professional author of novels.

After all, in 1978 U. C. Knoepflmacher could already write: "Today, we may still debate whether to call her narrator a 'he' or a 'she' or to view her/him as an 'androgynous' speaker, but the fact remains that we have learned from [W. J.] Harvey to regard this narrative voice as integral to the formal aspects of George Eliot's art." U. C. Knoepflmacher, "George Eliot," *Victorian Fiction: A Second Guide to Research*, ed. George H. Ford (New York: Modern Language Association, 1978), 235.

108. Eliot, letter to Charles Bray, Mar. 31, 1858, *Writings of George Eliot*, 24:83.

109. *Ibid.*, 81–82.

110. Eliot, "Silly Novels by Lady Novelists," in *George Eliot: Selected Essays, Poems, and Other Writings*, ed. A. S. Byatt and Nicholas Warren (London: Penguin, 1990), 140.

111. *Ibid.*, 162.

112. In a footnote surveying examples of this gesture, Zachary Samalin finds only two: Roland Barthes's "Writers, Intellectuals, Teachers" and John Brenkman's *Culture and Domination*; see Zachary Samalin, "Plumbing the Depths, Scouring the Surface: Henry Mayhew's Scavenger Hermeneutics," *New Literary History* 48 (Spring 2017): 408.

II: The King's Two Anuses

1. Freeman, *Time Binds*, 96.

2. Richard Rodgers and Oscar Hammerstein, "Something Good," featuring Julie Andrews, *The Sound of Music*, directed by Robert Wise, RCA Victor / Legacy, 1965.

3. This is a controversial nomenclature and one that most trans women avoid since it is bound up with attempts to pathologize and cure trans women, the explicit goal of Blanchard's 1991 article.

4. Rea Carey, the Acting Executive Director of the National Gay and Lesbian Task Force, made the following statement: "We are very concerned about these appointments. Kenneth Zucker and Ray Blanchard are clearly out of step with the occurring shift in how doctors and other health professionals think about transgender people and gender variance. It is extremely disappointing and disturbing that the apa appears to be failing in keeping up with the times when it comes to serving the needs of transgender adults and gender-variant children." https://radicaldoula.com/2008/06/05/dsmv-controversy/.

5. Ray Blanchard tweeted recently (@BlanchardPhD), "There is a popular narrative form that could fit desistance or detransition, namely demonic possession + successful exorcism. That needs a more complicated story, however, because there also exist real trans women who would be happier with reassignment," Twitter, October 30, 2018, 12:08 p.m., https://twitter.com/blanchardphd/status/1057303291535785985.

6. Freud, "Analysis Terminable and Interminable," 252.

7. Vera, Peter Capaldi's tragic drag queen, finally revealed as an even more tragic trans woman in *Prime Suspect 3* (1993), would exemplify the former; Buffalo Bill in Thomas Harris's novel *The Silence of the Lambs* (1988), of course, the latter.

8. By "public discourse" I mean, in this context, not merely the numerous editorials and articles published on trans issues in the last decade but the production of speech about trans people on social media, which seems to have spiked in the last five years. This spike is both a cause and an effect of the historical phenomenon sometimes referred to as the "trans tipping point," which might be understood variously as a moment of increased visibility of trans people, a profusion of public trans identifications, and an escalation of the legislative and cultural oppression of trans people. For historical and theoretical accounts of this convergence, see Tourmaline, Stanley, and Burton, *Trap Door*.

9. Terada, *Feeling in Theory*, 11.

10. Murphy, "Why I'm Suing Twitter."

11. A sense of exhaustion suffuses the writing of the trans critic Andrea Long Chu, for example. Chu's criticism synthesizes academic writing with the ethos of online trans community

and so enables a livelier sense of the utopian possibilities of trans feminism—its political urgency and personal revelation—than has sometimes been possible. The touchstone of that utopian prospect is a confrontational assertion of negative affect to the extent that Chu's work seems to drive toward something like a romance of depression. See Chu, "My New Vagina Won't Make Me Happy" and "On Liking Women."

12. Navratilova, "Rules on Trans Athletes."

13. Liddle, "Women's Sports."

14. Butler, *Excitable Speech*, 2.

15. Trans rage is literally field-founding; it is the avowed affective disposition and politics of the field's single most influential document: Susan Stryker's "My Words to Victor Frankenstein above the Village of Edelman." Like Copjec, he takes his reading of Freud's drive from Lacan, who in turn bases his theory of the drive on a reduction of sexual identity to an opposition of active and passive:

> There is no other pathway by which the impact of sexuality is manifested in the subject. A drive, insofar as it represents sexuality in the unconscious, is never anything but a partial drive. This is the essential failing [*carence*]–namely, the absence [*carence*] of anything that could represent in the subject the mode of what is male or female in his being. The vacillation that psychoanalytic experience reveals in the subject regarding his masculine or feminine being is not so much related to his biological bisexuality, as to the fact that there is nothing in his dialectic that represents the bipolarity of sex apart from activity and passivity; that is, a drive versus outside-action polarity, which is altogether unfit to represent the true basis of that bipolarity. (Lacan, "Position" 720)

16. Toomey, Syvertsen, and Shramko, "Transgender Adolescent Suicide Behavior."

17. Butler, *Bodies That Matter*, ix.

18. *Ibid.*, x.

19. Chu, "My New Vagina."

20. Quoted in Kantorowicz, *King's Two Bodies*, 7.

21. This term is explored at length in Foucault's *Fearless Speech*.

22. Foucault, *Fearless Speech*, 16.

23. Barbaro, "What Drives Donald Trump?"

24. Politi, "Milo Yiannopoulos."

25. *Tolman v. Underhill.*

26. Kantorowicz, *Fundamental Issue*, 1.

27. *Ibid.*, 6–7.

28. See Nolan, "Metaphoric History," 570, n13.

29. Ernst Kantorowicz, *The King's Two Bodies: A Study In Medieval Political Theology* (Princeton, NJ: Princeton University Press, 2016).The King's Two Bodies. Princeton, NJ: Princeton University Press, 1957.

30. Hayward, "Lessons from a Starfish," 249–64.

31. Freud, *Three Essays*, 176.

32. Laplanche and Pontalis, *Language of Psychoanalysis*, 235.

33. Copjec, "Sex and the Euthanasia of Reason," 22–23

34. Freud, "Analysis Terminable and Interminable," 252.

35. We notice not merely that Lacan's theory of the drive depends on the reduction of sexual identity to hydraulic force, a gesture that bypasses and, by bypassing, eradicates trans identification; but also that the suppression of trans identification entails the coeval suppression of the "biological" dimension that Freud discusses in "Analysis Terminable and Interminable."

36. Freud, *Beyond the Pleasure Principle*, 5.

37. The most serious partial exception is Patricia Gherovici's *Transgender Psychoanalysis: A Lacanian Perspective on Sexual Difference.* Gherovici registers the profound discomfort among psychoanalysts with trans patients, and she commits politically to "the transgender fight for equality" (2), taking the position opposite Slavoj Žižek's. Yet in other respects, Gherovici's work is somewhat clueless: the protagonist of the introductory chapter turns out to be Rachel Dolezal; and the book refers constantly to "transgenderism" as though trans people either shared or simply manifested a political philosophy. Gherovici does, however, point to the possibility of a Lacan capable of handling the question of trans feminism. She writes:

> The need to establish sex-segregated public restrooms was discussed by Lacan in a 1957 essay where he called it "urinary segregation," noting that "public life [is] subject [to] laws of urinary segregation." While Lacan was at the time discussing how language sets up sexual difference as an impasse, he had also foreseen the recent controversy when he observed that public life is subjected to the inequalities of "urinary segregation." Lacan illustrated it with an anecdote of transit. Perhaps it can be read today as a journey of transition: A brother and sister take a train journey, sitting across from each other in the compartment. When they pull in to the station, they look at the platform from their window, and the boy exclaims: "We have arrived at Ladies!" while the girl states: "You, idiot! Can't you see we are at Gentlemen?" As Lacan noted, it seems impossible that they would reach an agreement: "Gentlemen and Ladies will henceforth be two homelands toward which each of their souls will [take flight on divergent wings, and regarding which it will] be all the more impossible for them to reach an agreement since, being in fact the same homeland, neither can give ground regarding the one's unsurpassed excellence without detracting from the other's glory." (11–12; Gherovici misquotes Lacan, "The Instance of the Letter in the Unconscious," in *Écrits: A Selection*, trans. Bruce Fink [New York: Norton, 2002], 144.)

The possibility of a trans universalism for which a trans person might be a privileged subject, rather than the dupe who took the whole thing too seriously, or got on the wrong train, is at least implied here, though it is not, in general, the focus of Gherovici's study.

38. Žižek, "The Sexual Is Political."

39. Chiesa, *Not-Two*, 26.

40. *Ibid.*, 193.

41. Morel, *Sexual Ambiguities*, 4.

42. Zupančič, *What Is Sex?*, 7–8.

43. *Ibid.*, 8.

44. James Sturcke, "How the West Wing Helped Outsmart Labor Whips," *The Guardian*, February 2, 2006. https://www.theguardian.com/news/2006/feb/02/wrap.jamessturcke.

45. John Guillory, *Cultural Capital: The Problem of Literary Canon Formation* (Chicago, IL: University of Chicago Press, 1993), 236.

46. Stephen Sondheim, "I'm Still Here," with Elaine Stritch performing, *Follies* (1971).

47. David Kurnick, "A Few Lies: Queer Theory and Our Method Melodramas," *ELH* 87, no. 2 (Summer 2020): 349–74.

48. James Atlas, "The Case of Paul De Man," *New York Times*, August 28, 1988.

49. Paul de Man, "Autobiography as De-Facement," in *The Rhetoric of Romanticism* (New York: Columbia University Press, 1984), 69.

50. Gérard Genette, *Figures: Essais*, Collection Tel Quel, vols. 1–3 (Paris: Editions du Seuil, 1966), 50.

51. Roland Barthes, *Writing Degree Zero*, 1st American ed. (New York: Hill and Wang, 1968), 11.

52. Sharon Marcus, *The Drama of Celebrity* (Princeton, NJ: Princeton University Press, 2019).

53. Naomi Klein, *No Logo: Taking Aim at the Brand Bullies* (Toronto, ON: Knopf Canada, 2000).

54. *American Hustle* (2013), *Kung Fu Hustle* (2004), etc.

55. *The Hustle*, directed by Chris Addison (2019; Universal Pictures Home Entertainment).

56. "Trap" both as transsexual and as sex worker: see, for example, Tourmaline, Stanley, and Burton, *Trap Door*. See also "trap" in the film *Zola*, e.g.—but the "trap" is the same whether or not the woman in question is transsexual. *Zola*, directed by Janicza Bravo (Killer Films, 2020).

57. "Harassment, Assault Allegations against Moretti Span Three Campuses," *The Stanford Daily*, November 16, 2017, https://www.stanforddaily.com/2017/11/16/harassment-assault-allegations-against-moretti-span-three-campuses/. Franco Moretti pioneered a depersonalized empirical mode of literary criticism adapted from corpus linguistics, which he calls "distant reading." "Franco Moretti, *Distant Reading* (London, UK: Verso, 2013).

58. W. H. Auden, "The Platonic Blow," *Fuck You / A Magazine of the Arts* 5, no. 8 (March 1965); "Grace Lavery & Daniel M. Lavery (Joseph Lavery & Mallory Ortberg)," Kiwi Farms, accessed September 5, 2021, https://kiwifarms.net/threads/grace-lavery-daniel-m-lavery-joseph-lavery-mallory-ortberg.77242/page-95.

59. Zoe Greenberg, "What Happens to #MeToo When a Feminist Is the Accused?," *New York Times*, August 13, 2018, https://www.nytimes.com/2018/08/13/nyregion/sexual-harassment-nyu-female-professor.html; Colleen Flaherty, "Some Say the Particulars of the Ronell Harassment Case Are Moot, in That It All Comes Down to Power," *Inside Higher Ed*, accessed September 5, 2021, https://www.insidehighered.com/news/2018/08/20/some-say-particulars-ronell-harassment-case-are-moot-it-all-comes-down-power; Seo-Young Chu, "WOVEN: A Refuge for Jae-in Doe: Fugues in the Key of English Major," accessed September 5, 2021, https://entropymag.org/a-refuge-for-jae-in-doe-fugues-in-the-key-of-english-major/.

60. Avital Ronell and Richard Eckersley, *The Telephone Book: Technology—Schizophrenia—Electric Speech* (Lincoln: University of Nebraska Press, 1989).

61. See Melanie Klein on splitting and D. W. Winnicott on the reality principle.

62. Anna Kornbluh, "Ecocide and Objectivity: Literary Thinking in How the Dead Dream," in Anirudh Sridhar, Mir Ali Hosseini, and Derek Attridge, eds., *The Work of Reading: Literary Criticism in the 21st Century* (Palgrave Macmillan, 2021), 261–75. https://doi.org/10.1007/978-3-030-71139-9.

63. *Ibid.*, 263.

64. *Ibid.*, 266.

65. *Ibid.*

66. Philippe Lacoue-Labarthe and Jean-Luc Nancy, *The Literary Absolute: The Theory of Literature in German Romanticism*, Intersections (Albany: State University of New York Press, 1988); Michel Foucault, *Language, Counter-Memory, Practice: Selected Essays and Interviews* (Ithaca, NY: Cornell University Press, 1977).

67. Kornbluh, "Ecocide and Objectivity," 267.

III: Picaresque and Pornography in *The Old Curiosity Shop*

1. Bersani, "Is the Rectum a Grave?"

2. Linda Williams, *Hard Core: Power, Pleasure, and the "Frenzy of the Visible"* (Berkeley: University of California Press, 1999).

3. Eugenie Brinkema, "Rape and the Rectum: Bersani, Deleuze, Noe," *Camera Obscura* 20, no. 1 (2005): 32–57; and Kathleen Lubey, "Spectacular Sex: Thought and Pleasure in the Encounter with Pornography," *Differences: A Journal of Feminist Cultural Studies* 17, no. 2 (2006): 113–31.

4. Lubey, "Spectacular Sex."

5. Charles Dickens, *The Old Curiosity Shop: A Tale* (London, UK: Chapman and Hall, 1841).

6. Catherine Robson, *Men in Wonderland: The Lost Girlhood of the Victorian Gentleman* (Princeton, NJ: Princeton University Press, 2001).

7. Theodor W. Adorno, "On Dickens' *The Old Curiosity Shop*," in *Notes to Literature* (New York: Columbia University Press, 2019), 430–36.

8. Gustave Flaubert, *Madame Bovary* (New York: Penguin, 2002); Gustave Flaubert, *Bouvard et Pécuchet* (New York: Penguin, 1976); and Gustave Flaubert, *Salammbô* (New York: Penguin, 1977).

9. Jean-Francois Lyotard, *The Postmodern Condition: A Report on Knowledge* (Minneapolis: University of Minnesota Press, 1984).

10. Dickens, *Old Curiosity Shop*, 247.

11. *Ibid.*, 242.

12. *Ibid.*, 243.

13. *Ibid.*, 242.

14. Anonymous, "If I Had a Donkey," Grandma's Nursery Rhymes, accessed January 21, 2021, https://www.grandmasnurseryrhymes.com/ifIhadadonkey.html.

15. John Ashton, *Modern Street Ballads* (London, UK: Chatto & Windus, 1888), 94.

16. *Ibid.*

17. Steven Marcus, *The Other Victorians: A Study of Sexuality and Pornography in Mid-Nineteenth-Century England* (New York: Basic Books, 1966), 15.

18. Marquis de Sade, *Justine, or the Misfortunes of Virtue* (Oxford, UK: Oxford University Press, 2005).

19. Anonymous, "Sub-Umbra, or Sport among the She-Noodles," collected in *The Pearl: A Journal of Facetiae and Voluptuous Reading* (New York: Grove, 1968). The story is shared in eight installments beginning on page 2.

20. Oscar Wilde, Ada Leverson, and Robert Baldwin Ross, *Letters to the Sphinx from Oscar Wilde, with Reminiscences of the Author* (London, UK: Duckworth, 1930), 42.

21. Aldous Huxley, *Vulgarity in Literature: Digressions from a Theme* (London, UK: Chatto and Windus, 1930), 54, 55.

22. *Ibid.*, 56.

23. *Ibid.*, 54.

24. Charles Dickens, *Master Humphrey's Clock* (London, UK: Dover, 2020).

25. G. K. Chesterton, *Appreciations and Criticism of the Works of Charles Dickens* (London, UK: Dent, 1911), 231.

26. Charles Dickens, "Night Walks," in *The Uncommercial Traveler* (Boston, MA: Ticknor & Fields, 1868), 135–44.

27. Dickens, *Old Curiosity Shop*, 38–39.

28. Judith Walkowitz, *City of Dreadful Delight: Narrative of Sexual Danger in Late Victorian London* (London, UK: Virago, 1992), 99.

29. W. T. Stead, "*The Maiden Tribute of Modern Babylon III: The Report of Our Secret Commission," Pall Mall Gazette* (London, UK), July 8, 1885), 2.

30. Dickens, *Old Curiosity Shop*, 39.

31. *Ibid.*, 46.

32. *Ibid.*, 90.

33. William Morris, *The Collected Works of William Morris, vol. 16 (London, UK: Longmans Green & Co., 1912)*, 5.

34. Tony Giffone, "Putting 'Master Humphrey' Back Together Again," *Journal of Narrative Technique* 17, no. 1 (Winter 1987): 102–6.

35. Dickens, *Old Curiosity Shop*, 222.

36. *Edward Penishands*, directed by Paul Norman (Video Team, 1991).

37. Brendan O'Neill, "How the Trans Ideology Dehumanises Women," *spiked*, April 23, 2022, https://www.spiked-online.com/2022/04/23/how-the-trans-ideology-dehumanises-women/.

38. Charlie Markbreiter, "'Other Trans People Make Me Dysphoric': Trans Assimilation and Cringe," *The New Inquiry*, March 1, 2022, https://thenewinquiry.com/cringe/.

39. Michel Foucault, *This Is Not a Pipe*, trans. James Harkness (Berkeley, CA: University of California Press, 1983), 22.

40. Lily Woodruff alerted me to this resonance; she writes about it in *Disordering the Establishment: Participatory Art and Institutional Critique in France 1958–1981* (Durham, Duke UP: 2020) pp. 163–164.

IV: Fear of Commitment

1. A turning point in this discourse was Steven Carter and Julia Sokal's self-help classic, *Men Who Can't Love* (1987).

2. Stryker, "My Words to Victor Frankenstein."

3. Theodor Adorno, "Commitment," *New Left Review*, nos. 87–88 (1974): 76.

4. Stryker, Currah, and Moore, "Introduction," 11.

5. Hayward, "More Lessons from a Starfish," 255.

6. Hegel, preface to *Phenomenology of Mind*, §60.

7. Solanas, *SCUM Manifesto*, 37.

8. Adorno, "Commitment," 83.

9. *Ibid.*, 84.

10. *Ibid.*, 89.

11. *Ibid.*, 88.

12. *Ibid.*, 89.

13. Sianne Ngai, "The Cuteness of the Avant-Garde," *Critical Inquiry*, no. 31 (2005): 837.

14. Adorno, "Commitment," 75.

15. *Ibid.*, 76.

16. *Ibid.*, 81.

17. *Ibid.*, 87.

18. *Ibid.*, 83.

19. Chu and Drager, "After Trans Studies."

20. Sandy Stone, "The *Empire* Strikes Back: A Posttranssexual Manifesto," *Camera Obscura* 10, no. 2(29) (1992): 150–76.

21. Turner, "Man's Work," 483.

22. This queer utopian reading of Wilde and Pater I take from Sinfield and Dollimore—who I think are right in their diagnosis of Wilde and Pater but use that diagnosis to shore up the Adornian contempt for femininity. See Jonathan Dollimore, *Sexual Dissidence: Augustine to Wilde, Freud to Foucault* (Oxford: Clarendon Press, 1991), and Alan Sinfield, *The Wilde Century: Effeminacy, Oscar Wilde, and the Queer Moment* (New York: Columbia UP, 1994).

V: On Being Criticized

1. F. R. Leavis, *The Great Tradition: George Eliot, Henry James, Joseph Conrad* (Garden City, NJ: Doubleday, 1954), 7.

2. Joseph Conrad, "The Crime of Partition," *Collier's Illustrated Weekly*, June 14, 1919, 10.

3. *Ibid.*, 40.

4. Leavis, *Great Tradition*, 7.

5. These words are taken, as Arnold acknowledges, from the second of his three lectures in *On Translating Homer*, where the "critical effort" of European intellectuals is distinguished from the "eccentric and arbitrary spirit" of the English. However, as Arnold's editor, R. H. Super, acknowledges, in his *Complete Prose Works*, "Arnold may not have been upon oath in describing the reception of his proposition. Only one reviewer of the Homeric lectures seems to have quoted his sentence, and that with approbation: the author of 'Recent Homeric Critics and Translators,' *North British Review*, no. 36 (May, 1862): 348. Arnold had been much pleased with this article, as he told his mother on May 3. Matthew Arnold, *Lectures and Essays in Criticism*, ed. R. H. Super (Ann Arbor: University of Michigan Press, 1962), 474. Such bad faith on Arnold's part is neither, as we shall see, unusual nor inconsequential.

6. Arnold, "Function of Criticism," in Arnold, *Essays in Criticism*, 23.

7. See Rita Felski, *The Limits of Critique* (Chicago, IL: University of Chicago Press, 2015). See also Stephen Best and Sharon Marcus, "Surface Reading: An Introduction," *Representations* 108, no. 1 (2009): 1–21.

8. Felski, *Limits of Critique*, 4.

9. Heather Love, "Close but not Deep: Literary Ethics and the Descriptive Turn," *New Literary History* 41, no. 2 (2010): 371.

10. Arnold, *Essays in Criticism*, 1.

11. Lionel Trilling was the most vocal of Arnold's twentieth-century advocates and one of a handful cited here who treated him as the "father" figure of the new critical textual studies—we will see variations of the same idea in T. S. Eliot, William E. Cain, James Joyce, and others. Yet Trilling's ardor facing Arnold was deeply ambivalent, as he confesses in the introduction to *The Portable Matthew Arnold*:

> Of the literary men of the great English nineteenth century there are few who have stayed quite so fresh, so immediate, and so relevant as Matthew Arnold. It is not entirely easy to understand why this should be so. For, as we usually judge power, Arnold is not the most powerful of his contemporaries—he does not make anything like, say, Carlyle's bold and dramatic claim upon our attention. Nor does he hold his position by reason of a massive and ranging body of work. His poetic canon is relatively small; and of this canon it must be said that some of its most ambitious items are failures, and that, although almost every one of Arnold's poems is in some way interesting, only a few are perfect in their kind. Of his more extensive prose works, a considerable part—that which deals with religion—is likely to be disregarded by modern readers, not because of its subject but because of its way of dealing with its subject. His writing on literature and politics was carried on in the free moments allowed him by his burdened life as a civil servant, and the larger part of it consists of occasional essays and lectures, forms which do not easily establish their authority. (Lionel Trilling, introduction to *The Portable Matthew Arnold*, ed. Lionel Trilling [New York: Viking, 1949], 1)

12. Arnold, *Essays in Criticism*, 1.

13. *Ibid.*

14. *Ibid.*, vi.

15. *Ibid.*

16. *Ibid.*

17. *Ibid.*, vii.

18. *Ibid.*, ix, x.

19. *Ibid.*, xi.

20. Arnold to his mother, December 7, 1864, in *The Letters of Matthew Arnold*, ed. George W. E. Russell, vol. 1, 1848–1888 (London, UK: Macmillan, 1895), 243.

21. For an account of the complex relation to manliness in Arnold's prose, see Heather Ellis, "'This starting, feverish heart': Matthew Arnold and the Problem of Manliness," *Critical Survey* 20, no. 3 (2008): 97–115. My argument differs from Ellis's in two particulars: first, while I agree that Arnold's writing retains a "sensitivity to gendered criticism" (97), I do not think this allows us to diagnose "a desire to emulate his famously 'manly' father"; rather, I think Arnold's constant attempt was to make a virtue of his difference from that father. Second, and more consequently, I do not believe that any act of criticism can fully absent itself from the scene of penetration, which seems to produce an imbalance in the relation between text and critic. I therefore take Arnoldian criticism to exhibit precisely the problematic features of criticism as such.

22. Arnold, *Lectures and Essays*, 2.

23. *Ibid.*

24. *Ibid.*, 3.

25. Arnold, *Essays in Criticism*, 4.

26. *Ibid.*, 9.

27. *Ibid.*, 16 and *passim*. My own evocation of the language of Marxist feminism here takes its license from an implicit analogy, or echo, in Arnold's own prose, which distinctively recalls *The Eighteenth Brumaire of Louis Bonaparte*: "Powers must concur, the power of the man and the power of the moment, and the man is not enough without the moment; the creative power has, for its happy exercise, appointed elements, and those elements are not in its own control" (Arnold, *Essays in Criticism*, 5–6); "Man makes his own history, but he does not make it out of the whole cloth; he does not make it out of conditions chosen by himself, but out of such as he finds at hand" (Karl Marx, *The Eighteenth Brumaire of Louis Bonaparte*, trans. Daniel de Leon [Chicago, IL: Charles H. Kerr, 1913], 9).

28. Arnold, *Essays in Criticism*, 8.

29. *Ibid.*

30. *Ibid.*, 6.

31. In an eccentric, persuasive, and tantalizingly brief history of "anti-criticism," which he takes to be the position of critics who declare that literary criticism is "impossible," William E. Cain characterizes Arnold (whom he thinks "the father, or at least the presiding genius, of both criticism and anti-criticism") as standing in a position of "militant redundancy." William E. Cain, "Towards a History of Anti-Criticism," *New Literary History* 20, no. 1 (1988): 40. Arnold's frequent recourse to a set of "touchstone" writers, whose luminous truth neither requires nor brooks further elucidation, positions the critic outside the boundaries of that which he wishes to promote.

32. Arnold, *Essays in Criticism*, 11.

33. *Ibid.*, 12.

34. *Ibid.*, 15.

35. *Ibid.*

36. *Ibid.*, 21. For an account of Victorian effeminacy as a failure or refusal to participate in the practical business of civil society, see Thaïs Morgan, "Victorian Effeminacies," in *Victorian Sexual Dissidence*, ed. Richard Dellamora (Chicago, IL: University of Chicago Press, 1999), 109–26.

37. Arnold, *Essays in Criticism*, 12–13.

38. See Stefan Collini, *Matthew Arnold: A Critical Portrait* (Oxford, UK: Clarendon Press, 2008).

39. Lytton Strachey, *Eminent Victorians* (Garden City, NY: Garden City Publishing, 1918), 222.

40. Arnold, *Essays in Criticism*, 13; emphasis added.

41. Arnold to Campbell, in Russell, *Letters of Matthew Arnold*, 1:239. The letter is dated September 22, 1864; "The Function of Criticism" was delivered at Oxford on October 29, the following month.

42. *Ibid.*

43. Arnold to his mother, June 5, 1869, in Russell, *Letters of Matthew Arnold*, 347.

44. See Collini, *Matthew Arnold*.

45. Strachey, *Eminent Victorians*, 222.

46. T. S. Eliot, "Arnold and Pater," *The Bookman*, September 1930, 23–24.

47. Marc Redfield, *The Politics of Aesthetics: Nationalism, Gender, Romanticism* (Stanford, CA: Stanford University Press, 2003), 89.

48. Arnold, *Essays in Criticism*, 22.

49. *Ibid.*, 23.

50. *Ibid.*, Arnold's source for this passage initially proved somewhat mysterious, but the matter has been solved, and it is clear that Arnold must have encountered the report in the *Carlisle Express* on September 17, traveling back to London from the Highlands of Scotland in 1864. The report in the *Express* is nonetheless subtly different:

> A shocking child murder has been committed at Nottingham. A girl named Wragg left the Workhouse there on Saturday morning with her young illegitimate child. The child was after- wards found dead on Mapperley Hills, having been strangled. Wragg is in custody.

To this, Arnold added the intensifying adverbs "just [been committed]" and "soon [afterwards]," changed the spelling of "Mapperley," and de-capitalized "Workhouse." James Walter Caulfield has traced Arnold's quotation to "General News," *Carlisle Express*, September 17, 1864, 3. See Caulfield, *Overcoming Matthew Arnold: Ethics in Culture and Criticism* (London, UK: Routledge, 2016), 175n56.

51. Arnold, *Essays in Criticism*, 24.

52. Eliot, *Adam Bede*.

53. Arnold, *Lectures and Essays*, 536.

54. *Ibid.*, 391, 392.

55. *Ibid.*, 392.

56. Trilling, introduction to *Portable Matthew Arnold*, 2.

57. Arnold, *Essays in Criticism*, 150, 27, 35, 38. Arnold himself characterizes Guérin's writing as like "the sounds of the murmuring forest itself" (87).

58. Trilling, introduction to *Portable Matthew Arnold*, 3.

59. "The essay as an attack on Arnold is rather weak, both because it is late in the day, and because Mr. Eliot has no real point to bring out,—always excepting his own relation to Arnold, which is interesting." M. L. S. Loring, "T. S. Eliot on Matthew Arnold," *The Sewanee Review* 43, no. 4 (1935): 480.

60. Eliot, "Arnold and Pater," 2.

61. Trilling, *Portable Matthew Arnold*, 1.

62. Harold Bloom, *Poets and Poems* (Philadelphia, PA: Chelsea House, 2005), 203.

63. Amanda Anderson, *The Powers of Distance: Cosmopolitanism and the Cultivation of Detachment* (Princeton, NJ: Princeton University Press, 2001), 93.

64. Benjamin Jowett, *Letters of Benjamin Jowett*, ed. Evelyn Abbott and Lewis Campbell (London, UK: John Murray, 1899), 223.

65. Trilling, introduction to *Portable Matthew Arnold*, 2.

66. Arnold to Macmillan, August 2, 1864, in *Matthew Arnold's Books: Toward a Publishing Diary*, ed. William Earl Buckler (Paris: Librarie Minard, 1958), 67.

67. Redfield, *Politics of Aesthetics*, 90.

68. McLaughlin argues (relatedly) that "disinterestedness" in Arnold, which he characterizes as a return to Kant, also moves away from the lyrical mode (Kevin McLaughlin, *Poetic Force: Poetry after Kant* [Stanford, CA: Stanford University Press, 2014], 81). That argument amplifies one element of Herbert Tucker's influential critique of Trilling's account of Arnold's oeuvre as an organic whole: Trilling saw the prose as the "goal" of the poetry; Tucker as its lackluster

"institutionaliz[ation]." Herbert F. Tucker, "Arnold and the Authorization of Criticism," in *Knowing the Past: Victorian Literature and Culture,* ed. Suzy Anger (Ithaca, NY: Cornell University Press, 2001), 114.

69. Matthew Arnold, "Haworth Churchyard, April, 1855," *Fraser's Magazine,* May 1855, 527–30.

70. See Matthew Arnold, *Poems: Lyric, Dramatic, and Elegiac* (London, UK: Macmillan, 1877), 239–44.

71. Edward Young, *The Complaint; or Night Thoughts on Life, Death, and Immortality* (London, UK: Tegg, 1843), 249; Algernon Charles Swinburne, *Atalanta in Calydon: A Tragedy* (London, UK: John Camden Hotten, 1866), 90.

72. Arnold to Wightman, *The Letters of Matthew Arnold, ed. Cecil Y. Lang* (Charlottesville, VA: University Press of Virginia, 1996), 1:13.

73. Arnold to Arthur Hugh Clough, March 21, 1853, in Lang, *The Letters of Matthew Arnold,* 1:258.

74. Antony H. Harrison, *The Cultural Production of Matthew Arnold* (Athens: Ohio University Press, 2009), 72.

75. See, for example, Arnold to Arthur Hugh Clough, September 29, 1848, in *Selected Letters of Matthew Arnold,* ed. Clinton Machann and Forrest D. Burt (Basingstoke, UK: Macmillan, 1993), 46–48.

76. Brontë to James Taylor, January 15, 1851, in Elizabeth Gaskell, *The Life of Charlotte Brontë* (London, UK: Smith, Elder, 1857), 512–13.

77. Virginia Jackson, "The Function of Criticism at the Present Time," *Los Angeles Review of Books,* April 12, 2015, lareviewofbooks.org/article/function-criticism-present-time/.

78. Arnold, *Essays in Criticism,* 6.

79. See Freud, "On Narcissism," 67–102.

80. Arnold, *Essays in Criticism,* 6.

81. Cain, "Towards a History," 40.

82. F. J. Furnivall, "To the Editor of the *Pall Mall Gazette,*" quoted in *The Shelley Society's Note-Book* 1, no. 2 (1886): 20.

83. James Joyce, *Ulysses,* ed. Hans Walter Gabler (New York: Vintage, 1986), 7.

VI: The Egg and the Essay

1. Susan Sontag, "Notes on Camp," in *Against Interpretation and Other Essays* (New York: Farrar, Straus and Giroux, 1966), 290.

2. Sontag as reported by Joan Acocella, "The Hunger Artist," *The New Yorker,* March 6, 2000, https://www.newyorker.com/magazine/2000/03/06/the-hunger-artist.

3. Miller, *Bringing Out Roland Barthes,* 3.

4. I deploy the absurd term "gender critical" here to refer to that group of antitrans activists, academics, and journalists, including Kathleen Stock, Germaine Greer, Sophie Allen, Jane Clare Jones, Holly Lawford Smith, Mary Long, Rebecca Reilly-Cooper, and Graham Linehan. By using this term, I am avoiding the more value-neutral "TERF," an acronym for "trans-exclusionary radical feminist," partly on the grounds that exclusion is not the best word for the hostile actions of members of this group—the forced inclusion of trans men within the category

"adult human female," for example, is as objectionable as the repeated physical molestation and relentless vilification of trans women. But I also partly do so because the term "gender critical," which on its own distinguishes Stock et al. from precisely nobody, is conspicuously stupid enough that I think it is worth letting the group defend. For a concise digest of the position of the group, see Stock et al., "Doing Better."

5. Lamb, "You Best Never Ever Tr*nsition, Tr*nny."

6. Sedgwick, *Epistemology of the Closet*, 22.

7. Sedgwick, "White Glasses," 262.

8. *Ibid.*

9. *Ibid.*

10. *Ibid.*, 262–63.

11. *Ibid.*, 256.

12. Reed's "Axiomatic" has, fortunately, been removed from the Penn State University English Department website that was hosting it, and it is difficult to find. I have a private copy in my own personal archive, and I'm sure one can find it by searching Reddit—I'm not going to, though.

13. Reed, "Axiomatic," sec. 7.

14. LaFleur, "Fairy's Tale."

15. Freud, "Inhibitions, Symptoms, and Anxiety," 53.

16. Freud, "Psycho-Analytic Notes," 16.

17. *Ibid.*, 16–17.

18. Quoted in Etherington-Smith, *Persistence of Memory*, 222.

19. Stephin Merritt, songwriter, "Living in an Abandoned Firehouse," track 7 on The Magnetic Fields, *The Wayward Bus*, PoPuP, 1992.

20. Lauren Berlant, *The Female Complaint: The Unfinished Business of Sentimentality in American Culture* (Durham, NC: Duke University Press, 2008), 1.

21. Lauren Berlant, cover endorsement, Andrea Long Chu, *Females* (London, UK: Verso Books, 2019).

22. Solanas, *SCUM Manifesto*.

23. Lauren Berlant, "Structures of Unfeeling: *Mysterious Skin*," *International Journal of Politics, Culture, and Society*, no. 28 (2015): 191–213, https://doi.org/10.1007/s10767-014-9190-y.

24. Charlie Markbreiter, "Can't Take a Joke: An Interview with Lauren Berlant," *The New Inquiry*, March 22, 2019, https://thenewinquiry.com/cant-take-a-joke/.

25. Johnson, "Bringing Out D. A. Miller," 3–8; Miller, *Bringing Out Roland Barthes*; Lauren Berlant, "Eve Sedgwick, Once More," *Critical Inquiry* 34, no. 4 (2009): 1089, https://doi.org/10.1086/605402; Terry Castle, "Desperately Seeking Susan," *London Review of Books* 27, no. 6 (March 17, 2005), https://www.lrb.co.uk/the-paper/v27/n06/terry-castle/desperately-seeking-susan.

26. Johnson, "Bringing Out D.A. Miller," 3.

27. Since the publication in 2015 of the graduate student Cara Daggett's essay "Drone Disorientations: How 'Unmanned' Weapons Queer the Experience of Killing in War," the phrase "drones are queer" has become a perhaps rather unfair shorthand among online LGBT communities, signifying the tendency of academic queer theory to treat the term "queer" as migrating ever further from the lived experiences and commitments of queer people. Cara Daggett, "Drone Disorientations," *International Feminist Journal of Politics*, 17, no. 3 (2015): 361–79. The

LG-sorta-B movement, which seeks to excise trans people from queer communities altogether, exemplifies the political platform of the British charity "the LGB Alliance," whose founder Bev Jackson argued in 2020 that "[a] lesbian is a biological woman who is attracted to another biological woman. That's obvious. Or at least it was obvious until a few years ago." Any individual attraction, provided it is "biological," makes a lesbian, apparently. See Camilla Tominey, "Lesbians Facing Extinction as Transgenderism Becomes Pervasive, Campaigners Warn," *The Telegraph*, December 25, 2020. Happy Christmas!

28. Nicolas Scheffer, "Les lesbiennes n'aiment pas les pénis," *têtu*, June 26, 2021, accessed July 13, 2021, https://tetu.com/2021/06/28/pride-paris-2021-militante-trans-interpellee-altercation-feministes-anti-trans-terf/.

29. See Sophie Lewis, ""How British Feminism Became Anti-Trans," in the *New York Times*, February 7, 2019, https://www.nytimes.com/2019/02/07/opinion/terf-trans-women-britain.html.

30. See, for example, the conversation entitled "How Long Will the Gender Woo Movement Last?," on Ovarit, https://www.ovarit.com/o/GenderCritical/13360/how-long-will-the-gender-woo-movement-last.

31. "She'll Be Coming Round the Mountain" is a traditional American folk song, which I use here as shorthand for trochaic hexameter. See Carl Sandburg, *The American Songbag* (New York: Harcourt, Brace, &. Co., 1927), 372.

32. The lesbian feminist Monique Wittig famously distinguished "lesbians" from "women" along these lines, for example: "it would be incorrect to say that lesbians associate, make love, live with women, for 'woman' has meaning only in heterosexual systems of thought and heterosexual economic systems. Lesbians are not women." Monique Wittig, "The Straight Mind," *Feminist Issues* 1 (1980): 103–11.

33. Margalit Fox, "Susan Sontag, Social Critic with Verve, Dies at 71," *The New York Times*, December 29, 2004.

34. Brendan Lemon, "Why Sontag Didn't Want to Come Out: Her Words," *Out*, January 5, 2005.

35. Suzie Mackenzie, "Finding Fact from Fiction," *The Guardian*, May 27, 2000.

36. Patrick Moore, "Susan Sontag and a Case of Curious Silence," *The Los Angeles Times*, January 4, 2005.

37. Charles Dickens, *Bleak House* (Ware, UK: Wordsworth Editions, 1993).

38. Castle, "Desperately Seeking Susan."

39. Mackenzie, "Finding Fact from Fiction."

40. Helen Fielding, *Bridget Jones's Diary* (London, UK: Macmillan, 1996).

41. Walter Pater, *Studies in the History of the Renaissance* (London, UK: Macmillan, 1873); Oscar Wilde, *The Picture of Dorian Gray* (Philadelphia, PA: Lippincott's, 1890); Neil Bartlett, *Who Was That Man?: A Present for Mr. Oscar Wilde* (London, UK: Serpent's Tail, 1988).

42. Susan Sontag, "Notes on Camp," *Partisan Review* 31, no. 4 (Fall 1964): 515–30.

43. Sedgwick, *Epistemology of the Closet*.

44. Berlant, "Eve Sedgwick, Once More," 1089.

45. Patricia Highsmith, *The Price of Salt* (New York: W. W. Norton, 2004).

46. Lewis Carroll, "Jabberwocky," from *Through the Looking Glass* (London, UK: Macmillan, 1871).

47. Hans Christian Andersen, "*The Emperor's New Clothes," trans. Jean Hersholt, H. C. Andersen Centret (The Hans Christian Andersen Centre), Department for the Study of Culture at the University of Southern Denmark, September 19, 2019,* https://andersen.sdu.dk/vaerk/hersholt/TheEmperorsNewClothes_e.html.

48. The Danish: "'Men han har jo ikke noget paa,' sagde et lille Barn. 'Herre Gud, hør den Uskyldiges Røst,' sagde Faderen; og den Ene hvidskede til den Anden, hvad Barnet sagde.

> 'Men han har jo ikke noget paa,' raabte tilsidst hele Folket. Det krøb i Keiseren, thi han syntes, de havde Ret, men han tænkte som saa: 'nu maa jeg holde Processionen ud.' Og Kammerherrerne gik og bar paa Slæbet, som der slet ikke var."

49. Meredith Chivers et al., "A Sex Difference in the Specificity of Sexual Arousal," *Psychological Science* 15, no. 11 (2004): 736–44.

50. Dan Savage, "Savage Love," *The Stranger*, July 14, 2005.

51. Berlant, *Female Complaint*, 2.

52. Sarah Patterson, "Lauren Berlant, Preeminent Literary Scholar and CulturalTtheorist, 1957–2021," *University of Chicago News*, June 28, 2021.

VII: *The Cannibal's Diagnosis*

1. *Silence of the Lambs*, directed by Johnathan Demme (1991; Beverly Hills. CA: Metro-Goldwyn-Mayer Studios Inc.: 20th Century Fox Home Entertainment, 2008).

2. Gill-Peterson, *Histories of the Transgender Child*, 60.

3. *Ibid.*, 61.

4. Werther, *Autobiography of an Androgyne*; Torrey Peters, *Detransition, Baby* (New York: One World, 2021); Sybil Lamb, *I've Got a Time Bomb* (New York: Topside Press, 2014).

5. Emma Heaney, *The New Woman: Literary Modernism, Queer Theory, and the Trans Feminine Allegory* (Evanston, IL: Northwestern University Press, 2017).

6. Alfred W. Herzog, Introduction to Werther, *Autobiography of an Androgyne*, 11.

7. Sergius Pankejeff, *The Wolf-Man and Sigmund Freud* (London, UK: Hogarth Press and the Institute of Psychoanalysis, 1972).

8. Werther, *Autobiography of an Androgyne*; Bellwether, *Fucking Trans Women*.

9. Todd, "Feminism."

10. Cáel M. Keegan, "Getting Disciplined: What's Trans* About Queer Studies Now?," *Journal of Homosexuality* 67, no. 3 (2020): 384–397.

11. Rachel Mesch, *Before Trans: Three Gender Stories from Nineteenth-Century France* (Stanford, CA: Stanford University Press, 2020).

12. Jean-Paul Sartre, *Existentialism Is a Humanism* (New Haven: Yale University Press, 2007).

13. Harris, *Silence of the Lambs*, 150.

14. Marjorie Garber, *Vested Interests: Cross-Dressing and Cultural Anxiety* (New York: Routledge, 1992).

15. Harris, *Silence of the Lambs*, 164–165.

16. *Psycho*, directed by Alfred Hitchcock (1960, Paramount Pictures).

17. "Jonathan Demme Wins Best Directing: 1992 Oscars," Academy of Motion Picture Arts and Sciences, April 26, 2013, 5:19, https://youtu.be/1YS2ovtUveQ. See also Jeffrey Bloomer, "When Gays Decried Silence of the Lambs, Jonathan Demme Became an Early Student of

Modern Backlash," *Slate,* April 28, 2017, https://slate.com/human-interest/2017/04/director-jonathan-demme-faced-down-silence-of-the-lambs-gay-backlash.html.

18. Jeffrey Bloomer, "When Gays Decried Silence of the Lambs, Jonathan Demme Became an Early Student of Modern Backlash," *Slate,* April 28, 2017, https://slate.com/human-interest/2017/04/director-jonathan-demme-faced-down-silence-of-the-lambs-gay-backlash.html.

19. Larry Kramer, "Playwright and Gay Activist Larry Kramer Explains Why He Hated Jonathan Demme's 'Philadelphia'" *Los Angeles Times,* January 10, 1994. https://www.latimes.com/entertainment/movies/la-et-archives-jonathan-demme-philadelphia-20170426-story.html

20. Jonathan Demme, *Jonathan Demme: Interviews* (Jackson: University Press of Mississippi, 2009), 68.

21. Demme, interviewed by Marlow Stern, "Jonathan Demme on Gaza, Transphobia in 'The Silence of the Lambs,' and Meryl Streep as a Rock Star," *Daily Beast,* July 25, 2014, https://www.thedailybeast.com/jonathan-demme-on-gaza-transphobia-in-the-silence-of-the-lambs-and-meryl-streep-as-a-rock-star. Emphasis is Demme's.

22. Harris, *Silence of the Lambs,* 53.

23. Charles Dickens, *Oliver Twist* (New York: Penguin Classics, 2003).

24. Lee Edelman, *No Future: Queer Theory and the Death Drive* (Durham: Duke University Press, 2004), 33-66.

25. Harris, *Silence of the Lambs,* 19. In the television show, Lecter says this to Dr. Bloom.

26. Halberstam, *Skin Shows,* 167.

27. Harris, *Silence of the Lambs,* 123.

28. *Ibid.*

29. *Ibid.*, 149.

30. *Ibid.*, 22, 138, 149.

31. Halberstam, *Skin Shows,* 164.

32. *Ibid.*

33. Judith Butler, "Critically Queer," *GLQ: A Journal of Lesbian and Gay Studies* 1, no. 1 (1993): 21.

34. Melanie Klein, "Envy and Gratitude," in *The Writings of Melanie Klein,* vol. 3, *Envy and Gratitude and Other Works : 1946–1963* (New York : Free Press, 1975), 176–235.

35. Ted Tally, Screenplay of "The Silence of the Lambs," *Internet Movie Script Database,* https://imsdb.com/scripts/Silence-of-the-Lambs.html.

36. Charles Baudelaire, «Au Lecteur,» in *Les Fleurs du mal* (Paris : Poulet-Malassis et de Broise, 1857), 5–7.

37. Harris, *Silence of the Lambs,* 122.

38. Freud, "Fetishim," 155.

39. Heaney, *New Woman.*

40. D. A. Miller, "Hitchcock's Hidden Pictures," *Critical Inquiry* 37, no. 1 (2010): 106–30.

VIII: generic deductiveness

1. Tourmaline, Stanley, and Burton, *Trap Door.*

2. Gill-Peterson, *Histories of the Transgender Child.*

3. Che Gossett and Eva Hayward, "Trans in a Time of HIV/AIDS," *Transgender Studies Quarterly* 7, no. 4 (2020): 527–53.

4. Walter Benjamin, "On the Theory of .Knowledge, Theory of Progress," in *The Arcades Project*, trans. Howard Eiland and Kevin McLaughlin (Cambridge, MA: Harvard University Press, 1999), 462.

5. Michael Fried, "Three American Painters: Kenneth Noland, Jules Olitski, Frank Stella," in *Art and Objecthood: Essays and Reviews* (Chicago, IL: University of Chicago Press, 1998), 213–68.

6. Laing, *Knots.*

7. Freud, "On Narcissism."

8. Paul Ricœur, *Freud and Philosophy: An Essay on Interpretation*, trans. Denis Savage (New Haven, CT: Yale University Press, 1970), 65.

9. *Ibid.*, 66.

10. *Ibid.*, 92.

11. Freud, *Interpretation of Dreams*, 96–121.

12. Gay, *Freud*, 84–87; Alexander Welsh, *Freud's Wishful Dream Book* (Princeton, NJ: Princeton University Press, 1994), 23.

13. This is the subject of much scholarly analysis. For example, see Dianne Hunter, ed., *Seduction and Theory: Readings of Gender, Representation, and Rhetoric* (Urbana: University of Illinois Press, 1989).

14. J. Moussaieff Masson, ed., *The Complete Letters of Sigmund Freud to Wilhelm Fliess, 1887–1904* (Cambridge, MA: Harvard University Press, 1985), 184.

15. *Ibid.*, 264. See also K. R. Eissler, *Freud and the Seduction Theory: A Brief Love Affair* (Madison, CT: International Universities Press, 2001).

16. Jeffrey Moussaieff Masson, *Freud: The Assault on Truth; Freud's Suppression of the Seduction Theory* (London, UK: Faber and Faber, 1984). Masson addressed connections between his work and Rush's in his essay "A Personal Perspective: The Response to Child Abuse Then and Now," *Journal of Trauma & Dissociation* 18, no. 3 (2017): 476–82.

17. See Florence Rush, *The Best Kept Secret: Sexual Abuse of Children* (Englewood Cliffs, NJ: Prentice Hall, 1980).

18. Jean G. Schimek, "Fact and Fantasy in the Seduction Theory: A Historical Review," *Journal of the American Psychoanalytic Association* 35, no. 4 (1987): 937–65; Han Israëls and Morton Schatzman, "The Seduction Theory," *History of Psychiatry* 4, no. 13 (1993): 23–59.

19. Though neither is at all an orthodox Freudian, Žižek and Miller both explore Freudian classicism in their books on Hitchcock. A version of this argument is also outlined in Larry Gross's 1976 essay "Film après Noir," which first outlines the new noir of *The Long Goodbye* and *Chinatown* (as well as Jean-Luc Godard's *Alphaville*, John Boorman's *Point Blank*, and Nicholas Roeg's *Performance*). See Slavoj Žižek, ed., *Everything You Always Wanted to Know about Lacan (but Were Afraid to Ask Hitchcock)* (London, UK: Verso, 1992); D. A. Miller, *Hidden Hitchcock* (Chicago, IL: University of Chicago Press, 2017); and Larry Gross, "Film après Noir," *Film Comment* 12, no. 4 (1976): 44–49.

20. Gross, "Film après Noir," 45, 47.

21. Len Gutkin, "The Dandified Dick: Hardboiled Noir and the Wildean Epigram," *ELH* 81, no. 4 (2014): 1299–1326.

22. Adam Hibbert (@adhib), Twitter, March 8, 2021, 5:19 a.m., https://twitter.com/adhib/status/1368868882971246597.

23. Grant Morrison, *The Invisibles*, 3 vols. (New York: DC Comics, 1996–2000).

24. Jane Clare Jones (@janeclarejones), "So, a request for someone to write something - shortish - for the next issue of TRN. Ideally an American, or someone living/has lived in the States. Am interested in exploring the whole 'post truth left and right' thing, specifically of course QAnon/Trans ideology, and would be particularly interested in an analysis that could link this to any notable aspects of American culture, history or politics . . . for example, religiosity, lack of material class politics, conspiracy theories etc . . .", Twitter, September 17, 2021, 9:32 a.m., https://twitter.com/janeclarejones/status/1438858335701327877; https://twitter.com/janeclarejones/status/1438858337467211776.

25. Graham Linehan, "Just So It's Absolutely Clear," *The Glinner Update*, March 6, 2021, https://grahamlinehan.substack.com/p/just-so-its-absolutely-clear.

26. *Fritz the Cat*, directed by Ralph Bakshi (1972; Cinemation Industries).

27. For an argument about neo-noir as revenge against mid-century modernist architecture, see the video essay *Los Angeles Plays Itself*, directed by Thom Andersen (2014; Cinema Guild).

28. *Jackie Brown*, directed by Quentin Tarantino (1997; Miramax Films);, *Lock, Stock and Two Smoking Barrels*, directed by Guy Ritchie (1998; Gramercy Pictures); *The Big Lebowski*, directed by Joel and Ethan Coen (1998; Gramercy Pictures); *Pineapple Express*, directed by David Gordon Green (2008; Sony Pictures Releasing); *Inherent Vice*, directed by Paul Thomas Anderson (2014; Warner Bros. Pictures). All except for the British movie *Lock Stock* are set and filmed in Los Angeles, too.

29. The release of *Inherent Vice* in 2014 prompted an essay by the film critic Chris Wade on "slacker noir," which defines the genre according to a protagonist's "wish to remove themselves from the action." Yet while this might apply to *Pineapple Express*, and more tendentiously to *The Big Lebowski* (tendentious because the Dude does accept commissions from both Maude Lebowski and Jackie Treehorn to retrieve the missing briefcase), it can hardly apply to *Inherent Vice*, whose protagonist is a professional PI, albeit a stoned one; and even less to *Under the Silver Lake*, whose protagonist is an obsessive collator of clues and conspiracy theories. Chris Wade, "Inherent Vice, The Big Lebowski, and the Rise of 'Slacker Noir,'" *Slate*, January 9, 2015, https://slate.com/culture/2015/01/inherent-vice-the-big-lebowski-and-the-rise-of-slacker-noir-video.html.

30. *The Year's Work in Lebowski Studies*, edited by Aaron Jaffe and Edward P. Comentale (Bloomington: Indiana University Press, 2009).

31. *The Big Lebowski*.

32. *Forrest Gump*, directed by Robert Zemeckis (1994; Paramount Pictures).

33. Preciado, *Testo Junkie*, 11–12.

34. Roland Barthes, *The Pleasure of the Text*, trans. Richard Miller (New York: Hill and Wang, 1975), 9.

35. Ironically, or not, I was kicked off Her in 2017 for looking too masculine. In order to get back on the app, I would have needed to supply them with a passport, or state ID illustrating the change in my gender markers. I didn't have such ID obviously, I just wanted to date people.

36. Butler, "The Lesbian Phallus and the Morphological Imaginary," in *Bodies That Matter*, 28–57.

37. *Under the Silver Lake*, directed by David Robert Mitchell (2018; A24).

38. "I mean, I've just been thinking, why do we assume that all of this infrastructure and entertainment and open information beaming all over the place into every home on the planet

is exactly what people tell us it is. Maybe there are people more important, more powerful or wealthier than us that communicate things or see things in the world that are meant for them and not for us. I think it's fucking ridiculous to assume that media only has one purpose . . . right?" (*Under the Silver Lake*).

39. Freud, *Interpretation of Dreams*, 107. Emphasis added.

Epilogue

1. Edmund Burke, *A Philosophical Enquiry into the Origin of Our Ideas of the Sublime and Beautiful* (London, UK: A. Robertson, 1824).

2. Alexander Gottlieb Baumgarten, *Aesthetica* (Traiecti cis Viadrum: Kleyb, 1750); Walter Pater, *Studies in the History of the Renaissance* (London, UK: Macmillan, 1873).

3. Immanuel Kant, *The Critique of the Power of Judgement*, trans. Paul Guyer (Cambridge, UK: Cambridge University Press, 2000), 111–20 (*Kritik der Urteilskraft* 5:226–36).

4. *Ibid.*, 102–4, 175 (5:217–19, 295).

5. Kojin Karatani, *Transcritique: On Kant and Marx*, trans. Sabu Kohso (Cambridge, MA: MIT Press, 2003), 113.

6. Janet Mock, *Redefining Realness: My Path to Womanhood, Identity, Love & So Much More* (New York: Atria, 2014), 33–34.

7. Kevin Rowland, *My Beauty*, Creation Records, 1999.

8. See "WHOARGH! STEADY LADS!," *NME*, May 17, 1999, https://www.nme.com/news/music/kevin-rowland-7-1386737; Victoria Segal, review of *My Beauty*, *NME*, September 12, 2005, https://www.nme.com/reviews/reviews-nme-1399-339198.

9. "Kevin Rowland: The 'My Beauty' Story," Cherry Red Records, September 25, 2020, 16:09, https://youtu.be/k3cQbc_pAxk.

10. Quoted in the liner notes of Rowland, *My Beauty*.

11. Angela Morley, arrangement and orchestration, *The Little Prince: Original Soundtrack*, score by Frederick Loewe, lyrics by Alan Jay Lerner, Decca Broadway, 2004; arrangement, *Scott*, by Scott Walker, Philips Records, 1967; arrangement, *Scott 2*, by Scott Walker, Philips Records, 1968; arrangement, *Scott 3*, by Scott Walker, Philips Records, 1969. Compare RuPaul's debut studio album, *Supermodel of the World*, Tommy Boy Records, 1993, with his Christmas album, *Ho Ho Ho*, Rhino, 1997. SOPHIE, producer, *Vroom Vroom*, by Charli XCX, Vroom Vroom Recordings, 2016; SOPHIE, Diplo, producers, "Bitch I'm Madonna," featuring Nicki Minaj, track 6 on Madonna, *Rebel Heart*, Interscope Records, 2015.

12. Track 4 on *Scott 3*.

13. Track 8 on *Scott 2*. Wait until Dark, directed by Terence Young (1967; Warner Bros./Seven Arts).

14. Marmalade, "Reflections of My Life," Decca Records, 1969; Whitney Houston, "The Greatest Love of All," written Michael Masser and Linda Creed, Arista Records, 1986.

15. Theodor Adorno, "Theses against Occultism," in *The Stars Down to Earth, and Other Essays on the Irrational in Culture*, ed. Stephen Crook (London, UK: Routledge, 1994), 174.

16. Roland Barthes, "The Grain of the Voice," in *Image Music Text*, trans. Stephen Heath (London, UK: Fontana Press, 1977), 179–89.

17. Bruce Springsteen, "Thunder Road," track 1 on *Born to Run*, Columbia Records, 1975.

18. Silvia Federici, "Marx and Feminism," *tripleC* 16, no. 2 (2018): 468–75.

19. Rita Felski, *The Gender of Modernity* (Cambridge, MA: Harvard University Press, 1995), 92.

20. Silvia Federici, *Caliban and the Witch* (Brooklyn, NY: Autonomedia, 2004).

21. Silvia Federici, *Beyond the Periphery of the Skin: Rethinking, Remaking, and Reclaiming the Body in Contemporary Capitalism* (Oakland, CA: PM Press, 2020), 56. Cory Austin Knudson, review of *Beyond the Pierphery of the Skin*, *Full Stop*, May 28, 2020, https://www.full-stop.net/2020/05/28/reviews/cory-austin-knudson/beyond-the-periphery-of-the-skin-silvia-federici/.

22. bell hooks, "An Aesthetic of Blackness: Strange and Oppositional," *Lenox Avenue: A Journal of Interarts Inquiry* 1 (1995): 65–72. Sierra Mannie, "Dear White Gays: Stop Stealing Black Female Culture," *Time*, July 9, 2014, https://time.com/2969951/dear-white-gays-stop-stealing-black-female-culture/.

23. *Paris Is Burning*, directed by Jennie Livingston (1990; Off-White Productions).

24. Hannah Arendt, *Lectures on Kant's Political Philosophy*, ed. Ronald Beiner (Chicago, IL: University of Chicago Press, 1992).

25. Arendt, *Lectures on Kant's Political Philosophy*, 70–75.

26. Grace E. Lavery, *Quaint, Exquisite: Victorian Aesthetics and the Idea of Japan* (Princeton, NJ: Princeton University Press, 2019), 10–11.

27. For the debate, see Eva Schaper, *Studies in Kant's Aesthetics* (Edinburgh: Edinburgh University Press, 1979); Paul Guyer, *Kant and the Claims of Taste*, 2nd ed. (Cambridge, UK: Cambridge University Press, 1997), 218; and Paul Guyer, "Free and Adherent Beauty: A Modest Proposal," *The British Journal of Aesthetics* 42, no. 4 (2002): 357–66.

28. Guyer, "Free and Adherent Beauty," 358–59.

29. Kant, *Critique of Judgment*, 115. (*Kritik der Urteilskraft*, 5:230).

30. David Kazanjian, *The Colonizing Trick: National Culture and Imperial Citizenship in Early America* (Minneapolis: University of Minnesota Press, 2003).

31. Kant, *Critique of Judgment*, 115. (*Kritik der Urteilskraft*, 5:230).

32. Gayatri Chakravorty Spivak, *A Critique of Postcolonial Reason: Toward a History of the Vanishing Present* (Cambridge, MA: Harvard University Press, 1999).

33. Émile Benveniste, "The Nature of Pronouns," in *Problems in General Linguistics*, trans. Mary Elizabeth Meek (Coral Gables, FL: University of Miami Press, 1971), 217–22.

34. Segal, review of *My Beauty*.

35. *Austin Powers: International Man of Mystery*, directed by Jay Roach (1997; New Line Cinema).

36. Freud, "Fetishism," 147–57.

37. Kevin Rowland, "I Was Nuts," https://www.theguardian.com/music/2003/sep/19/2.

38. "Kevin Rowland on the *My Beauty* Furore: 'I Wasn't Cracking Up. I Just Wanted to Wear a Dress,'" interview by Tim Jonze, July 21, 2020, https://www.theguardian.com/music/2020/jul/21/kevin-rowland-interview-dexys-midnight-runners-covid-19-my-beauty-dress-stockings.

39. *Ibid.*

40. The claim that Cobain was trans was most recently advanced by the writer Magdalene Visaggio (@MagsVisaggs), "Kurt Cobain was a trans girl. she is ours now. we will not be returning her", Twitter, January 23, 2022, https://twitter.com/MagsVisaggs/status/1485329749387972608. See also Niko Stratis, "Kurt Cobain Pushed the Boundaries of Gender and Made Room for Us

All," *Catapult*, March 1, 2022, https://catapult.co/stories/niko-stratis-everyone-is-gay-nirvana-kurt-cobain-pushed-boundaries-gender-masculinity-queerness-rock-grunge.

41. For example: Jane Clare Jones (@janeclarejones), "Here's [referring to an attached photograph of the artist Prince] a male person 'breaking through the boundaries of gender.' The minute you say that this male person is thereby not male, you reinforce the male = masculinity box. You think we are objecting to gender non-conformity. We're not. We're objecting to you essentialising gender." Twitter, March 2, 2021, https://twitter.com/janeclarejones/status/1366662007680811009.

42. Rowland, "Rag Doll," Cherry Red Records, June 1, 2020, 6:13, https://youtu.be/Xo9SbrsV3T8.

BIBLIOGRAPHY

Adorno, Theodor. "Commitment." *New Left Review*, nos. 87–88 (1974): 75–89.

Aizura, Aren. "Kill Your Dads: On Reed and Castiglia's Response to Grace Lavery." *Medium*, December 13, 2018. medium.com/@aren.aizura/kill-your-dads-on-reed-and-castiglias-response-to-grace-lavery-28857b636a2c.

Alcoholics Anonymous Big Book. 4th ed. New York: Alcoholics Anonymous World Services, 2001.

Arnold, Matthew. *Essays in Criticism*. New York: Macmillan, 1883.

Barbaro, Michael. "What Drives Donald Trump? Fear of Losing Status, Tapes Show." *New York Times*, October 25, 2016. https://www.nytimes.com/2016/10/26/us/politics/donald-trump-interviews.html.

Baudelaire, Charles. 1997. *Complete Poems: Charles Baudelaire*. Manchester, UK: Carcanet Press, 1997.

Bellwether, Mira. *Fucking Trans Women (FTW): A Zine about the Sex Lives of Trans Women*. Self-published, CreateSpace, 2013.

Bersani, Leo. "Is the Rectum a Grave?" In *Is the Rectum a Grave? and Other Essays*, 3–31. Chicago, IL: University of Chicago Press, 2010.

Blanchard, Ray. "Clinical Observations and Systematic Studies of Autogynephilia." *Journal of Sex and Marital Therapy* 17, no. 4 (1991): 235–51.

Buchanan, Blu. "A Burning White Ga(y)ze: On 'Free Speech' and White Gay Men." *BLARB, Los Angeles Review of Books* (blog), December 19, 2018. https://blog.lareviewofbooks.org/essays/burning-white-gayze-free-speech-white-gay-men/.

Butler, Judith. *Bodies That Matter: On the Discursive Limits of "Sex."* London, UK: Routledge, 1993.

———. *Excitable Speech: A Politics of the Performative*. London, UK: Routledge, 1997.

Carter, Steven, and Julia Sokal. *Men Who Can't Love: When a Man's Fear Makes Him Run from Commitment (And What a Smart Woman Can Do about It)*. New York: M. Evans, 1987.

Castiglia, Christopher, and Christopher Reed. "Conversion Therapy v. Re-education Camp: An Open Letter to Grace Lavery." *BLARB, Los Angeles Review of Books*, December 11, 2018. https://blog.lareviewofbooks.org/essays/conversion-therapy-v-re-education-camp-open-letter-grace-lavery/.

Chiesa, Lorenzo. *The Not-Two: Logic and God in Lacan*. Cambridge, MA: MIT Press, 2016.

Chu, Andrea Long. "My New Vagina Won't Make Me Happy." *New York Times*, November 24, 2018. https://www.nytimes.com/2018/11/24/opinion/sunday/vaginoplasty-transgender-medicine.html.

———. "On Liking Women." In "Motherland," special issue, *n+1*, no. 30 (Winter 2018). https://nplusonemag.com/issue-30/essays/on-liking-women/.

Chu, Andrea Long, and Emmett Harsin Drager. "After Trans Studies." *Transgender Studies Quarterly* 6, no. 1 (2019): 103–16.

Copjec, Joan. "Sex and the Euthanasia of Reason." In *Supposing the Subject*. Edited by Joan Copjec, 16–44. London, UK: Verso, 1994.

Diagnostic and Statistical Manual of Mental Disorders, Fifth Edition (DSM-5). American Psychiatric Association. Washington, DC: American Psychiatric Publishing, 2013.

Edelman, Lee. *No Future: Queer Theory and the Death Drive*. Durham, NC: Duke University Press, 2004.

Etherington-Smith, Meredith. *The Persistence of Memory: A Biography of Dalí*. New York: Random House, 1993.

Foucault, Michel. *Fearless Speech*. Los Angeles, CA : Semiotext€, 2001.

Freeman, Elizabeth. *Time Binds: Queer Temporalities, Queer Histories*. Durham, NC: Duke University Press, 2010.

Freud, Sigmund. "Analysis Terminable and Interminable." 1937. In *The Standard Edition of the Complete Psychological Works of Sigmund Freud*, vol. 23, edited by James Strachey and Anna Freud, 209–54. London, UK: Hogarth, 1964.

———. *Beyond the Pleasure Principle*. 1920. In *The Standard Edition of the Complete Psychological Works of Sigmund Freud*, vol. 18, edited by James Strachey, Alix Strachey, and Alan Tyson, 1–64. London, UK: Hogarth, 1955.

———. "Fetishism." 1926. In *The Standard Edition of the Complete Psychological Works of Sigmund Freud*, vol. 21, edited by James Strachey, Alix Strachey, and Alan Tyson, 147–57. London, UK: Hogarth, 1958.

———. "Inhibitions, Symptoms, and Anxiety." 1926. In *The Standard Edition of the Complete Psychological Works of Sigmund Freud*, vol. 20, edited by James Strachey, Alix Strachey, and Alan Tyson, 75–176. London, UK: Hogarth, 1958.

———. *The Interpretation of Dreams*. Vol. 4 of *The Standard Edition of the Complete Psychological Works of Sigmund Freud*, edited by James Strachey, Anna Freud, Alix Strachey, and Alan Tyson. London, UK: Hogarth, 1953.

———. "On Narcissism." 1914. In *The Standard Edition of the Complete Psychological Works of Sigmund Freud*, vol. 14, edited by James Strachey, Alix Strachey, and Alan Tyson, 67–102. London, UK: Hogarth, 1957.

———."Psycho-Analytic Notes on an Autobiographical Account of a Case of Paranoia (Dementia Paranoides)." In *The Standard Edition of the Complete Psychological Works of Sigmund Freud*, vol. 12, edited by James Strachey, Alix Strachey, and Alan Tyson, 3–84. London, UK: Hogarth, 1958.

———. *Three Essays on the Theory of Sexuality*. 1905. In *The Standard Edition of the Complete Psychological Works of Sigmund Freud*. vol. 7, edited by James Strachey, Anna Freud, Alix Strachey, and Alan Tyson, 125–248. London: Hogarth, 1953.

———. *The Wolfman and Other Cases*. London, UK: Penguin Classics, 2003.

Garber, Marjorie. *Vested Interests: Cross-dressing and Cultural Anxiety*. New York: Harper Perennial, 1992.

Gay, Peter. *Freud: A Life for Our Times*. New York: Norton, 1988.

Gherovici, Patricia. *Transgender Psychoanalysis: A Lacanian Perspective on Sexual Difference.* New York: Routledge, 2017.

Gill-Peterson, Jules. *Histories of the Transgender Child.* Minneapolis: University of Minnesota Press, 2018.

Halberstam, Jack. *Skin Shows: Gothic Horror and the Technology of Monsters.* Durham, NC: Duke University Press, 1995

Harris, Thomas. *The Silence of the Lambs.* New York: St. Martin's Press, 1988.

Hayward, Eva. "Lessons from a Starfish." In *Queering the Non/human,* edited by Noreen Giffney and Myra J. Hird, 249–63. Aldershot, UK: Ashgate, 2008.

———. "More Lessons from a Starfish: Prefixial Flesh and Transspeciated Selves." *Women's Studies Quarterly* 36, nos. 3–4 (2008): 64–85.

Heaney, Emma. *The New Woman: Literary Modernism, Queer Theory, and the Trans Feminine Allegory.* Evanston, IL: Northwestern University Press, 2017.

Hegel, G. W. F. Preface to *The Phenomenology of Mind* (1807). Marxists Internet Archive. https://www.marxists.org/reference/archive/hegel/works/ph/phprefac.htm.

Johnson, Barbara. "Bringing Out D. A. Miller." *Narrative* 10, no. 1 (2002): 3–8.

Kantorowicz, Ernst. *The Fundamental Issue: Documents and Marginal Notes on the University of California Loyalty Oath.* Berkeley, CA: Parker, 1950.

———. *The King's Two Bodies.* Princeton, NJ: Princeton University Press, 1957.

Kapsis, Robert E. *Jonathan Demme Interviews.* Jackson: University Press of Mississippi, 2009.

Kermode, Frank. *The Sense of an Ending: Studies in the Theory of Fiction.* 2nd ed. Oxford, UK: Oxford University Press, 2000.

Kramer, Larry. "From the Archives: Playwright and Gay Activist Larry Kramer Explains Why He Hated Jonathan Demme's 'Philadelphia.'" *Los Angeles Times,* January 10, 1994. Accessed January 19, 2021. https://www.latimes.com/entertainment/movies/la-et-archives-jonathan-demme-philadelphia-20170426-story.html.

Lacan, Jacques. "Les non-dupes errent." Radio Lacan. Recorded November 13, 1973. http://www.radiolacan.com/en/topic/215/2.

———. "Position of the Unconscious." In *Écrits.* Translated by Bruce Fink, 703–21. New York: Norton, 2006.

LaFleur, Greta. "A Fairy's Tale." *Public Books,* July 10, 2019. www.publicbooks.org/a-fairys-tale/.

Laing, R. D. *Knots.* Harmondsworth, UK: Penguin Books, 1970.

Lamb, Sybil. "You Best Never Ever Tr*nsition, Tr*nny." Tranny Punk. Accessed January 15, 2020. www.trannypunk.com/TSPX/detransition.html.

Laplanche, Jean, and Jean-Bertrand Pontalis. *The Language of Psychoanalysis.* Translated by Donald Nicholson-Smith. Oxford, UK: W. W. Norton, 1973.

Lavery, Grace. "We Will Need to Remember This Hole." December, 2018. Berkeley, CA.

Liddle, Rod. "Women's Sports May One Day Soon Consist Entirely of Men." *Spectator,* February 8, 2019. https://spectator.us/womens-sports-consist-men/.

Lind, Earl. *Autobiography of an Androgyne.* New York: Medico-Legal Journal, 1918.

Mesch, Rachel. *Before Trans: Three Gender Stories from Nineteenth-Century France.* Stanford, CA: Stanford University Press, 2020.

Miller, D. A. *Bringing Out Roland Barthes.* Berkeley: University of California Press, 1992.

Morel, Geneviève. *Sexual Ambiguities: Sexuation and Psychosis*. Translated by Lindsay Watson. London, UK: Karnac, 2011.

Murphy, Meghan. "Why I'm Suing Twitter." *Quillette*, February 26, 2019. https://quillette.com/2019/02/26/why-im-suing-twitter/.

Navratilova, Martina. "The Rules on Trans Athletes Reward Cheats and Punish the Innocent." *Sunday Times*, February 17, 2019. https://www.thetimes.co.uk/article/the-rules-on-trans-athletes-reward-cheats-and-punish-the-innocent-klsrq6h3x.

Ngai, Sianne. *Ugly Feelings*. Cambridge, MA: Harvard University Press, 2005.

Nolan, Maura. "Metaphoric History: Narrative and New Science in the Work of F. W. Maitland." *PMLA* 118, no. 3 (2003): 557–72.

Politi, Daniel. "Milo Yiannopoulos Loses CPAC Invite, Book Deal after Pedophilia Defense." *Slate*, February 20, 2017. https://slate.com/news-and-politics/2017/02/milo-yiannopoulos-loses-cpac-invite-book-deal-after-pedophilia-defense.html.

Preciado, Paul. *Testo Junkie: Sex, Drugs, and Biopolitics in the Pharmacopornographic Era*. New York: Feminist Press, 2013.

Samuels, Ellen. "Remember Who the Real Enemy Is: In Support of Trans Existence." *Medium*, December 12, 2018. medium.com/@ellensamuels/remember-who-the-real-enemy-is-in-support-of-trans-existence-4bed6d489a27.

Sedgwick, Eve Kosofsky. *Epistemology of the Closet*. Berkeley: University of California Press, 1990.

———. "How to Bring Your Kids Up Gay." *Social Text*, no. 29 (1991): 18–27.

———. "White Glasses." In *Tendencies*, 252–66. Durham, NC: Duke University Press, 1993.

Solanas, Valerie. *SCUM Manifesto*. 1967. London, UK: Verso, 2006.

Spade, Dean. "Mutilating Gender." In *The Transgender Studies Reader*, edited by Susan Stryker and Stephen Whittle, 315–32. New York: Routledge, 2006.

Stern, Marlow. "Jonathan Demme on Gaza, Transphobia in 'The Silence of the Lambs,' and Meryl Streep as a Rock Star." *The Daily Beast*, July 25, 2014. Accessed January 19, 2021. https://www.thedailybeast.com/jonathan-demme-on-gaza-transphobia-in-the-silence-of-the-lambs-and-meryl-streep-as-a-rock-star.

Stock, Kathleen, Sophie Allen, Jane Clare Jones, Holly Lawford-Smith, Mary Leng, and Rebecca Reilly-Cooper. "Doing Better in Arguments about Sex, Gender, and Trans Rights." *Medium*, May 23, 2019. medium.com/@kathleenstock/doing-better-in-arguments-about-sex-and-gender-3bec3fc4bdb6.

Stopes, Marie Carmichael. *Married Love, or, Love in Marriage*. New York: The Critic and Guide Co., 1918.

Stryker, Susan. "My Words to Victor Frankenstein above the Village of Chamounix: Performing Transgender Rage." *GLQ: A Journal of Lesbian and Gay Studies* 1, no. 3 (1994): 237–54.

Stryker, Susan, Paisley Currah, and Lisa Jean Moore. "Introduction: Trans-, Trans, or Transgender?" *Women's Studies Quarterly* 36, nos. 3–4 (2008): 11–22.

Sullivan, Lou. Letter to Judy Van Maasdam, May 21, 1987, box 2, folder 45, Louis Graydon Sullivan Papers (1991–07). The Gay, Lesbian, Bisexual, Transgender Historical Society, San Francisco, CA.

Terada, Rei. *Feeling in Theory: Emotion after the "Death of the Subject."* Cambridge, MA: Harvard University Press, 2003.

Todd, Selina. "Feminism, Postmodernism and Women's Oppression." Speech given at A Woman's Place, London, UK, May 21, 2019. Accessed January 19, 2021. https://womansplaceuk.org/2019/05/21/feminism-postmodernism-and-womens-oppression/.

Toomey, Russel B., Amy K. Syvertsen, and Maura Shramko. "Transgender Adolescent Suicide Behavior." *Pediatrics* 142, no. 4 (2018). https://pediatrics.aappublications.org/content/142.

Tourmaline, Eric A. Stanley, and Johanna Burton, eds. *Trap Door: Trans Cultural Production and the Politics of Visibility*. Cambridge, MA: MIT Press, 2017.

Turner, Benedick. "A Man's Work Must She Do: Female Manliness in Tennyson's *Gareth and Lynette*." *Victorian Poetry* 52, no. 3 (2014): 483–507.

Werther, Ralph. *Autobiography of an Androgyne (Subterranean lives)*. New Brunswick, NJ: Rutgers University Press, 2008.

Žižek, Slavoj. "The Sexual Is Political." *Philosophical Salon* 1, Aug. 2016. https://thephilosophicalsalon.com/the-sexual-is-political/.

Zupančič, Alenka. *What Is Sex?* Boston, MA: MIT Press, 2017.

INDEX

Page numbers in *italics* denote figures.

A NOTE ON THE TYPE

This book has been composed in Arno, an Old-style serif typeface in the classic Venetian tradition, designed by Robert Slimbach at Adobe.